Herman Hueg

Ornamental confectionery

And practical assistant to the art of baking in all its branches, with numerous illustrations

Herman Hueg

Ornamental confectionery

And practical assistant to the art of baking in all its branches, with numerous illustrations

ISBN/EAN: 9783337727222

Printed in Europe, USA, Canada, Australia, Japan

Cover: Foto ©ninafisch / pixelio.de

More available books at **www.hansebooks.com**

ORNAMENTAL CONFECTIONERY

AND

PRACTICAL ASSISTANT

TO

The Art of Baking

IN ALL ITS BRANCHES,

WITH

NUMEROUS ILLUSTRATIONS.

BY

HERMAN HUEG,

Practical Cake Baker and Confec^r

PRINTED IN ENGLISH AND GERMAN.

1892.

INTRODUCTION.

In offering this book to the public and trade in general, I take the opportunity of expressing my grateful thanks to my numerous customers for their very liberal patronage and their testimonial of approbation and encouragement extended to me during the short period of my business relation with them.

My first attempt at writing a book, which you probably bought, was but a beginning, and I hope that all purchasers of it have received the worth of their money; and I am thankful for the many kind letters of gratitude received from them. From the many inquiries which I have had about recipes I can now say that I have a book which will satisfy the purchaser and exceed all his expectations.

The recipes that follow are not copied from other books, or written down from memory, but each one of them have been repeatedly tested and found correct in the course of many years of practice. They comprise the most saleable and popular forms of Cake and Confectionery, such as is generally found in first class establishments. Many books have been written on the various branches of our trade ; but none, I believe, treat on the subject with which I propose to deal in this book. I have classed these mixtures in an honest spirit, and to the best of my knowledge and ability.

It would not be possible to give recipes for all kinds of Cake and Confectionery in so small a work, as in many cases the ingredients are very simple, and the success of the experiment depends altogether on the skill of the workman, and years are often necessary to attain the requisite proficiency.

Any one with a fair share of courage and intelligence can, with this book in hand, produce in a short time better and purer Cake and Candies than are generally offered for sale

In order to keep this book in the reach of all, I will have to divide the Cake baking into three parts, which we may call thus:

"RUBBING", "MIXING" & "BEATING".

Best paying recipes are marked "*".

CONTENTS.

Page.	PART I.	No.
1	Rubbing	1
1	Drop Cakes	1—13
2	Wine Cakes	14—18
3	Cup Cakes	19—21
3	Rough and Ready	22—23
3	Plain Pound Cakes	24
3	Citron Pound Cake	25
3	Raisin Pound Cake	26
3	Silver Cake	27
3	Gold Cake	28
3	Lady Wine Cakes	29
3	Lady and Marble Cakes	30—33
4	Common Raisin Cake	31—42
4	Fruit Cake	43 45
5	Springerle	46—47
5	Corn Muffins	45—51
5	Cocoanut Cakes	52—53
5	Metropolitan Cakes	54
5	White Mountain Cakes	55—56
5	Croton Cakes	57
6	Union and Shilling Cakes	58—59
6	Penny Pound Cakes	60
6	Strawberry Short Cakes	61
6	Lunch Cakes	62
6	Diamond and Jelly Squares	63
6	Raisin Cake	64—65
6	Washington Slice	66
6	Soda and Madeira Cakes	66—67
6	Self-raising Flour	68
7	Currant and Heart Cakes	60—70
7	Genoa and Madeira Cakes	71—75
7	Wedding Cakes	76
7	Patent Flour	77
7	Currant and Rice Cakes	78—80
7	Intermediate	81
8	Heart Cakes	82
8	Rice Buns	83
8	Dandy and Cheese Cakes	84—85
8	Seed and Teameeting Cakes	86—87
8	Rice Buns	88
8	Genoa, Madeira and Penny Cakes	89—92
8	Rocks and Rice Buns	93—94
9	Intermediate	95
9	Wedding and Mahary Cakes	96—97
9	Parisiens	98
9	Butter Scotch and Domestic Cakes	99—100
9	German Wine Cakes	101
9	Duchess and Lunch Cakes	102—103
9	Claremont & Codrington Buns	104 105
10	Cotton Seed Oil	106
10	Almond & Cocoanut Jumbles	107—100
10	French Snaps	110—111
10	Layer, White, Marble and Jelly Cakes	112—115

Page.	PART II.	No.
11	Mixing	116
11	Genuine Scotch Short Cakes	117—120
12	Sugar Cakes Shrewsberry	121—134
13	Vanilla, Cinnamon and Wafer Jumbles	135—144
14	Tea Biscuit & Baking Powder	145—148
14	Sponge Cakes and Jelly Roll	149—151
14	Crullers and Sponge Biscuits	152—162
15	Mol. Fruit Cake & Mol. Cakes 163—166	
15	Bolivars and Sugar Bolivars	167—171
16	Gingernuts and Spice Cakes	172—178
16	Ginger Snaps & Ginger Bread	179—190
17	Ginger Pound Cakes	191
17	New Years Cakes and Lemon Snaps	192—202

Page.		No.
18	Lemon Crackers, Brandy and Wine Snaps	203—207
18	Cocoanut Balls & Macaroons	208—211
19	Cinnamon Stars and French Macaroons	212—214
19	French Gingernuts & Pie Pastry	215—218
19	Puff Paste and Cream Tarts	219—221
20	Cream Cakes and Eclairs	222—225
21	Vanilla Creams & Doughnuts	226—229
21	Wine Biscuits & Queens Drops	230—231
21	Collet and Credition Buns	232—233
21	Africans and Lemon Drops	234—235
21	Scones and Bath Buns	135—238
22	Jumbles, Puff Paste and Cinnamon Stars	239—241
22	Cocoanut & Lemon Fingers	242—249
22	Golden Drops & Ginger Jumbles	246—246
22	Prince Albert and Cantones	247—248
22	Domestic Cakes and Shrewsberry	249—251
23	Lemon Snaps. Dips & Cantones	252—254
23	Queen Cakes and Scones	255—256
23	Santa Claus and Jelly Roll	257—260
23	Spice Rings & Pumpernicle	261—262
23	Chocolate Rings	263
24	Cocoanuts Pyramids	264
24	Napoleons & Chocolate Beses	255—266
24	Neapolitan and Bisqne Cake	267—268
24	Brazil Molasses Cakes	269
24	French Crullers and Cocoanut Cakes	270—271
25	Cinnamon and Italian Fruit Drops	272—273
25	Crumb and Lemon Cakes	274—275
25	Brandy Snaps & Spice Cakes	276—277
25	French Crullers & Gold Cakes	278—281
26	Cream Roll & Vanilla Slices	282—285
26	Turn Overs & Puff Paste Tarts	285—286
26	Patties or Tarts	287

	PART III.	
27	Beating	288
27	Meringue Work & Jenny Lind	284—291
28	Kisses and Cocoanut Kisses	292—293
28	Meringue, Tarts, Pies & Tartlets	294—297
29	Angel Cakes & Lady Fingers	298—302
29	Lady, Marble and White Cakes	303—307
29	Brides and Sponge Cakes	308—310
30	Charlotte Russe & Anise Drops	311—315
30	Spanish Macaroons and to test Eggs	316—317
30	Fancy Cakes	320—343

	PART IV.	
35	Pie Baking	344
35	Dried Fruits and Mince Meats	345—350
36	Oyster Pie and Canned Fruits	351—353
36	Lemon Cream and Custards	354—361

	PART V.	
37	Icing & Glazing	362
36	Two Colors	363
38	All kinds of Icings	364—375
39	Ornamenting Butter and Lard	375
39	How to Ice Large Cakes	376
39	Confectioners Paste	377

	PART VI.	
40	Jelly	378
40	All kinds of Colors	379—389
40	How to make Colored Sugars	385

CONTENTS

PART VII.

Page		No.
41	About Bread...............	386
41	London Snow Flake Yeast....	387
42	Celebrated Dry Hop Yeast...	388
42	Glycerine Bread.............	389
43	Croll System	390
43	Stock Yeast Liquid..........	391
43	Stock Yeast Dry............	392
44	How to make Ferment.......	393
44	How to make Bread.........	394
44	Valuable Hints..............	395
45	Best method of making Ferment........	296
46	Fine Bread without Ferment.	397
46	Malt Stock Yeast............	398
46	London Stock Yeast.........	399
46	American Plain Yeast........	400
47	Genuine Snow Flake Yeast...	401
47	Compressed Yeast...	402
47	Rolls, Buns, Rusk & Doughnuts	403—406

PART VIII.

| 48 | Egg Preserving. | |
| 50 | Best Methods..... ....| 407—410 |

PART IX.

| 50 | Flavoring Extracts........... | 411 |
| 51 | How to make all kinds of flavors................ | 412—423 |

PART X.

| 51 | Ice Creams. | |
| 52 | How to make all kinds of Ice Creams................. | 423—430 |

PART XI.

53	Syrup for Soda Water.	
53	All kinds of Syrups	430—436
53	Foam on Soda Water.........	437

PART XII.

54	Gum Paste	438
54	How to make Moulds........	439
55	How to make Ornaments.....	440
55	Icing and Gum Paste Roses..	441
56	Gum Paste Easter Eggs......	442

PART XIII.

57	Ornamental Confectionery....	
57	List of Tools.................	443
57	Clarifying...................	444
57	Finger Test and Thermometer	445—446
59	Ice Cream Candy, all kinds	447—449
59	All kinds of Caramels........	450—451
59	Imitation Eggs in grained Sugar	452
60	Mallow Cups.................	453
60	Butterines...................	454
60	Caramels........	455—457
61	Peanut and Almond Bars.....	458—460
61	Cocoanut Cakes.............	461
61	Cocoanut Cream Bars........	462
61	Cream for Chocolate Drops..	463
61	Walnut Candy...............	464
61	Lemon Acid Drops..........	465

Page.		No.
62	Old Fashioned Mol. Candy .	466
62	Mol. Taffy and Everton Candy	467—469
62	Chocolate Paste.............	470
62	Cream Chocolate............	471
62	Starch Room....	472
62	Cream Bonbons.............	473
63	Crystalization	474
63	Sugar Spinning.............	475
63	Saccharometer	476
64	Nougat or Croquant.........	477
64	New England Taffy..........	478
64	Soft Fondant................	479
65	Paraffine	480
65	Caramel Ornaments..........	481
65	Vanilla Sugar...............	482
66	Papier Mache...............	483
66	Pastillage	484
66	Rock Sugar..................	485
66	Almond Paste for ornaments	486
66	Panorama Eggs..............	487
67	Conserve Sugar..............	488
68	Apple Sugar	489
68	Cream Mint Drops	490
68	Pink Burnt Almonds........	491
69	Praline Cups................	492
69	To spin a silver or gold web..	493
70	Blow Candy.................	494
70	Cream Candy...............	495
71	Saccharine..................	496
71	Beehives and Pyramids......	397
71	Chocolate Caramels..........	498
71	Easter Cards.................	499
72	Spun Sugar Bee Hive........	500
72	Lozenges....................	501—502
73	Fruit Juices.................	503
73	Fruit Preserving.............	504
73	The Thermometer............	505
73	Behandlung der I Abtheilung	506
74	" " II. "	507
74	" " III. "	508
75	Miscellaneous Recipes.	
75	Fritters.	
75	All kinds of Fritters.	
75	Batter.	
75	Crumpets.	
75	Butter Cakes.	
75	Sausage Rolls.	
76	Butter Cakes.	
76	Johnny Cakes.	
76	Buckwheat Cakes.	
76	Bath Buns.	
76	Domestic Bread.	
76	No more dry bakers bread.	
77	White and Graham Bread.	
77	Potato Yeast.	
77	Golden Cottolene.	
78	Notes about flavoring, baking, &c.	
78	Composition Cake.	
79	Silver Cake.	
79	The proper Baking Heat.	
	250 Designs and Illustrations.	
	Representing the Bakers' and Confectioners' art in all its branches.	

Inhalts-Verzeichniss.

Seite.		No.
1	Conditorei.	
	I. THEIL.	
1	Das Läutern	1
1	Die Zuckerprober	2—7
2	Conserven und Früchte	8—10
4	Zucker-Coleur	12
4	Nougat oder Croquant	13
4	Candiren	14
5	Carmeliren	15
	II. THEIL.	
6	Torten-Bäckerei	16
6	Mandel- und Nuss-Torte	17—18
7	Apfelsinen- und Wiener Torte	19—20
7	Punch- und Brod-Torte	21—22
7	Imperial u. Chocoladen-Torte	23—24
7	Biscuit- und Aleanca-Torte	25—28
8	Eisenbahn- u. Berliner Torte	29—30
8	Sand- und Macronen-Torte	31—32
8	Baiser- und Eis-Torte	33—34
9	Baiser Berg	35—36
9	Schaum- und Elisen-Torte	37—38
10	Marschall-Torte	39
	III. THEIL.	
10	Tafel-Aufsätze.	
10	Macronen-Fruchtkorb	40
11	Baumkuchen	41
13	Kranzkuchen	42
13	Aufsatz auf Baumkuchen	43
13	Caramel-Figuren	44
13	Mandelspähne	45
14	Aufsatz von Bonbon	46
14	Macronen-Aufsatz	47
14	Füllhorn	48
15	Macronen-Pyramide	49
15	Felsen-Zucker	50
15	Pousier-Wachs	51
15	Glasur-Spähne	52
	IV. THEIL.	
15	Thee- und Tafel Bäckerei	53
16	Mürbe Teig	54
16	Zimmt-Sterne	55
16	Anis-Plätzchen	56
16	Gewürz-Ringe	57
17	Pumpernickel	58
17	Theestengel	59
17	Chocoladenringe	60
17	Macronen-Törtchen	61
17	Anis-Zwieback	62
17	Vanilla-Bretzeln	63
17	Thee-Kuchen	64
17	Napoleons	65
17	Creme-Törtchen	66
17	Maserinen	67
18	Leipziger Kuchen	68
18	Marschall-Kuchen	69
18	Porzellan-Schnitte	70
18	Schaum-Torte	71
18	Thee-Bretzeln	72

Seite.		No.
18	Vanilla-Bretzeln	73
18	Vanilla Thee-Biscuit	74
18	Zimmtstangen	75
18	Mandelberge	76
18	Congress-Kuchen	77
19	Devrient	78
19	Domino-Steine	79
19	Backwerk aus Kapsel	80
19	Strohhüte	81
19	Schmetterlinge	82
19	Bohnen	83
20	Aprikosenschnitte	84
20	Johannisbrod	85—86
20	Mohrenköpfe	87
21	Spritzkuchen	88
21	Sahnenküchelchen	89
21	Theeschlangen	90
21	Punschringe	91
21	Windbeutel	92
22	Chau d'eau-Körbchen	93
22	Anischius zu Chocolade	94
	V. THEIL.	
22	Macronen-Bäckerei.	
22	Belegte Macronen	95
23	Gefüllte Macronen	96
23	Rosen-Macronen	97
23	Zimmet-Macronen	98
23	Chocoladen-Macronen	99
23	Vanilla-Macronen	100
23	Citronen-Macronen	101
23	Bestreute Macronen	102
23	Mandelbogen	104—105
24	Zimmetstange	106
24	Mandelschlangen	107
24	Mandelringe	108
24	Mandelbogen	109
24	Macronenschnitte	110
24	Mandel-Bretzeln	111
25	Zimmetstangen	112
	VI. THEIL.	
25	Marzipan.	
26	Königsberger Marzipan	113
26	Marzipan-Torte	114
26	Marzipan-Confect	115
26	Backwaaren von Marzipan	116
	VII. THEIL.	
27	Hefen- und Schmalz-Bäckerei	117
27	Zwieback	118—121
27	Muskuchen	122
27	Pressburger Zwiebäcke	123
28	Plunderbretzeln	124
28	Martinshörner	125
28	Gries- und Speckkuchen	126—127
28	Zwiebel- und Kirschenkuchen	128
28	Pflaumen- und Apfelkuchen	129—130
29	Topf- und Zimmetkuchen	131—132
29	Streusel- und Käsekuchen	133—135
29	Quark- und Mohnkuchen	136—137
30	Rädergebackenes	138

Inhalts-Verzeichniss.

Seite		No.	Seite		No.
	VIII. THEIL.			**XIII. THEIL.**	
30	Leb- u. Honigkuchen-Bäckerei.		42	Glasuren.	
30	Dünner Honigkuchen	140	42	Wasser-Glasur	191
31	Pflastersteine	140	42	Rosen- "	192
31	Weisse Lebkuchen	141	42	Citronen- "	193
31	Verschiedene Lebkuchen	142	42	Apfelsinen-Glasur	194
31	Citronenkuchen	143	42	Chocolade "	195
31	Scheveletten	144	43	Gekochte "	196
31	Braunschweiger Confect	145	43	Eiweiss- "	197
32	Weisser Marzipan	146	43	Eiweiss-Chocolade-Glasur	198
32	Wasser-Marzipan	147	43	Spritz-Glasur	199
32	Geduldskuchen	148	43	Ersatz für Eiweiss	200
	IX. THEIL.			**XIV. THEIL.**	
32	Schaumsachen.		44	Ueber den Traganth.	
33	Warme Schaummasse	149	44	Traganth-Lack	201
33	Kalte "	150	44	Bonbon-Lack	202
33	Gerührte "	151	44	Chocoladen-Lack	203
33	Figuren aus Schaummasse	152	44	Traganthteig	204
34	Conserve-Formen	153	45	Verarbeitung des Traganths	205
	X. THEIL.		45	Formen zu Traganth	206
34	Mandel-Auflauf	154		**XV. THEIL.**	
34	Weisser "	155	46	Garniren und Schablonen	207
35	Rother "	156	46	Ornamente aus Spritz-Glasur	208
35	Chocoladen-Auflauf	157	47	Aufsätze auf Gauze	209
35	Gespritzter "	158	47	Tafel-Aufsätze	210
35	Traganth "	159			
35	Baiserschalen	160		**XVI. THEIL.**	
36	Spanischer Wind	161			
36	Porzellan-Bretzeln	162	48	Früchte in Dunst,	
	XI. THEIL.		48	Blanchiren	211
36	Cremes und Wein-Gelees.		48	Behandlung	212
36	Schlagsahne	163—165	48	Birnen in Dunst	213
37	Creme von Pistatien	166	49	Erdbeeren in Dunst	214
37	" " Marasquino	167	49	Himbeeren " "	215
37	" " Chocolaee	168	49	Kirschen " "	216
37	" " de Rose	169	49	Bemerkung	217
37	" zu verzieren	170		**XVII. THEIL.**	
37	" von Chocolade	171			
38	Citronen-Creme	172	49	Gelees und Marmelade	218
38	Gelees	173	50	Marmelade	219
38	Wein-Gelees	174	50	Apfel-Gelee	220
38	Farbiger Gelee	175	50	Himbeer-Gelee	221
39	Blanc Mange	176	51	Johannisbeeren-Gelee	222
	XII. THEIL.		51	Kirsch-Marmelade	223
39	Liqueur-Fabrikation.		51	Erdbeer-Marmelade	224
39	Verschiedene Liqueure	177	51	Himbeer-Marmelade	225
39	Kräuter-Bitters	178	51	Johannisbeeren-Marmelade	226
39	Punsch-Extract	179	51	Pflaumen-Marmelade	227
40	Glühwein-Essenz	180		**XVIII. THEIL.**	
40	Bonekamp	181	51	Croquant-Aufsatz	228
40	Marasquino di Sara	182	51	Erklärung zu Tafel I	229
40	Marasquino Liqueur	183		**XIX. THEIL.**	
40	Rosen-Liqueur	184	54	Das Mischen der Farben	230
40	Vanilla-Liqueur	185	54	Farben-Harmonie	231
41	Bishoff	186	54	Vom Zuckerfärben	232
41	Bishoff-Essenz	187		Technische Ausdrücke.	
41	Cardinal	188		250 Illustrationen und Vorlagen zu Cakes, Torten-Aufsätzen, Macaronen, Traganth u. Wind-Confect.	
41	Limonade-Extract	189			
41	Höllen-Punsch	190			

RUBBING.

The ingredients of all recipes in this book are written the way they are used one after the other, this you will find very handy, as you can start on a mixture without reading the whole recipes.

One of the most important things is to know how to rub, and also to know when it is rubbed enough; I will try my best to explain this matter to you.

Scale your sugar and butter in the bowl, place your right hand flat down to the bottom of the bowl, in this position keep rubbing steadily, until your mixture is a perfect cream, add 2 eggs every 2 minutes until all used up, this is taken from the size of mixture mentioned in this book; larger or smaller mixtures you will have to take in proportion; after your eggs are all used up, add flour, milk and soda, stir it up, now is the time to sift your flour and cream of tartar into it, mix it easy, and the dough is ready for baking. If you like to have large heads on your cakes you can work the dough a little more, but whenever you do not find any soda, cream of tartar, baking powder, or ammonia in the mixture you are making, do not work it with the flour at all. Butter and sugar of these recipes require plenty of rubbing, but as soon as you add the flour mix as little as you can possibly help, then the less you work the dough the nicer the cake will be.

All recipes in this part have to be rubbed up, and worked as mentioned above.

1. DROP CAKES. *

1½ lb sugar, ¾ lb butter and lard, 10 eggs, 1 pt milk, 1 oz ammonia, 2½ flour. Hot oven. 10 cents a doz.

2. DROP CAKES.

2¼ lbs sugar, 1½ lb butter and lard, 18 eggs, 1 qt milk, 2 oz ammonia, 4½ lbs flour.

3. DROP CAKES.

3 lbs sugar, 1½ lb butter, 15 eggs, 1 qt milk, 1⅓ oz ammonia, 4½ flour.

4. DROP CAKES

2 lbs sugar, 12 oz butter, 17 eggs, 2 oz ammonia, 1 qt milk, 4 lbs flour.

5. DROP CAKES.

3 lbs sugar, 1¼ lb butter, 15 eggs, ⅔ oz ammonia, ½ oz soda, 1 qt milk, 4½ lbs flour.

6. DROP CAKES.

¾ lb sugar, ½ lb butter, 8 eggs, ½ oz ammonia, 1 pt milk, 1½ lb. flour.

7. DROP CAKES.

2¼ lbs sugar, 18 oz butter, 18 eggs, 2 oz ammonia, 1 qt milk, 4½ lbs flour.

8. DROP CAKES.

2½ lbs sugar, 1¼ lb butter, 15 eggs, 1 qt milk, 1 oz ammonia, 4 lbs flour. ⅓ oz soda.

9. DROP CAKES.

3 lbs of sugar, 2 lbs butter, 24 eggs, 1 qt milk, ⅔ oz soda, ⅔ oz ammonia, 5 lbs flour.

10. DROP CAKES.

2½ lbs sugar, 1¼ lb butter, 14 eggs, 1 qt milk, ⅔ oz ammonia, ⅔ oz soda, 4 lbs flour.

11. DROP CAKES.

2 lbs sugar, 1 lb butter, 10 eggs, 1 oz soda, 1 qt milk, 4¼ lbs flour, 2 oz cream of tartar.

12. DROP CAKES.

2½ lbs sugar, 1½ lb butter, 15 eggs, 1 qt milk, 1⅛ oz ammonia, 4½ lbs flour.

13. DROP CAKES.

2 lbs sugar, 2 lbs butter, 16 eggs, 2 oz ammonia, 1 qt milk, 4¾ lbs flour.

14. WINE CAKES.*

2½ lbs sugar, 1¼ lb butter, 15 eggs, 1 qt milk, ⅔ oz ammonia, 1⅓ oz cream of tartar, 4½ lbs flour.   5, 10, and 25 cts. cakes.

15. WINE CAKES.*

3 lbs sugar, 2 lbs butter, 20 eggs, 1 qt milk, 1 oz soda, 2 oz cream of tartar, 4½ lbs flour.

16. WINE CAKES.

1½ lb sugar, 1⅛ lb butter, 15 eggs, ⅔ oz soda, 1⅓ cream of tartar, 1 qt milk, 4½ lbs flour.

17. WINE CAKES.*

2½ lbs sugar, 1½ lb butter, 20 eggs, 1 oz soda, 2 oz cream of tartar, 1 qt milk, 4½ lbs flour.

18. WINE CAKES.

5 lbs sugar, 2⅓ lbs butter, 30 eggs, 1 oz soda, 2 oz cream of tartar, 1⅛ qt milk, 6¼ lbs flour.

19. CUP CAKES.*
2 lbs sugar, 1 lb butter, 12 eggs, 1 oz soda, 2 oz cream of tartar, 1 qt milk, 4 lbs flour. 3 for 5 cents.

20. CUP CAKES.
1 lbs sugar, $\frac{1}{2}$ lb butter, 8 eggs, $\frac{1}{2}$ oz soda, 1 oz cream of tartar, 1 pt milk, 2 lbs flour.

21. CUP CAKES.
$1\frac{1}{4}$ lb sugar, $\frac{3}{4}$ lb butter, 9 eggs, $\frac{1}{8}$ oz soda, $\frac{2}{3}$ oz cream of tartar, 1 pt of milk, $2\frac{1}{8}$ lbs flour.

22. ROUGH AND READY.*
$1\frac{1}{4}$ lb sugar, $\frac{3}{4}$ lb butter, 4 eggs, $\frac{2}{3}$ oz soda, $1\frac{1}{3}$ oz cream of tartar, 1 pt milk, $2\frac{3}{4}$ lbs flour. 3 for 5 cents.

23. ROUGH AND READY.
$\frac{3}{4}$ lb sugar, 6 oz butter, 2 eggs, $\frac{1}{8}$ oz ammonia, $\frac{3}{4}$ pt milk, 1 lb 10 oz flour.

24. PLAIN POUND CAKE.*
2 lbs sugar, 2 lbs butter, 20 eggs, 2 lbs flour. Rub well. Up to 45 get sold by lb or piece.

25. CITRON POUND CAKE.*
2 lbs sugar, 2 lbs butter, 20 eggs, $2\frac{1}{2}$ lbs flour, 3 lbs citron. Rub well.

26. RAISIN POUND CAKE.*
2 lbs sugar, 2 lbs butter, 20 eggs, $2\frac{1}{2}$ lbs flour, 3 lbs raisins. Rub well.

27. SILVER CAKE*
1 lb sugar, $\frac{1}{2}$ lb butter, 8 white of eggs, $\frac{1}{6}$ oz soda, $\frac{1}{3}$ oz cream of tartar, $\frac{1}{4}$ pt milk, 1 lb flour, vanilla; baked in square tins.

28. GOLD CAKE *
1 lb sugar, $\frac{1}{2}$ lb butter, 12 yolks, $\frac{1}{6}$ oz soda, $\frac{1}{3}$ oz cream of tartar, $\frac{1}{4}$ pt milk, 1 lb flour.

29. LADY WINE CAKES.*
$1\frac{1}{4}$ lb sugar, $\frac{3}{4}$ lb butter, 10 eggs, $\frac{1}{3}$ soda, $\frac{2}{3}$ oz cream of tartar, 1 pt milk, 2 lbs flour.

30. LADY CAKE.
$1\frac{1}{2}$ lb sugar, 1 lb butter, 2 white of eggs, $\frac{1}{6}$ oz soda, $\frac{1}{3}$ oz cream of tartar, $1\frac{3}{4}$ flour, almond flavor.

31. LADY CAKE.
$1\frac{1}{2}$ lb sugar, $1\frac{1}{4}$ lb butter, 22 white of eggs, $1\frac{1}{2}$ lb flour, almond flavor.

32. LADY OR MARBLE CAKE.
$3\frac{3}{4}$ lbs sugar, 3 lbs butter, $1\frac{1}{4}$ qt white of eggs, 4 lbs flour. $\frac{1}{4}$ of the mixture color with chocolate, the other $\frac{1}{4}$ with cochenille, and work the same as 114.

33. LADY CAKE.
1½ lb sugar, 1 lb butter, 24 white of eggs, 1½ lb flour, almond flavor.

34. COMMON RAISIN CAKE.
2⅓ lb sugar, 2 lbs butter, 20 eggs, 3 lbs flour, 4 lbs raisins.

35. COMMON RAISIN CAKE.*
4 lbs sugar, 2½ lbs butter, 25 eggs, 3 pts milk, ⅓ oz soda, ⅔ oz cream of tartar, 6 lbs flour, 6 lbs raisin, equal to pound cake.

36. COMMON RAISIN CAKE.
4½ lbs sugar, 3 lbs butter, 35 eggs, ½ oz soda, 1 oz cream of tartar, 3 pts milk, 9 lbs flour, 6 lbs raisins.

37. COMMON RAISIN CAKE.
6 lbs sugar, 4 lbs butter, 62 eggs, ¼ oz soda, 1 oz cream of tartar, 8½ lbs flour, 7 lbs raisins, flavor.

38. COMMON RAISIN CAKE.
7½ lbs sugar, 4 lbs butter, 3 qts milk, 45 eggs, 1 oz soda, 2 oz cream of tartar, 14 lbs flour, 8 lbs raisins.

39. COMMON RAISIN CAKE.
3 lbs sugar, 2¼ lbs butter, 30 eggs, 2 qts milk, ⅔ oz soda, 1⅓ oz cream of tartar, 9 lbs flour, 6 lbs raisins.

40. COMMON RAISIN CAKE.
2 lbs sugar, 1½ lb butter, 16 eggs, 1 pt milk, ⅓ oz soda, ⅔ oz cream of tartar, 2¼ lb flour, 3 lbs raisins.

41. COMMON RAISIN CAKE.
1½ lb sugar, 1¼ lb butter, 16 eggs, 1 lb 10 oz flour, 3 lbs raisins.

42. COMMON RAISIN CAKE.
11 lbs sugar, 4½ lbs butter, 3 lbs lard, 7½ pts eggs, 7½ pts milk, 1½ oz soda, 3 oz cream of tartar, 20 lbs flour, 18 lbs raisins. Of course you can use any other kind of fruit in place of raisins, such as citron, currants, lemon and orange peel.

43. FRUIT CAKE.
6½ sugar, 5½ lbs butter, 54 eggs, 1 pt molasses, ½ pt brandy, 5 lbs flour, 17 lbs currants, 13 lbs raisins, 5 lbs citron spices.

44. FRUIT CAKE.
4 lbs sugar, 4 lbs butter, 32 eggs, 3½ lbs flour, 10 lbs raisins, 12 lbs currants, 1 pt molasses, ½ pt brandy, spices.

45. FRUIT CAKE.
1 lb sugar, 1 lb butter, 10 eggs, 1 lb flour, 1 lb citron, 4 lbs raisins and currants, ½ pt brandy, spices.

46. SPRINGERLE *
2 lbs sugar, 9 eggs, rub well, 1 oz anise, ⅓ oz ammonia, 2½ lbs flour, press well into the moulds, let them dry about 2—3 hours and bake them in a cool oven.

46a. SPRINGERLE.
3 lbs sugar, 18 eggs, 4½ lbs flour, ¾ oz ammonia; worked as above.

47. CORN MUFFINS.*
10 oz sugar, 6 oz lard, 1 oz soda, 2 oz cream of tartar, 5 eggs, 1½ lb flour, 1 lb corn meal, 1 qt milk.

48. CORN MUFFINS.*
1½ lb sugar, 10 oz butter, 8 eggs, ⅔ oz soda, 1⅓ oz cream of tartar, 1 qt milk, 1 lb corn meal, 2 lbs flour, makes 75 corn cakes.

49. CORN MUFFINS.
1½ lb sugar, ¼ lb butter, 4 eggs, ⅔ oz soda, 1⅓ oz cream of tartar, 1 qt milk, 1½ lb flour, ½ lb corn meal. 1 ct. each.

50. CORN MUFFINS.
1¼ lb sugar, ¾ lb lard, 1 lb corn meal, 3½ lbs flour, 2 qts milk, 1⅓ oz soda 2⅔ oz cream of tartar.

51. CORN MUFFINS.
1¼ lb sugar, ¾ lb butter, 10 eggs, 2 qts milk, 2⅔ lbs flour, 1 oz soda, 2 oz cream of tartar, little of salt, hot oven.

52. COCOANUT CAKES.
1 lb sugar, 1 lb butter, 12 eggs, 1 lb flour, ¼ lb cocoanut; hot oven.

53. COCOANUT CAKES.*
2 lbs grated cocoanut, 1 lb sugar, 2 oz butter, ½ lb flour, ⅙ oz soda, ⅓ oz cream of tartar, and yolks enough to make a stiff dough, hot oven, lemon flavor. 6 for 5 cents.

54. METROPOLITAN CAKES.
Made out of a wine cake mixture and baked in cup cake tins, ice the bottom, jelly the sides, and dip in cocoanut.

55. WHITE MOUNTAIN CAKES.*
3 lbs sugar, 1½ lb butter, 12 egg whites, 1 pt milk, 1 oz soda, 2 oz cream of tartar, 2 lbs 2 oz flour, orange flavor. 15—20 cents each.

56. WHITE MOUNTAIN CAKES.
1¼ lb sugar, 1 lb butter, 1 pt whites of eggs, 1 pt milk, 2 lbs flour.

57. CROTON CAKES.*
1¼ lb sugar, 12 oz butter, 4 eggs, ½ pt milk, ⅓ oz soda, ⅔ oz cream of tartar, 2½ lbs flour.

58. UNION CAKES.*
1 lb sugar, ¾ lb butter, 6 eggs, ½ pt milk, 2½ lbs flour, ½ oz ammonia.

59. SHILLING CAKES.*
4 lbs sugar, 2 lbs butter, 24 eggs, 1 qt milk, 1 oz soda, 2 oz cream of tartar, 6 lbs flour, flavor.

60. PENNY POUND CAKES.
You can make out of wine or pound cake dough.

61. STRAWBERRY SHORT CAKES.
You can make out of wine, sponge or scones dough.

62. LUNCH CAKES.
Gets made from wine or cup cake mixture.

63. DIAMOND OR JELLY SQUARES.
You can make out of sponge or wine cake mixture.

NOTICE.
The recipes that follow I have gathered in London, England, and Glasgow, Scotland, but as they belong in this part, I will let them follow :

64. RAISIN CAKE.
6 lbs sugar, 4 lbs butter. 62 eggs, ¼ oz soda, 1 oz cream of tartar, 8½ lbs flour, 7 lbs raisins. Sold by pound.

64a. RAISIN CAKE.
4 lbs sugar, 2¼ lbs butter, 25 eggs, 3 pts milk, ⅓ oz soda, ⅜ oz cream of tartar, 6 lbs flour, 6 lbs raisins.

65. WASHINGTON SLICES.*
1 lb sugar, 1 lb butter, 9 eggs, 1 oz ammonia, 2¼ lbs flour, roll the dough ¼ inch thick, then roll up like jelly roll, cut them in 3 equal lenghts, put on a flat cake pan, wash with eggs, sprinkle some chopped almond on top, bake hot, ice them with water icing and cut in diamond shape. 1 cent each

66. SODA CAKES.
2½ lbs sugar, 2½ lbs butter, 9 lbs self-raising flour, 4½ lbs currants, 1 lb citron. 10 eggs, 2 qts milk; baked in square tins. Sold by pound.

67. MADEIRA CAKES.*
1 lb sugar, ¾ lb butter, 9 eggs, ⅙ oz ammonia, 1 lb 2 oz flour; work it like pound cake. 10 cent cakes.

68. SELF-RAISING FLOUR.
30 lbs flour, 10 oz soda, 7 oz tartaric acid; mix and sift 3 times.

69. CURRANT CAKE.

14 oz sugar, $\frac{3}{4}$ lb butter, 8 eggs, $2\frac{3}{4}$ lbs of the above self-raising flour, 2 lbs currants. Sold by pound.

70. HEART CAKES.*

$\frac{1}{2}$ lb sugar, $\frac{1}{2}$ lb butter, 4 eggs, $\frac{1}{2}$ oz ammonia, $\frac{1}{2}$ pt milk, $1\frac{1}{4}$ lb flour, are about the same as fancy cakes. 1 cent each.

71. GENOA CAKE.*

$1\frac{1}{4}$ lb sugar, 1 lb butter, 10 eggs, $1\frac{1}{2}$ lb flour, 2 lbs currants and citron. Sold by pound.

72. GENOA CAKE.

$2\frac{1}{2}$ lbs sugar, 2 lbs butter, 20 eggs, 4 lbs flour, 4 lbs raisins, 1 lb citron.

73. GENOA CAKE.

$1\frac{3}{4}$ lb sugar, $1\frac{3}{4}$ lb butter, 18 eggs, 3 lbs flour, 4 lbs citron and raisins.

74. GENOA CAKE.

$1\frac{1}{2}$ lb sugar, $1\frac{1}{2}$ lb butter, 18 eggs, $2\frac{1}{4}$ lbs flour, 4 lbs citron, raisins and currants.

75. MADEIRA CAKES.*

1 lb sugar, 1 lb butter, 12 eggs, 1 lb patent and 1 lb vienna flour, little milk. 10 cents each.

76. WEDDING CAKE.

1 lb sugar, 1 lb butter, 10 eggs, $1\frac{1}{2}$ lb flour, 4 lbs currants, 2 lbs raisins, 1 lb citron, $2\frac{1}{2}$ lb chopped almonds, 1 gill sherry wine, spices.

77. PATENT FLOUR.

$\frac{1}{4}$ lb soda, $\frac{1}{2}$ lb cream of tartar, 24 lbs flour, mix and sift 3 times. This is what we call patent flour in London, and is used in those recipes under the name of patent flour in this part only.

78. COMMON CURRANT CAKE.

1 lb sugar, $\frac{3}{4}$ lb butter, 2 oz soda, 1 oz tartaric acid, 7 lbs flour, 7 lbs currants, spices; one large cake.

79. RICE CAKES.*

2 lbs sugar, $1\frac{1}{4}$ lb butter, 10 eggs, 1 qt milk, 2 oz rice, 5 lbs patent flour: about the same as wine cakes. 10 cent cakes.

80. SMALL CURRANT CAKES.

$1\frac{1}{4}$ lb sugar, $1\frac{1}{4}$ lb butter, 8 eggs, 1 pt milk, 3 lbs currants, 5 lbs patent flour; same as lunch cakes. 1 cent each.

81. INTERMEDIATE.*

$1\frac{1}{4}$ lb sugar, $1\frac{1}{4}$ lb butter, 10 eggs, 1 pt milk, $3\frac{1}{2}$ lbs patent flour, 1 lb currants, 1 lb raisins, 1 lb citron. 10 cents each.

82. HEART CAKES.

1¼ lb sugar, 1¼ lb butter, 12 eggs, 2½ lbs flour, ½ oz ammonia, little milk. 1 cent each.

83. RICE BUNS.*

¾ lb sugar, ¼ lb butter, 6 eggs, ½ pt milk, 2 oz ammonia, 4 lbs flour; break the dough into 1 oz pieces, wash them with eggs, dip in coarse sugar and bake hot, very nice cakes, never seen them in this country. 1 cent each.

84. DANDY CAKES.

¾ lb sugar, ¾ lb butter, 7 eggs, 1¼ lb flour, 1½ lb currants.

85. CHEESE CAKES.*

¼ lb sugar, ¼ lb butter, ¼ lb powdered sponge cakes, rub well, 3 eggs, fill this mixture in fancy cake pans, which are laid out with pie paste. 1 cent each.

86. SEED CAKES.

1½ lb sugar, 1 lb 2 oz butter, 15 eggs, 1 qt milk, ⅔ oz soda, 1⅓ oz cream of tartar, 4½ lbs flour, 2 oz caraway seed. 10 cents each.

87. TEA MEETING CAKES.

2½ lbs sugar, 2½ lbs butter, 15 eggs, ⅓ oz soda, ⅔ oz cream of tartar, 5 lbs flour, 3 lbs raisins, 4 lbs currants and citron. 10 cents each.

88. RICE BUNS.*

1½ lb sugar, 1 lb butter, 14 eggs, 1 pt milk, ½ lb rice, 3 lbs patent flour.

89. SULTANA GENOA.

2 lbs sugar, 2 lbs butter, 25 eggs, 2½ lbs flour, 3 lbs sultanas. Sold by pound.

90. CARAWAY SEED DEVONS.

1 lb sugar, 1 lb butter, 10 eggs, ½ lb patent flour, 2½ lb flour.

91. MADEIRA CAKES.

3 lbs sugar, 2½ lbs butter, 32 eggs, ½ lb patent flour, 3 lbs flour. 10 cents each.

92. PENNY CAKES.

1½ lb sugar, 1½ lb butter, 1 qt milk, ⅔ oz soda, 1⅓ oz cream of tartar, 4 lbs flour, 2½ lbs currants.

93. ROCKS.

10 oz sugar, 10 oz butter, 1½ pt water, ⅔ oz soda, 1⅓ oz cream of tartar, 4 eggs, 2 lbs flour, ¾ lb currants. 1 cent each.

94. RICE BUNS.*

½ lb sugar, 1 lb butter, 9 eggs, 2 oz ammonia, ½ pt milk, 4 lbs flour.

95. INTERMEDIATE.

1½ lb sugar, 1 lb 2 oz butter, 15 eggs, ⅔ oz soda, 1⅓ oz cream of tartar, 1 qt milk, 4½ lbs flour, 4½ lbs raisins and currants.

96. WEDDING CAKE.

2½ lbs sugar, 2½ lbs butter, 2½ lbs eggs, 2½ lbs flour, 2½ lbs citron, 2½ lbs almonds, 10 lbs currants, ¼ pt brandy.

97. MAHARY CAKES.

2 lbs sugar, ¾ lb butter, 2 lbs eggs, ⅙ oz soda, ⅓ oz cream of tartar, ½ pt milk, 2½ lbs flour.

98. PARISIENS.*

¾ lb sugar, ¾ lb butter, 10 eggs, little milk, 1½ oz soda, 2⅔ oz cream of tartar, 4 lbs flour, lay out in 2 oz pieces, wash with eggs, dip in coarse sugar, let stand ½ hour, bake hot.

99. BUTTER SCOTCH CAKES.*

1 lb brown sugar, 1 lb butter, 9 eggs, ½ pt N. O. molasses, ⅛ oz soda, ⅛ oz cream of tartar, 1 gill milk, 1½ lb flour, spices, lemon oil; baked in oblong tins.

100. DOMESTIC CAKES.*

4 lbs sugar, 2 lbs butter, 18 eggs, 1½ oz ammonia, 1 qt milk, 5¼ lbs flour, lemon oil.

101. GERMAN WINE CAKES.*

5 lbs sugar, 2 lbs butter, 20 eggs, 2 qts milk, 1 oz soda, 2 oz cream of tartar, 6 lbs flour; baked in square tins and sprinkle some cinnamon and sugar on top.

102. DUCHESS CAKES.

1½ lb sugar, 1 lb butter, 8 eggs, ⅓ oz soda, ⅔ oz cream of tartar, 1 pt milk, 2 lbs 2 oz flour; baked and iced. 10 cents each.

103. LUNCH CAKES.

1 lb sugar, ¾ lb butter, 10 eggs, ½ oz soda, 1 oz cream of tartar, 1¾ lb flour, ¾ lb currants; baked in corn cake tins. 3 for 5 cents.

104. CLAREMONT BUNS.*

1 lb sugar, ½ lb butter, 3 eggs, 1 oz ammonia, 2½ lbs flour, little milk, lay out like ginger nuts on greased pans, rather rough, wash with egg, dredge a little sugar on top, bake hot.

105. CODRINGTON BUNS.*

½ lb sugar, ½ lb butter, ½ oz ammonia, 4 eggs, little milk, 1¾ lb flour; lay out like drop cakes, put a slice of citron on top, bake hot.

106. COTTON SEED OIL.

Cotton seed oil, if you take the very best, is a good substitute for lard, it got into the bakeries on account of being cheaper and richer, and can be used in most all of the common cakes in place of lard. You can fry a good cruller in it, and make a first-class cream cake, but it is not advisable to use it in fancy cakes. The best way to use it is half and half

107. ALMOND JUMBLES.

1 lb butter, $1\frac{1}{2}$ lb sugar, 4 whites of eggs, $\frac{1}{3}$ oz soda, $\frac{2}{3}$ oz cream of tartar, $1\frac{1}{2}$ lb flour, wash with milk and dip them in chopped almonds and sugar; open damper.   1 cent each.

108. COCOANUT JUMBLES.

$1\frac{1}{2}$ lb grated cocoanut, $1\frac{1}{2}$ lb sugar, 1 lb butter, 4 eggs, $\frac{1}{6}$ oz soda, $\frac{1}{3}$ oz cream of tartar, $1\frac{3}{4}$ lb flour.   1 cent each.

109. COCOANUT JUMBLES.

$1\frac{1}{2}$ lb sugar, 1 lb butter, 4 whites of eggs, $\frac{1}{3}$ oz soda, $\frac{2}{3}$ oz cream of tartar, $\frac{1}{4}$ lb cocoanut, $1\frac{1}{2}$ lb flour.   1 cent each

110. FRENCH SNAPS.

1 lb sugar, 1 lb butter, 1 pt molasses, 1 lb flour.   1 cent each.

111. FRENCH SNAPS.

1 lb sugar, 1 lb butter, 1 lb flour, 6 eggs.

112. LAYER CAKES.*

2 lbs sugar, 2 lbs butter, 2 oz baking powder, 6 eggs, $1\frac{1}{2}$ pt water, 2 lbs flour, lemon oil; baked in layers, fill with cream or jelly, and ice over.

113. WHITE CAKES.*

3 lbs sugar, 1 lb butter, 2 oz baking powder, 24 whites of eggs, 1 qt water, 3 lbs flour, lemon oil; worked and baked like pound cakes, ice over when cool, and mark in 10 cents squares.

114. MARBLE CAKES.*

As above. $\frac{1}{4}$ of the dough color with chocolate, $\frac{1}{4}$ with cochineal, and $\frac{1}{2}$ keep white, first put a thin layer of the white all over the bottom, then with two spoons drop in the two mixtures alternately in such a manner as to form the desired combination.

115. JELLY CAKES.*

1 lb sugar, $\frac{1}{2}$ lb 1 oz baking powder, 6 eggs, $\frac{1}{2}$ pt milk, 1 lb flour; baked in layers, fill with jelly, ice or sprinkle cocoanut on top.

PART SECOND.

116. MIXING.

Always knead your butter and lard before using; always have your sugar and flour sifted; always have your ammonia good and fine; always put your flavors in the wet part of your mixtures; always be careful with scaling, as too much or too little of anything will spoil your cakes.

Now we are ready to mix.

First scale your butter, sugar and lard in the bowl and put ammonia into the mortar, pound and dissolve them, then mix your sugar and butter, add your eggs, work them through and put in your milk, ammonia and flavor, take the pallet-knife, scrape it altogether nicely, stir it up and mix in the flour easy; the less you work the dough the nicer the cakes. Take care that you don't work your dough too much on the bench, cut your cakes out close, and do not use too much flour for dusting. Molasses mixture gets handled about the same way, the only difference is, that you commence to mix with molasses and lard instead of butter and sugar.

By reading the recipes you will find that I did not mention any lard, flavors and spices; this is done to keep the book as small as possible, so that it will be in the reach of all.

Explanation of lard, flavors, spices and cotton seed oil.

In every recipe mentioned in this book you can use half lard in place of butter, also in the common cakes you can use cotton seed oil in place of lard; spices and flavors I leave to your own taste, and the name of the cake will tell you a good many times what flavor or spices to take; for lemon snaps take lemon; for ginger snaps take ginger; but cloves and allspices are very nice for molasses mixture; for vanilia jumbles take vanilla, etc., etc. All the recipes in this part must be mixed and worked as mentioned above.

117. GENUINE SCOTCH SHORT CAKE.*

2 lbs flour, 1 lb butter, ¼ lb lard, ½ lb sugar, mix into a very stiff dough, and bake in a very cool oven; this is the genuine scotch short cake recipe and only known by a very few bakers, always has been a great secret.

118. SCOTCH SHORT CAKES.

¾ lb sugar, 10 oz butter, 1½ lb flour, 3 eggs, little milk and ammonia. Cool oven.

119. SCOTCH SHORT CAKES.

¾ lb sugar, ¼ lb butter, 4 eggs, ⅙ oz ammonia, 1½ pt milk, 3 lbs flour. Very common.

120. SCOTCH CAKES.

1 lb sugar, 1½ lb butter, 4 eggs, 2¼ lbs flour, flavor. 10, 15, 25 cents each. Cool oven.

121. SUGAR CAKES.*

6 lbs sugar, 4 lbs butter, 3 oz ammonia, 3 pts milk 20 eggs, 12 lbs flour. Hot oven.

122. SUGAR CAKES.

4 lbs sugar, 3 lbs butter, 2 oz ammonia, 1 qt milk, 8 eggs, 8 lbs flour. 1 cent each. Hot oven.

123. SUGAR CAKES.

12 lbs sugar, 7½ lbs butter, 30 eggs, 6 oz ammonia, 3 qts milk, 24 lbs flour. Cut round, leaf and diamond shape.

124. SUGAR CAKFS.

2 lbs sugar, 1½ lb butter, 1 pt milk, 5 eggs, 1 oz ammonia, 2½ lbs flour. Granulated sugar on top.

125. SUGAR CAKES.

1½ lb sugar, ¾ lb butter, 4 eggs, ½ pt milk, ½ oz ammonia, 2½ lb flour.

126. SUGAR CAKES.*

2 lbs sugar, 1 lb butter, 1 oz ammonia, 7 eggs, ½ pt milk, 4 lbs flour.

127. SUGAR CAKES.

9 lbs sugar, 5 lbs lard, 18 eggs, 3 qts milk, 18 lbs flour, 6 oz ammonia

128. SUGAR CAKES.

lb sugar, ¾ lb butter, 4 eggs, ½ oz ammonia, ½ pt milk, 2 lbs flour.

129. SUGAR CAKES.

1½ lb sugar, 1 lb butter, 1 pt milk, 5 eggs, ½ oz ammonia, 3 lbs flour. Rich sugar cakes don't need any washing.

130. SUGAR CAKES.

1½ lb sugar, ½ lb butter, 4 eggs, 1 pt milk or water, ½ oz ammonia, 4 lbs flour.

131. SUGAR CAKES WITHOUT EGGS.

15 lbs sugar, 7½ lbs butter, 5 oz ammonia, 5 qts milk, 30 lbs flour. Wash with milk and egg and dip in sugar.

132. SUGAR CAKES WITHOUT EGGS.

12 lbs sugar, 4 lbs lard, 4 qts water, 5 oz ammonia, 24 lbs flour.

133. SHREWSBERRY.

1 lb sugar, 1 lb butter, 4 eggs, ½ pt milk, ½ oz ammonia, 2½ lbs flour.

134. SHREWSBERRY.

1 lb sugar, 1 lb butter, 4 eggs, ⅛ oz ammonia, ½ gill milk, 2¼ lbs flour.

135. ROCK CAKES.

1 lb sugar, ¾ lb butter, 4 eggs, ½ pt milk, ½ oz ammonia, 2½ lbs flour.

136. VANILLA JUMBLES.

5 lbs sugar, 4 lbs butter, 16 eggs, ⅓ oz ammonia, 7½ lbs flour, vanilla.

137. VANILLA JUMBLES.

2 lbs sugar, 1 lb butter, 6 eggs, 1/6 oz ammonia, 2¼ lbs flour. 1 cent each.

138. VANILLA JUMBLES.

10 oz sugar, ½ lb butter, ½ gill milk, ¼ oz ammonia, 4 eggs, 14 oz flour.

139. CINNAMON JUMBLES.

1½ lb brown sugar, 6 oz butter, 8 eggs, ⅓ oz soda, ⅔ oz cream of tartar, 2 lbs flour.

140. WAFER JUMBLES.

1 lb sugar, 1 lb butter, 1¼ lb flour, 6 eggs, flavor. 1 cent each.

141. WAFER JUMBLES.

2 lbs sugar, 2 lbs butter, 12 eggs, 3 lbs flour, flavor.

142. WAFER JUMBLES.

1¼ lb sugar, 1 lb butter, 3 eggs, 1 lb flour, flavor.

143. JUMBLES.

1½ lb sugar, 1¼ lb butter, 6 eggs, 3 lbs flour, 1 oz ammonia, 1 pt milk.

144. JUMBLES.

1 lb sugar, 14 oz butter, 5 eggs, ⅛ oz ammonia, ½ pt milk, 2⅛ lbs flour.

145. TEA BISCUIT.

3 lbs flour, 6 oz lard, 2 oz sugar, ½ oz soda, 1 oz cream of tartar, 1 qt milk, little salt.

146. TEA BISCUIT.

10 lbs flour, 1¼ lb lard, 2 oz soda, 4 oz cream of tartar, 3 qts milk, ¼ lb sugar, a pinch ammonia, little salt; mix well, and let them stand about 5 minutes before baking, hot oven. 1 cent each.

147. TEA BISCUIT.

3 lbs flour, 6 oz lard, ⅔ oz soda, 2 oz cream of tartar, 1 qt milk, salt. Mix well.

148. BAKING POWDER.

1 lb soda, 1 lb flour, 2 lbs cream of tartar, sift 3 times.

149. SPONGE CAKE.

1 lb sugar, 11 eggs, 1¼ lb flour, 1 oz of the above baking powder.

150. JELLY ROLL.

1 lb sugar, 1½ lb flour, 5 eggs, ½ pt milk, 1 oz baking powder.

151. JELLY ROLL.

1 lb sugar, 1½ lb flour, ⅓ oz soda, ⅔ oz cream of tartar, 5 eggs, ½ pt milk, mix, no beating. 10, 15 cents each.

152. CRULLERS.*

1 lb sugar, ¼ lb butter, ½ oz soda, 1 oz cream of tartar, 4 eggs, 1 qt milk, 4 lbs flour; this is the best paying recipe.

153. CRULLERS.

1¼ lb sugar, 6 oz butter, 6 eggs, 1 qt milk, ½ oz soda, 1 oz cream of tartar, 4 lbs flour, flavor.

154. CRULLERS.

1½ lb sugar, ¼ lb butter, ⅓ oz ammonia, ⅙ oz soda, ⅓ oz cream of tartar, 1 qt milk, 6 eggs, 4½ lbs flour. 1 cent each.

155. CRULLERS.

1 lb sugar, 6 oz butter, 6 eggs, ⅓ oz ammonia, 1 qt milk, 4 lbs flour.

156. CRULLERS.

3 lbs sugar, 1 lb butter, 20 eggs, 2 qts milk, 2 oz soda, 4 oz cream of tartar, 10 lbs flour.

157. CRULLERS.

1½ lb sugar, 6 oz butter, 8 eggs, ⅔ oz soda, 1⅓ oz cream of tartar, 1 qt milk, 5 lbs flour.

158. CRULLERS.

1 lb sugar, ½ lb butter, 6 eggs, ½ oz soda, 1 oz cream of tartar, 1 qt milk, 4 lbs flour.

159. SPONGE BISCUIT.

4 lbs sugar, 44 eggs, 6 lbs flour, 2 oz soda, 2 oz cream of tartar, flavor.   1 cent each.   Ice on bottom.

160. SPONGE BISCUIT.

1 lb sugar, 12 eggs, $\frac{1}{3}$ oz ammonia, 1 lb 6 oz flour, flavor.

161. SPONGE BISCUIT.

2 lbs sugar, 12 eggs, 1 qt milk, $1\frac{1}{2}$ oz ammonia, $3\frac{1}{2}$ lbs flour, flavor.   Ice on bottom.

162. SPONGE BISCUIT.

1 lb sugar, $1\frac{1}{4}$ lb flour, 10 eggs, $\frac{1}{3}$ oz soda, $\frac{1}{3}$ oz cream of tartar.

163. MOLASSES FRUIT CAKE.*

1 qt molasses, 1 qt water, 1 lb lard, 1 lb sugar, 5 lbs flour, 4 lbs raisins, 4 lbs currants, $\frac{1}{2}$ lb citron, $\frac{2}{3}$ oz soda, 2 oz spices; if the cake is 2 inches thick will bake about 2 hours, cool oven, never touch the cake until it is $1\frac{1}{2}$ hour in the oven.   Sold by the pound.

164. MOLASSES FRUIT CAKE.

1 qt molasses, $\frac{1}{2}$ lb sugar, 1 lb lard, $\frac{1}{2}$ oz soda, 1 qt water, 5 lbs flour, 4 lbs currants, 2 lbs raisins, $\frac{1}{2}$ lb citron, 3 eggs.

165. MOLASSES CAKES.

1 qt molasses, 1 qt water, $\frac{3}{4}$ lb lard, $\frac{3}{4}$ lb flour, 2 oz soda, 1 egg.

166. MOLASSES CAKES.

1 qt molasses, 1 qt water, $\frac{3}{4}$ lb lard, 2 oz soda, $3\frac{1}{2}$ lbs flour, 2 oz sugar, 4 eggs.

167. BOLIVARS.

1 qt molasses, 1 pt water, $\frac{3}{4}$ lb lard, 2 oz soda, 4 lbs flour, spices.   1 cent each.

168. BOLIVARS.

2 qt molasses, 1 qt water, 6 oz soda, 1 lb lard, 8 lbs flour, spices.

169. BOLIVARS.

1 qt molasses, $\frac{1}{4}$ lb lard, 2 oz soda, 1 pt water, $4\frac{1}{2}$ lbs flour, spices.

170. SUGAR BOLIVARS.

4 lbs sugar, 2 lbs lard, 3 oz ammonia, 2 qts milk, 8 lbs flour, flavor.

171. SUGAR CRACKERS.

10 lbs sugar, 3 lbs butter, 2 oz ammonia, 3 qts water, 12 lbs flour.

172. GINGER NUTS.*
2 qts molasses, 1 pt water, 4 oz soda, 2 lbs lard, 1 lb sugar 8 lbs flour.

173. GINGER NUTS.
2 qts molasses, 1 pt water, 4 oz soda, 7 lbs flour, $1\frac{1}{2}$ lb lard, spices.

174. GINGER NUTS.
2 qts molasses, 1 pt water, 4 oz soda, $1\frac{1}{2}$ lb lard, 8 lbs flour, $\frac{1}{2}$ lb sugar.

175. SPICE CAKES.
1 qt molasses, 1 qt water, $\frac{1}{4}$ lb lard, $\frac{1}{4}$ lb sugar, 1 lb crumbs, $2\frac{3}{4}$ lbs flour, $\frac{2}{3}$ oz soda, $1\frac{1}{3}$ oz cream of tartar, 3 eggs.

176. SPICE CAKES.*
$1\frac{1}{4}$ lb crumbs, $\frac{1}{2}$ lb lard, $\frac{1}{2}$ lb sugar, 7 eggs, 1 pt molasses, $\frac{1}{3}$ oz soda, $\frac{2}{3}$ oz cream of tartar, 1 pt water, $1\frac{1}{2}$ lb flour.

177. SPICE CAKES.
2 lbs crumbs, 1 pt molasses, $\frac{2}{3}$ oz soda, 1 pt water, $1\frac{1}{4}$ lb flour, $\frac{1}{2}$ lb sugar. Grease the tins heavy.

178. SPICE CAKES.
1 qt molasses, 1 pt water, 2 oz soda, $\frac{1}{2}$ lb crumbs, $\frac{3}{4}$ lb lard, 3 lbs flour, 1 egg; ice top with chocolate icing.

179. GINGER SNAPS.*
1 qt molasses, 1 pt water, 2 oz soda, 3 lbs sugar, 1 lb lard, $5\frac{1}{2}$ lbs flour; wash them with water.

180. GINGER SNAPS.
1 qt molasses, 1 pt water, $\frac{3}{4}$ lb lard, 2 oz soda, $\frac{1}{2}$ lb sugar, 4 lbs flour; bake as soon as washed.

181. GINGER SNAPS.
4 qt molasses, 1 qt water, $1\frac{1}{2}$ lb lard, 6 oz soda, 3 oz ammonia, 2 lb corn meal, 4 lbs sugar, 16 lbs flour, spices; washed with water; medium oven.

182. GINGER SNAPS.
1 qt molasses, $1\frac{1}{2}$ lb brown sugar, 2 lbs lard, $1\frac{1}{3}$ oz soda, $\frac{1}{2}$ pt water, 5 lbs flour, spices.

183. GINGER SNAPS.
1 qt molasses, 1 gill water, $\frac{1}{2}$ lb sugar, $\frac{1}{2}$ lb lard, 1 oz soda, $\frac{1}{2}$ oz ammonia, 2 lbs flour, spices.

184. GINGER SNAPS.
2 qts molasses, $1\frac{1}{2}$ pt water, $2\frac{1}{4}$ lb lard, 9 lbs flour, 3 lbs crumbs, 3 lbs sugar, $2\frac{1}{2}$ oz soda.

185. COMMON GINGER BREAD.*

1 qt molasses, 1 qt water, 1⅓ lb crumbs, ¾ lb lard, 1 oz soda, 1 oz cream of tartar, 4 lbs flour; put all the dough on a flat cake pan, put a stick on the open end, so it won't run off, have the pan greased heavy, spread the dough level about 1 inch thick, bake in moderate heat, ice with water icing, and mark the icing in penny squares.

186. GINGER BREAD.

1 qt molasses, ¾ lb lard, ½ lb sugar, 1⅓ oz soda, 1 qt water, 3½ lbs flour, 4 eggs.

187. GINGER BREAD.

1 qt molasses, ½ lb lard, 2 oz soda, 1 pt water, ½ lb sugar, 4½ lbs sugar, spices.

188. GINGER BREAD.

1 pt molasses, ½ pt water, 1 oz soda, 5 oz lard, 2 lbs flour, spices.

189. GINGER BREAD.

¾ pt molasses, ¾ pt water, 4 oz lard, 1 oz soda, 2 lbs flour, spices.

190. GINGER BREAD.

1 pt molasses, 1 pt water, 6 oz lard, 1 oz soda, 2 lbs 6 oz flour.

191. GINGER POUND CAKE.*

1 pt molasses, ½ lb lard, 1 oz soda, ½ lb sugar, ½ pt water, 5 eggs, 2½ lbs flour.

192. NEW YEARS CAKES.*

5 lbs sugar, 3 lbs butter, 1½ qt water, 1 oz ammonia, ⅔ oz soda, 2 oz caraway seed, 12 lbs flour; hot oven, wash with egg and water.

193. NEW YEARS CAKES.

5 lbs sugar, 3 lbs butter, 3 pts water, 2 oz ammonia, 2 oz caraway seed, 12 lbs flour; cut while warm, work the dough well.

194. NEW YEARS CAKES.'

¾ lb butter, 1¾ lb sugar, 6 oz lard, 1 pt water, ½ oz ammonia, ½ oz caraway seed, 4 lbs flour; break up the butter in the water and sugar, that is the rule for new years cakes.

195. NEW YEARS CAKES.

7 lbs sugar, 4 lbs butter, 2 qts water, 1¾ oz ammonia, 16 lbs flour.

196. NEW YEARS CAKES.

5 lbs sugar, 4 lbs butter, 1 oz ammonia, ⅓ oz soda, 1¼ qt water, 13 lbs flour.

197. LEMON SNAPS.*
5 lbs sugar, 2 lbs butter, 5 lbs flour, 15 eggs, 1 oz ammonia, lemon oil.

198. LEMON SNAPS.
12 lbs sugar, 14 lbs flour, 48 eggs, 3 oz ammonia, 4 lbs butter, lemon oil.

199. LEMON SNAPS.
$7\frac{1}{2}$ lbs sugar, 3 pts milk, $2\frac{1}{4}$ lbs lard, 8 lbs flour, 2 lbs orn meal, 2 oz ammonia.

200. LEMON SNAPS.
1 bbl flour, 60 lbs sugar, 30 lbs lard, 2 lbs ammonia, 24 qts water.

201. LEMON SNAPS.
$1\frac{1}{4}$ lb sugar, $\frac{1}{2}$ lb butter, 4 eggs, $\frac{1}{3}$ oz ammonia, $1\frac{1}{4}$ lb flour; open door and damper as soon as they done spreading.

202. LEMON SNAPS.
$2\frac{1}{2}$ lb sugar, $\frac{3}{4}$ lb butter, 10 eggs, $\frac{2}{3}$ oz soda, $1\frac{1}{4}$ cream of tartar, $2\frac{1}{2}$ lbs flour. Cool oven.

203. LEMON CRACKERS.
6 lbs sugar, $2\frac{1}{2}$ lbs lard, 1 oz ammonia, 2 qts water, 12 lbs flour. Moderate oven.

204. SUGAR CRACKERS.
1 lb sugar, $\frac{3}{4}$ lb butter, 3 lbs flour, $\frac{3}{4}$ qt milk, $\frac{1}{3}$ oz ammonia, $\frac{1}{6}$ oz soda.

205. BRANDY SNAPS.*
1 lb sugar, 1 lb butter, 1 lb flour, 1 pt molasses. Bake, cut loose and roll up on small rolling-pins while hot.

206. BRANDY SNAPS.
1 pt molasses, 1 lb sugar, lb butter, $1\frac{1}{4}$ lb flour. Roll them hot, same as above.

207. WINE SNAPS.
$\frac{3}{4}$ lb sugar, 8 eggs, $\frac{1}{3}$ lb flour. Work the same as brandy snaps.

208. COCOANUT BALLS.
4 lbs grated cocoanut, $1\frac{3}{4}$ lb sugar, 1 oz traganth gum.

209. COCOANUT BALLS.
1 lb grated cocoanut, $\frac{1}{2}$ lb sugar, 2 oz flour, 3 or 4 white of eggs.

210. MACAROONS.*
1 lb almond paste, $1\frac{1}{4}$ lb sugar, 1 oz corn meal, whites of eggs.

211. MACAROONS.

1 lb ground blanched almonds, 1½ lb sugar. Whites of eggs, enough to get the right thickness.

212. CINNAMON STARS.

1 lb sugar, 1 lb butter, 4 eggs, ½ pt milk, ½ oz ammonia, 2 lbs flour. Medium oven.

213. CINNAMON STARS.

1 lb sugar, 1 lb butter, 4 eggs, ⅓ oz soda, ⅔ oz cream of tartar, ⅛ pt milk, 2 lbs flour. Wash with milk and dip in coarse sugar.

214. FRENCH MACAROONS.

1 lb sugar, ¾ lb sweet ground blanched almonds, 5 eggs, 1 lb flour.

215. FRENCH GINGER NUTS.

1 qt molasses, 1 pt water, 5 eggs, 1 oz soda, 3 lbs crumbs, 4 lbs flour, 1 lb lard, 1 lb sugar. Wash with eggs and dip them in coarse sugar.

216. FRENCH GINGER NUTS.

2 lbs crumbs, 1½ sugar, 1 pt molasses, 2 eggs, 1 oz soda, ½ pt water, 2 lbs flour. Bake hot.

217. PIE PASTRY.

1 lb flour, ¾ lb butter, little sa.t and water for top.

218. PIE PASTRY.

1 lb flour, ¾ lb butter, little salt and water for top.

219. PUFF PASTE.

The common American formular is to use ½ pt water to each pound of flour and to each pound of flour 1 lb butter.

220. GERMAN PUFF PASTE.

Mix 1 lb of spring flour, 2 yolks, 1 whole egg, pony rum, ½ oz butter, ½ pt water to a smooth dough, form into a flat square and let it lay ½ hour in a cool place, now roll the dough ¼ inch thick, place 1 lb of good washed butter formed in a square in the centre, turn the dough over the butter from all sides, roll 1 inch thick and turn over again, then roll it 3 times more in the same manner, but give it 15 minutes rest between each roll. By rolling the paste always brush off your flour, cut the dough out very close and bake in hot oven. Out of this paste any kind of shapes can be made, such as squares, ovals, stars, turn overs, different kinds of tarts and a good many more, too numerous to mention.

If you want to have your paste not so rich, you can leave the yolks, eggs, and the rum, out of it, it will work just as well.

221. CREAM TARTS.

Cut out the size of a sugar cake in pie paste, put a ring around it from cream cake dough, after baked ice the ring with chocolate-icing and fill the centre with vanilla cream.

222. CREAM CAKES.

Before you start on this mixture you must have every thing in its place such as:

I. Have your eggs broke and put them near the bowl.
II. Have your ammonia powdered before you start.
III. Have your bag, pans and bowl clean and ready.
IV. Never take too much ammonia or they will not raise at all; a pinch to a qt is plenty.
V. Always have your lard melted before it comes to a boil.
VI. Let water and lard boil $\frac{1}{2}$ minute, stir in the spring flour, quick, until the paste gets loose from the sides, dump the whole in the bowl, add 1 egg and stir it into the paste; keep a stiring quick and add about 2 eggs every $\frac{1}{2}$ minute until the paste gets the right thickness, than mix in your ammonia and the paste is ready to bake in a hot oven. Wash with eggs before baking. The thickness of cream cake dough depends on the kind of eggs you are using; if eggs are fresh you can have the dough so soft, that it will run the least bit, if you are using lime eggs dough must be stiffer. A hollow bottom shows that your dough has been too soft, if the dough is too stiff they will not get hollow in the centre, too much ammonia or not scald enough will do the same thing. Pans ought to be greased light, no dusting. Cream cake wants a hot and steady oven. Never touch them until very near done.

ECLAIRS.

Keep the cream cake dough a little stiffer, lay them out with jumble bag and plain tube about 5 inches long and of a thickness of your large finger. Bake and fill same as cream cakes and ice them with chocolate-icing.

223. CREAM CAKES.*

$1\frac{1}{4}$ lb lard, $1\frac{1}{2}$ lb spring flour, about 25 eggs, 1 qt water, $\frac{1}{4}$ oz ammonia.

224. CREAM CAKES.

1 lb lard, 1 qt water, $1\frac{1}{4}$ lb flour, $\frac{1}{4}$ oz ammonia, about 24 eggs.

225. CREAM CAKES.

$1\frac{1}{2}$ lb lard, 2 lbs flour, 1 qt water, $\frac{1}{4}$ oz ammonia, about 32 eggs.

226. VANILLA CREAM.

Mix 1½ lb sugar; ¾ lb flour, 12 eggs to a paste and stir this into 3 qts of boiling milk quick.

227. VANILLA CREAM.

1 lb sugar, 8 eggs, 2 qts milk, 5 oz corn starch, vanilla.

228. VANILLA CREAM.

3 qts milk, 1½ lb sugar, 6 oz corn starch, 12 eggs.

229. DOUGHNUTS.

4 qts water, 4 qts milk, 4 oz soda, 8 oz cream of tartar, 1 lb lard, 5 lbs sugar, little salt. Add flour sufficient to make a dough stiff enough to roll and cut.

230. WINE BISCUIT.

1 lb sugar, 1 lb butter, 4 eggs, 2 lbs flour, 1/6 oz ammonia.

231. QUEENS DROPS.

1 lb sugar, 1 lb butter, 2 lbs flour, 10 eggs, 1/6 oz ammonia.

232. COLLET BUNS.

¾ lb sugar, 9 oz butter, 2 eggs, little milk, 4½ oz soda, ¼ tartaric acid, 2½ lbs flour, lay out like ginger nuts, wash with eggs, dip in granulated sugar, lay a slice of citron on top and bake hot.

233. CREDITION BUNS.

1 lb sugar, 6 oz butter, 2 eggs, little milk, 1½ lb flour, ½ ammonia, wash as above mentioned, cocoanut on top in place of sugar.

234. AFRICANS.

1⅓ lb sugar, 1 lb butter, 8 eggs, 2½ lbs flour 1/6 oz. ammonia.

235. LEMON DROPS.

2 lbs flour, ½ lb butter, 2 lbs sugar, 6 eggs 1/6 oz. ammonia.

236. SCONES.*

4 lbs flour, 1 lb butter, 1 lb sugar, 2 oz. soda, 4 oz. cream of tartar, 1¼ pt. milk.

237. SCONES.

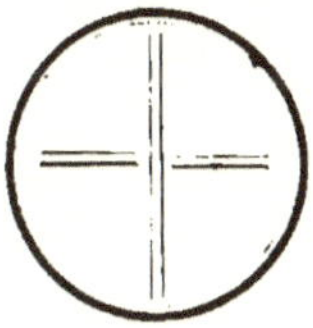

4 lbs flour, ½ lb butter, ½ sugar, 1 pt, milk, 1⅓ oz. soda, 2⅔ oz cream of tartar, work the dough well and quick, scale off 1 lb pieces, mould them round, roll ½ inch thick, cut crossways, wash with eggs, let them stand ½ hour and bake hot.

238. BATH BUNS.

3 lbs flour. 1 lb butter, 1 lb sugar, 1 lb raisins 6 oz citron, 1½ lb bread dough.

239. JUMBLES.

5 lbs sugar, 3 lbs butter, 12 eggs, 1½ oz ammonia, 12 lbs flour, milk to make a nice dough.

240. PUFF PASTE.

1 lb flour, 1 yolk, ½ pt water, 1 lb butter, roll 4 to 5 times. 15 minutes rest between each roll.

241. CINNAMON STAR.

1 lb sugar, 1 lb butter, 4 eggs, ½ pt milk, ½ oz ammonia, 2 lbs flour, flavor.

242. COCOANUT FINGERS.*

1½ lb sugar. 1 lb butter, 4 eggs, little milk, 3 lbs flour, ½ oz ammonia; cut out oval like sugar cake, wash with milk, dip in cocoanut, and bake in medium heat.

243. LEMON FINGERS.

2 qts water, 1½ oz ammonia, 8 lbs granulated sugar, 18 lbs flour, 2 lbs lard.

244. LEMON FINGERS.

2 qts water, 1½ oz ammonia, 8 lbs powdered sugar, 18 lbs flour, 2 lbs butter.

245. GOLDEN DROPS.

12 lbs flour, 1 lb butter, 5 lbs sugar, 1¼ qt milk, 1 oz ammonia, flavor.

246. GINGER JUMBLES.

1 lb lard, 1 lb sugar, 6 eggs, 1 pt water, 1 oz soda, 1 qt molasses, 4 lbs flour.

247. PRINCE ALBERT

1 lb sugar, 6 oz butter, 5 eggs, ¼ oz ammonia, 2 lbs flour, citron in the centre.

248. CANTONES.

1 lb sugar, 1 lb butter, 8 eggs, ½ oz ammonia, 2 lbs flour, dip in coarse sugar and bake.

249. DOMESTIC CAKES.

1 lb sugar, ½ lb butter, ¼ lb lard, ¾ pt milk, ¼ oz ammonia, 5 eggs, 2½ lbs flour; cut out with square cutter, set close together, ¼ inch thick.

250. DOMESTIC CAKES.

4 lbs sugar, 2 lbs butter, 18 eggs, 1½ oz ammonia, 1 qt milk, 5½ lbs flour as above, cut after baked.

251. SHREWSBERRY.

2 lbs sugar, 2 lbs butter, 4 lbs flour, 24 eggs, ¼ oz ammonia.

252. LEMON SNAPS.

½ oz ammonia, ¼ pt water, 16 eggs, 6½ lbs flour, 4½ lbs sugar, 2½ lbs butter; cut them out like ginger snaps.

253. DIPS.

½ lb butter, 1 lb sugar, 4 eggs, ½ pt milk, ½ oz ammonia, 2⅛ lbs flour.

254. CANTONES.

2 lbs sugar, 2 lbs butter, 16 eggs, ½ oz ammonia, 4 lbs flour, coarse sugar on top.

255. QUEEN CAKES.

9 lbs flour, 2 oz ammonia, 1 qt milk, 16 eggs, 2½ lb butter, 4 lbs sugar, flavor.

256. SCONES BAKED ON THE OVEN BOTTOM.

9½ lbs flour, ½ lb sugar, ½ lb lard, 2 oz soda, 5 oz cream of tartar, 3 qts milk.

257. SANTA CLAUS.*

3 lbs flour, 2 lbs sugar, 1 lb butter, ⅓ oz soda or potash, little milk. Can be cut in all shapes and figures.

258. SANTA CLAUS.

10 lbs sugar, 13½ lbs flour, 4 lbs butter, ½ oz soda, flavor, milk as above.

259. LEMON SNAPS.

2½ lbs sugar, ¾ lb butter, 10 eggs, ⅔ oz soda, 1¼ oz cream of tartar, 2½ lbs flour.

260. JELLY ROLL.

2 lbs sugar, 3 lbs flour, 12 eggs, 1 oz soda, 2 oz cream of tartar, 1 qt milk; 3 sheets.

261. SPICE RINGS.

2 lbs stale cakes, powdered, ½ lb sugar. 2 oz butter, 6 eggs, ½ pt molasses, 1 lb flour, ½ oz ammonia.

262. PUMPERNICLE.*

2 lbs stale cakes, powdered, 2 lbs sugar, 3 lbs flour, 12 eggs, ⅓ oz ammonia, spices, wash over with eggs.

263. CHOCOLATE RINGS.*

1 lb sugar, 2 oz butter, 4 eggs, ¼ lb grated chocolate, 1 lb flour, ⅙ oz ammonia, vanilla.

264. COCOANUT PYRAMIDS.*

1 lb grated cocoanut, ½ lb sugar, a little corn starch, and whites of eggs enough to make a medium dough, form the dough into small pyramids and bake hot.

265. NAPOLEONS.*

Bake a thin sheet of puff paste, cut it in two, spread vanilla cream over the one, and lay the other half on top, ice with water icing, and cut to suit.

266. CHOCOLATE BESES.*

2 lbs sugar, 6 whites of eggs, ¼ lb chocolate, set on fire, keep stirring until it is quite warm, take off, and put all little drops on a dusted pan, let them dry 1½ hour, and bake cool.

267. NEAPOLITAN CAKE.*

Make a sponge cake mixture, divide it into 4 parts, leave one part plain, and color the others, one pink, one yellow, one chocolate, bake in sheets 1 inch thick, after baking put the 4 layers together with jelly and cocoanut, ice the cake pink and white in strips, and mark the cake with the pallet knife cross ways.

268. BISQUE CAKE.*

1¼ lb sugar, 1 lb butter, 1¼ pt white of eggs, ½ lb powdered macaroons, almond flavor; baked like pound cake, and iced when cool.

269. BRAZIL MOLASSES CAKES.*

Make a good molasses cake mixture, add a few brazil nuts and figs, cut in lenghts, mix and bake.

270. FRENCH CRULLERS.*

This mixture is made the same way as cream cake, boil ½ lb butter with 1 pt water, and stir in ¾ lb flour, add about 10 to 12 eggs, mix it up good, now fill your jumble bag with star tube, and cut about 2 or 3 papers the size of cruller pot, grease the paper, put round rings on to it, take the paper, turn it upside down, and put it in your boiling cruller grease, you can take the paper out in less then a minute, and bake the same as crullers, in this way you continue until done.

271. COCOANUT CAKE.*

Take 1 lb sweet almonds, blanched and dried, pound them in a stone mortar to a fine smooth paste with the whites of 8 eggs; then add and pound into it 3 lbs of fine white pulverized sugar; now mix and stir well into it 1 lb of freshly-grated cocoanut, form this mixture with the hands into small balls or steeples, place them at a little distance apart on sheets of paper laid on baking tins. Bake them in a moderate oven. As soon as the tops begin to brown take them from the oven and let them stand till cold. These are a most delicious little cocoanut cake, suitable to go with the best assortment of mixed cakes for parties.

272. CINNAMON DROPS.*

$1\frac{1}{4}$ lb sugar, 6 oz butter, 1 pt molasses, 1 pt water, 4 eggs, $\frac{1}{2}$ soda, $\frac{1}{2}$ oz cinnamon, $2\frac{1}{2}$ lb flour, mix and drop with a spoon on greased pans; medium oven.

273. ITALIAN FRUIT DROPS.*

3 lbs C sugar, $\frac{3}{4}$ lb butter, $\frac{1}{2}$ oz almonds, 9 eggs, $1\frac{1}{2}$ lb chopped raisins, $3\frac{1}{2}$ lbs flour, $\frac{1}{3}$ oz cinnamon; handle and bake like ginger nuts.

274. CRUMB CAKES.*

2 lbs C sugar, 1 lb butter, 1 lb lard, 2 oz soda, 1 oz cinnamon, 4 eggs, 1 qt molasses, $\frac{1}{2}$ pt water, 3 lbs crumbs, $4\frac{1}{2}$ lb flour, work as above and put a raisin in centre of cake.

275. LEMON CAKES*.

2 lbs C sugar, $\frac{3}{4}$ lbs butter, $\frac{1}{2}$ almond, 6 eggs, 2 lbs flour, lemon oil, cut out like sugar cakes, and wash with eggs.

276. BRANDY SNAPS.*

2 lbs C sugar, 6 oz butter, 1 pt molasses, 2 lbs flour, lay out like ginger nuts, they spread very thin, roll up while hot.

277. SPICE CAKES.*

$\frac{1}{2}$ lb sugar, $\frac{1}{2}$ lb lard, 4 eggs, 1 pt molasses, $\frac{1}{2}$ pt water, $3\frac{1}{2}$ lbs flour, spices.

278. FRENCH CRULLERS.

$\frac{1}{2}$ butter, 2 oz sugar, 1 pt water, 1 lb flour, 14 eggs, work the same as above.

279. FRENCH CRULLERS.

$\frac{1}{4}$ lb butter, $\frac{1}{3}$ lb sugar, $\frac{3}{4}$ pt water, 1 lb flour, 10 to 12 eggs, the same as above.

280. FRENCH CRULLERS.

$\frac{1}{2}$ lb butter, 2 oz sugar, $\frac{3}{8}$ qt water or milk, 10 oz flour, about 6 eggs.

281. GOLD CAKE.*

1 lb sugar, $\frac{1}{2}$ lb butter, 8 yolks, $\frac{1}{2}$ pt milk $1\frac{1}{2}$ flour, 1 oz baking powder, mix and bake in pans in slow heat.

282. CREAM ROLLS.*

Roll out puff paste to the thickness of one-eighth of an inch, then cut in pieces four inches wide and five inches long, and wash them with water. Now take turned sticks, perfectly round and about 6 inches long, and $\frac{3}{4}$ of an inch thick; lap your paste (the four inch side) round it up to one inch. Now dip or roll it in granulated sugar and place them at about 4 inches apart on baking-pans. Bake well, then remove the sticks and fill the rolls with meringue so as to look out at both ends. This can be done nicely by means of a large meringue bag. They are now ready for use.

283. CREAM ROLLS.*

Cut long strips, about one inch wide and 12 inches long, wind them around turned sticks, lap over a little and work as above.

284. VANILLA SLICES.*

Take a sheet of puff-paste and roll down to $\frac{3}{4}$ inch in thickness, cut off slips 4 inches wide, and then cut up into pieces $\frac{1}{2}$ inch wide, that will give you slips 4 inches long, $\frac{1}{2}$ inch wide. Set then on tins, the cut side down, and bake. Instead of rising up they will flow out wide. Bake a very pale color.

285. TURN OVERS.*

May be cut out in square ovals or rounds, roll them with a rolling pin a little thinner in centre, fill with marmalade, turn over, wash with eggs and bake hot.

286. PUFF PASTE TARTS.*

Cut out in puff paste the size of sugar cake, then cut out another one, and cut with an smaller cutter a 1 inch hole in the centre, wash the first one with water and lay the one with the hole in centre on top, wash with eggs, bake hot and fill with jelly of different colors, they also can be filled with meringue, vanilla-cream and charlotte russe batter.

287. PATTIES OR TARTS.*

Tarts are, however, usually made by lining small patty-pans with the pastry rolled out thin, and filling them with any kind of marmalade or stewed fruit, such as cranberries, strawberries, cherries, apricots, peaches, &c.

PART III.

288. BEATING.

All the recipes in this part must be worked as follows: The principal thing in beating is to keep your tools very clean, and keep away from grease, beat steadily without stops, and do not always beat one way, change hands if you can. The whites of eggs for meringue or kisses should be beaten steadily. After they are beaten up stiff add 1 table spoon of your XXXX sugar and beat up again, put in another spoon full of sugar, and now beat all you can until it sticks up like pickets, put in the rest of your sugar, mix as little as you possible can help, now it is ready to lay out, in case the whites should not beat very well, add a few drops of lemon juice or acided acid. The right way to beat is to start very slow and keep increasing your speed until done. White of eggs, if kept for a day or two in a clean basin, are the best for meringue or icings.

289. MERINGUE WORK.

Pieces in meringue are easy of execution for any one familiar with the use of the cornet, but you cannot expect to make with meringue such complicated and regular pieces as with icing sugar; moreover the styles differ essentially and a difference is necessary between them, for they are not required for the same purpose. Pieces in meringue may be decorated like other pieces; but are executed in detached parts; that is, each piece is made separate with the cornet on buttered or floured baking pans, the drawing being sketched on the surface of the pan, with the point of a pencil, and from a pattern. When all the details are done the meringue is baked in a very moderate oven, but not allowed to get brown; the pieces are removed with care, and put together with icing, and decorated with roses, leaves, flowers, etc.

290. JENNY LIND.

Bake a thin sheet of pound cake, lady or sponge cake, or the following recipe can be used also: ¾ lb sugar, ¾ lb butter, 8 eggs, 1 lb flour, pinch ground mace, a few drops oil of lemon, ½ oz ammonia; rub sugar, butter and flavor light, as for pound cake; then the eggs in the same way.

Dissolve the ammonia in a tablespoonful of milk, and stir in with the flour lightly to make a soft batter; spread the mixture evenly on a papered sheet pan and bake in a moderate oven. Cut into slices as long as the cake may be; let the slices be three inches wide, which will be 4 pieces to the pan, spread a little currant jelly on the cake. Now beat up 20 white of eggs, and while beating add a little sugar now and then to give a body to the foam; take the sugar that you add from the 2 lbs, let this be icing sugar, then mix all in slowly with a spaddle; then lay out on these slices, with a a bag and star tube, 6 rows as long as the cake, then 5 rows, then 4 rows; next put 3, and continue in this manner until you have it tapered to an edge, and have the batter about 2 inches high. Let this sheet be on a pan on paper, then do the same to the other 3 pieces; sift over some fine sugar and put into a cool oven to let it get brown on top; take out, and when it has stood five minutes, cut these slices across, so that each piece will be only 1½ inches one way and 3 inches the other.

291. MERINGUE.

1 lb XXXX sugar, 1 pt white of eggs, 2 drops of acided acid.

292. KISSES.

1 lb XXXX sugar, 8 whites, 2 drops acided acid.

293. COCOANUT KISSES.

The above mixture laid out through a star tube in round rings, on dusted pans, sprinkle some desiccated cocoanut on top and bake cool.

294. MERINGUE TARTS.*

Lay out 24 fancy cake pans with rich pie paste, put a little marmalade in centre; after baked, decorate the tarts with meringue and bake again.

295. MERINGUE PIES.

Cover the plates with pie paste, fill them with lemon cream; after baked cover the whole pie with meringue and decorate.

296. ALMOND SACKS.

1 lb XXXX sugar, 8 whites, ½ lb chopped almonds, 2 oz flour, 3 oz chopped citron, little cinnamon.

297. TARTLETS MERINGUE.

Lay out 20 small rosette pans with pie paste, put a little marmalade into them, after baked fill them up with meringue, sprinkle some desiccated cocoanut on top and bake again.

298. ANGEL CAKES.*
1 qt whites, 1¾ lb sugar, 1¼ flour, ½ oz cream of tartar.

299. ANGEL FOOD.
1½ pt whites, 1½ lb sugar, 1 lb flour, 1 oz cream of tartar.

300. ANGEL CAKES.
1 qt whites, 2 lbs sugar, 1 lb flour, 1 oz cream of tartar.

301. LADY CAKE.
1½ sugar, 1 lb butter, rub to a cream, beat up 20 whites, ⅕ oz soda, ⅓ oz cream of tartar, 1¾ lb flour.

302. LADY FINGERS.
1 lb sugar, 12 eggs beat warm, 1 lb 2 oz flour, little soda and cream of tartar.

303. LADY CAKE.
1¼ lb butter, 1½ lb sugar, 22 whites, 1½ lb flour, almond.

304. LADY CAKE.
1½ lb sugar, 1 lb butter, 24 whites, 1½ lb flour, flavor.

305. LADY OR MARBLE CAKE.
3¾ lbs sugar, 3 lbs butter, 1½ pt whites, 4 lbs flour, divided in 3 parts, 1 part color with chocolate, 1 with cochenille and one plain; form the desired combination with spoon or bag.

306. ANGEL FOOD.*
Beat 20 whites of eggs with ½ oz cream of tartar to a stiff snow, add 12 oz sugar, little at the time, flavor with vanilla and mix in 7 oz flour lightly.

307. WHITE CAKE.*
Cream, 1½ lb sugar, 1¼ lb butter, and beat up 18 whites to a stiff snow, then mix it altogether with 1½ lb flour lightly, medium oven.

308. BRIDES CAKE.*
1½ lb sugar, 1 lb butter, 15 whites, ½ gill brandy, 1¼ lb flour; work and bake as above.

309. SPONGE CAKES.*
1 lb sugar, 12 eggs, beat warm, 1 lb flour, flavor.

310. SPONGE CAKES.
1 lb sugar, 12 eggs, beat warm, 1¼ lb flour, ⅓ oz baking powder.

311. SPONGE BISCUIT.
1 lb sugar, 10 eggs, 1 lb 2 oz flour, ⅙ oz ammonia.

312. CHARLOTTE RUSSE.*

Lay out the cups with sponge cake, then dissolve 1 oz gelatine and weigh ½ lb XXXX sugar, now beat up 1 qt sweet cream, add the sugar, gelatine and vanilla, mix easy and fill the cups.

313. CHARLOTTE RUSSE.

10 whites, 1 qt sweet cream, ½ lb XXXX sugar, ½ oz gelatine.

314. CHARLOTTE RUSSE.

1 qt sweet cream, ¼ lb XXXX sugar, ½ oz gelatine, vanilla.

315. ANISE DROPS.

1 lb sugar, 8 eggs, 1 lb flour, beat warm, lay out like sponge biscuit, let them stand 3 hours and bake in a cool oven.

316. SPANISH MACAROONS.

3 lbs XXXX sugar, 6 whites, beat up, mix, roll out ¼ inch thick, cut them out, let them stand ½ hour and bake in a cool oven, ice when cold. If you want to make red spanish macaroons add a little cochenille, if brown, add grated chocolate.

317. VANILLA ZWIEBACK.

Beat up 1 lb sugar, 9 eggs, skin of 2 lemons, and add 1 lb flour, form 2 long rolls on a dusted pan; when baked, ice with water icing, sprinkle some granulated sugar on top and cut to suit.

318. TO TEST EGGS.

In order to be certain that your eggs are good and fresh, put them in water; if the butts turn up, they are not fresh.

319. FANCY CAKES.

(See Designs.)

No. I.—For the moulded pieces, avoid the crust parts of trimmings. Now pass a desired quantity through a fairly coarse sieve, say quarter-inch mesh. Heat some strawberry, raspberry, or pineapple syrup, or boil some apple juice, as for apple jelly, only not quite so strong, and saturate your crumbs slightly, using about 1 pt of liquid to about 2 lbs of crumbs, over which may have been previously sprinkled a little brandy, rum, maraschino or some other fancy cordial. By all means, don't work your combination too much, lest you turn it into a pasty substance, which would be unfit for use; simply get it so that it practically takes form when worked into shape.

320.

No. II.—Soak 2 lbs of crumbs with ½ pt of sherry, 1 gill of rose or orange-flower water, and one cup of milk or cream.

Next, stir 2 lbs of sugar, 1¾ lb of butter, creamed; gradually add 18 whites of eggs and 8 yolks; beat the whites of the eggs to a stiff froth; add a pinch of mace, a pinch of ground cardamom, half a teaspoonful of cinnamon, and a little lemon or orange juice; then add the soaked crumbs, and, last, 1½ lb flour. This is for a sheet cake, to be cut up. Into a part of it may be put a proportionate quantity of melted chocolate, or some may be tinted a light red.

321.

No. III.—JUMBLE CAKE.—Grind ½ lb of roasted almonds with one cup of milk; add a good pinch of soda. Now pass 1 lb of crumbs through a *coarse flour* sieve. Next, stir 1 lb of sugar, 14 oz of butter, creamed; gradually add 18 yolks. Now add your ground almonds, next 1¼ lb flour, and, last, the fine crumbs.

322.

No. IV.—Take 3 lbs of sugar, 3 lbs of butter, 4 lbs of flour, 3½ lbs of crumbs, 1 pt of molasses or honey, ½ pt of milk, ½ pt of brandy or rum, 1½ pt of yolks, 1 teaspoonful of cloves, 2 teaspoonfuls of allspice, 3 teaspoonfuls of cinnamon, 2 grated nutmegs, and ½ teaspoonful of soda. Soak the crumbs about half an hour before using with the milk, rum and molasses, also, mix in the yolks. Stir the butter and sugar light, add the crumbs, and, last, the flour. If desirable, 1 lb of browned and ground almonds can be added to this mixture, which will tend to improve its flavor very much. This dough should be placed in a cool place for some time before using it.

323.

A RICH NUT FILLING.—Grind in a mortar 1 lb of walnuts, ½ lb of almonds, with 1½ pt of milk or cream; add 1½ lb of sugar and a glass of rum or brandy. Now take this and roast it, stirring constantly over the fire until it gets to a stout paste, then put aside to cool for future use. Filberts, chestnuts and roasted almonds may be done in the same way. When too stout, thin down with syrup or cordial.

324.

The pieces numbered from 1 to 10 (see design) are of composition No. I. They are moulded by hand about the size of a pigeon's egg, so that about 12 to 15 goes to a pound when done; into each is put a small quantity of some kind of jelly or marmalade, or some nutfilling, like, for instance, the chestnut potato and croquette. Fondant icing is the best kind of material to coat these with.

325.

Nos. 1, 2, 3 (see design) are done in vanilla; when dry, tint one side of them a little with dry carmine and starch mixture, applied with a small ball of cotton wadding; insert a whole clove into the blossom side of apple and pear, and a stem cut from orange peel or citron; for the peach the frosting may be a little light yellow.

326.

No. 4.—Strawberry; use a bright red icing flavored with strawberry juice; the bud and stem for this fruit can be bought from any supply firm for $1 a 1,000. The chestnut is filled with nut filling and coated with chocolate frosting of a light shade; when dry, brush the end over with syrup, and dip into a mixture of ground chocolate and powdered sugar. For the carrot the icing should be of an orange color; the greens may be drawn with a small leaf tube, of very stiff green royal icing.

327.

No 7.—The potato; instead of frosting, coat it with thin, warm macaroon paste, applied very sparingly; then roll it into the ground chocolate and sugar dust; then insert here and there sprouts which are cut from fresh blanched almonds.

328.

Frost No. 8 with a yellow lemon or pineapple frosting.

329.

No. 9.—Fill with orange marmalade and coat with a light pistachio icing of a light green shade; insert a stem.

330.

No. 10.—Fill with a nut filling; coat it with currant or apricot jelly, and roll into lightly-browned and crushed macaroon dust. This will give it a perfect appearance of a croquette.

331.

Nos. 11 and 12 are made from the sheet mixture No. II set together with jelly, and cut out with a cutter or knife, and each frosted over individually and garnished in an appropriate shape.

332.

No. 13.—Either model top part from first mixture, or use the second recipe, and bake it in small Madelein moulds; then fill with jelly and set upon bottoms which have been baked separately; cut out with an oval cutter from following recipe:

333.

No. VI.—Mix 1 lb sugar with $1\frac{3}{4}$ lb well-washed butter, not very light; add 12 yolks, $\frac{1}{2}$ cup milk, pinch of bicarbonate soda, pinch of cinnamon, pinch of nutmeg, and pinch of ground cardamom; now incorporate 3 lbs of flour; don't work your dough too much, but set it in a cool place a good while before using. This serves as an excellent bottom part for similar small cakes.

334.

Finish No. 13 by frosting it with a nice coffee frosting; sprinkle over each a pinch of browned and chopped almonds.

335.

No. 14 —Dress these cakes up from mixture No. III with a lady-finger tube, on greased and floured baking tins; wash over with egg with a soft brush, and sprinkle either with shreded almonds or pignolia nuts; bake in a warm oven; when taken out dust with sugar dredger.

336.

No. 15.—Take a half inch sheet of No. II mixture, fill with raspberry marmalade, cut in strips 1½ inch wide, and set on the edges ⅛ inch thick marzipan strips or rollable macaroon paste, which is then ribbed with a paste pincer; then shove these strips in a hot oven so as to lightly brown the marzipan, which is then gummed over with a brush, and the inner space is filled out with tart lemon juice icing, which should be quite stiff.

337.

No. 16.—Between two thin, white layers of mixture No. II a filling similar to No. I is put in, only the crumbs are supposed to be from dark fruit or wedding cake, with a small share of crushed macaroons and walnuts; put this under pressure for one or two hours; then cut these into narrow strips; frost with a raspberry frosting, and garnish with a red cherry and two sprays of almonds or angelique.

338.

No. 17.—Cut out and bake some scalloped bottoms from mixture No. VI. Put some kind of nut filling on it, mount it with a disc of the light sheet and cap it with a small macaroon, and frost the whole with a very thin but lukewarm vanilla icing. Decorate with a small red icing top and a silver bead.

339.

No. 18.—Cut ¾ or ½ inch strips of three different colored sheets of No. II mixture; coat one side of them lightly with currant jelly and set them together as indicated. Now roll out a sheet of marzipan or macaroon paste, converted to similar material; coat the four surfaces of cake also with a thin layer of jelly, and envelope it with the marzipan; now cut small squares, ½ inch in thickness, and frost over the surface with a thin coat af maraschino frosting.

340.

No. 19.—Form little pyramids of composition No. I. Frost these with pistachio icing, sprinkle over with even-chopped almonds or filberts. Now bake on thin bottoms, of mixture No. VI, rings dressed with small lady-finger tube of mixture No. III. Sprinkle these over with granulated sugar and bake in a pretty warm oven. When done, place a little nut· filling into the centre of each and mount with the pistachio-iced pyramids.

341.

Nos. 20 to 25 are made of mixture No. IV, rolled out about ¼ of an inch thick, washed over, when cut with the respective cutters, with egg, and either dusted with granulated sugar or fine-chopped almonds, or trimmed up with half almonds and round discs of citron. Desiccated cocoanut is a handy substitute for almonds. A dent may be made in some with the point of the finger, into which is put a little raspberry preserves, which is baked with the cakes.

342.

Nos. 26 to 30.—These cakes are all baked on bottoms made of mixture No. VI. No. 26 and 29 are made in long strips, and cut to suitable size after being baked. Mixture No. III is forced through medium star tube, either with aid of a bag or the regular jumble machine. The creases are then filled out, as well as the interior, of individual cakes, with some kind of jelly and fancy frosting, and garnished up a little, as shown in sketch.

343.

The recipes for these cakes may puzzle some a little, but after a fair trial they will prove themselves a valuable acquisiton both from an economical and palatable point of view. A little hitch is always experienced with every new recipe, and it greatly depends on the practical knowledge of the nature of the stock to be handled. If things don't exactly turn out as you desire, stop and think where the fault may lie, and whether an improvement can be made by adding or leaving out something. Perseverance is the greatest conqueror of all seeming obstacles or temporary mishaps. If you are gratified with your own success in what you undertake, you certainly reap your merits from your employer; or, if you are in business, from the patrons of your establishment.

PART IV.

344. PIE BAKING.

Apple Pie, Peach Pie, Rhubarb Pie, Cherry Pie, Gooseberry Pie, Raspberry Pie, Currant Pie, Grape Pie, Cranberry Pie, Orange Pie, Quince Pie, Raisin Pie, Cocoanut Pie, Sweet Potato Pie, Pine Apple Pie, Pumpkin Pie, Rice Pie, Custard Pie, Lemon Pie, Mince, and many others.

To explain every kind of pie to you would make this book too expensive, I will therefore explain them to you in general.

Pies can be made of either green, dried or evaporated fruits. Pies made out of green fruit generally run out in the oven, it is therefore better to stew green fruit before using. Take sugar and flavor to suit your taste.

345. DRIED FRUIT.

Dried or evaporated fruits boil soft in some water, add sugar and flavor to suit.

346. MINCE MEAT.

3 lbs currants, ½ lb suet, 4 lbs apples, 6 lbs beef, cook mutton, beef and suet, 1½ lb sugar, 2 lbs raisins, ¼ pt brandy, 1 pt cider, 2 oz allspice, 2 oz cloves; all meats for mince ought to be cooked.

347. LENTEN MINCE PIES.

1 lb hard boiled whites of eggs, 1½ apples, peeled, 1 lb raisins, 1 lb currants, ¼ lb sugar, ⅔ lb orange, citron and lemon peel, ½ oz mace, ½ oz cloves, ¼ oz nutmegs, 1 pt brandy, juice of 6 oranges.

348. MINCE MEAT.

5 lbs beef, 1 lb suet, 11 lbs apples, 3 lbs currants, 3 lbs raisins, ¼ lb citron, 5 lbs sugar, 1 qt molasses, 1 pt brandy, 1 oz cloves, 1 oz allspice, ½ oz pepper.

349. MINCE MEAT.

24 lbs currants, 12 lbs sugar, 12 lbs suet, 12 lbs tripe, 4 lbs citron, 2 lbs lemon peel, 2 oz orange peel, 16 lbs apples, 4 lbs sultanas, 6 oz spices, 1 oz ammonia, 2 oz nutmeg, 1 pt brandy, skin and juice of 12 lemons.

350. MINCE MEAT.

1 lbs soupmeat, 2 pecks apples, 1 lb suet, 1½ lb citron, 5 lbs raisins, 5 lbs currants, 4 lbs sugar, 3 oz cinnamon, 2 oz cloves, 1 pt brandy, cider.

351. OYSTER PIE.

1 qt oysters, dry measure, add 1 pt milk, cook 5 minutes, then add 3 oz cracker dust, ¼ oz pepper, little sage; fill the pies, cover and bake.

352. LEMON CREAM.

Boil 1 qt water with ¾ lb sugar, and mix 2½ oz corn starch, 4 yolks and stir this in the boiling sugar, take off the fire quick and mix in skin and juice of 2 lemons and 1 oz of butter.

353. CANNED FRUITS.

How to make a good apple pie from canned apples.— Put the apples, juice and all into a bowl or pail; put in a little salt; then put in a flavor mixture of mace and cinnamon,—one third mace and two-thirds cinnamon; sugar to taste, and you have a pie as good as if made of green apples.

All canned pie-fruit needs salt, as salt brings back and restores the flavor lost in canning and from age.

Plum and peach pies are improved by adding a little cinnamon.

Rhubarb should be boiled with sugar before using.

354. LEMON PIE FILLING.

1¼ lb sugar, 4 oz flour, 4 eggs, 1 qt water, 4 lemons.

355. LEMON PIE FILLING.

10 qts water, 8 lbs sugar, 20 eggs, 25 lemons, 1½ lb corn starch.

356. LEMON PIE FILLING.*

7 qts water, 5 lbs sugar, 1 lb corn starch, ½ lb lard, ½ lb butter, lemons and eggs to suit your taste.

357. LEMON PIE FILLING.

5 lbs sugar, 10 eggs, 10 oz corn starch, ¼ lb butter, 5 qts water, skin and juice of 16 lemons.

358. CUSTARD

1 lb sugar, 18 eggs, ¼ flour, 4 qts milk, salt.

359. CUSTARD.

5¼ lbs sugar, 4 qts eggs, 20 qts milk, 1¼ lb corn starch, salt.

360. CUSTARD.*

1½ lb sugar, 36 eggs, 8 qts milk, ½ lb corn starch, salt.

361. CUSTARD.

1 lb sugar, 15 eggs, 2 qts milk, 2 oz flour, salt.

PART V.

362. HINTS ABOUT ICING AND GLAZING.

I.   Use china or enamelled bowls to make icing.

II. Have spatula dry, and bowl very clean.

III. Never use whites or gelatine icing unless it is beaten up well.

IV. Always keep a damp cloth on top of your icing bowl.

V.   Do not keep icings in the bake shop.

VI. Always sift your XXXX sugar through a clean sieve on paper.

VII. Cakes iced on a board can not be moved onto another board until finished and dried.

VIII. Use as little colors as possible on cakes; light shades is the latest.

IX. Do not fasten gum paste ornaments, put them on when dry.

X.   Piping must not be covered with ornaments.

XI. Always put a lace paper under large cakes.

XII, My ornamenting machine stands at the head.

363. TWO COLORS.

Ornamenting with two colors is done by putting the colored icing with a small knife on one side of the bag or machine and the white on the other, always put more white than colored icing into your bag; for very small writing or ornamenting use ornamenting paper with no tubes at all; to make a paper bag cut a piece as shown in cut and start to roll up on corner No. 1, after all is rolled up turn corner No. 2 over to the inside of the bag and the bag will not unroll any more, and so is ready for use by filling, closing and cutting point to suit. A piece of ornamenting paper 6 by 12 inches will make two bags by cutting crossways like cut.

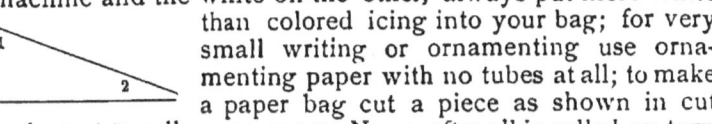

364. WATER ICING.

Water icing is simply XXXX sugar and water, this icing can be colored and flavored with most any kind of flavor.

365. ORNAMENTING ICING.

Is nothing but XXXX sugar, beat up with some whites of eggs and a few drops of acided acid or lemon juice.

366. ICING FOR CAKE.

Is the same as above, only not quite as thick; all icing made out of whites of eggs ought to be beat up well, as it makes it whiter and will not run. The proportion for a good icing are about 4 whites to every pound of sugar.

367. CHEAP ICING.

4 oz gelatine dissolved in 1 qt of warm water, when all melted skim it off, put in XXXX sugar and $\frac{1}{4}$ oz alaun, to make a nice icing beat well with spatula, common glue will answer as well as gelatine.

368. CHOCOLATE ICING.

$\frac{1}{2}$ lb chocolate, $\frac{1}{2}$ pt water, set in a warm place until melted, then mix in XXXX sugar, enough to get the right thickness.

369. CHEAP CHOCOLATE ICING.

5 pounds of your best cocoa, to which add from $1\frac{1}{2}$ to 2 pounds of cocoa butter, and enough well dried and sifted lozenge sugar to make it to the consistency you require. You may also use a heavy chocolate fondant to cover with.

370. TRANSPARENT ICING.

1 pound pulverized white sugar, $\frac{1}{2}$ pt water. Boil to the consistency of mucilage, rub the sugar with a wooden spatula against the sides of the pan until it assumes a white, milky appearance, stir in two table spoons extract vanilla, mix well together; pour while hot over the top of the cake, so as to completely cover it.

371. CHOCOLATE ICING.

Stir into white or royal icing, when ready for use, chocolate that has been melted over the fire; stir in a sufficient quantity to give the required color, at the same time moisten it with the whites of eggs.

372. BOILED CHOCOLATE ICING.

Put 1 pt hot water onto $\frac{1}{2}$ pt chocolate, add 1 lb sugar, stir it up and let it boil about 10 minutes, take a spatula and keep a rubbing on the sides of your pan to cause granulation.

373. BOILED CHOCOLATE ICING.

Melt 1 lb chocolate in a vessel, add $\frac{1}{2}$ pt of warm strong syrup, stir it up, and it is ready for use. All boiled chocolate icing must be applied while hot.

374. BOILED ICING.

Boil 2 lbs sugar, 1 pt water to a hard ball, beat up 12 whites stiff and pour the boiling sugar onto the whites in a long gentle stream, stir the whites while you are pouring in the sugar.

375. ORNAMENTING BUTTER OR LARD.

Mix 1 oz corn starch with 1 lb butter, work it well without softening the butter more than is needed. This kind of work ought to be done in a cool place. It is used to ornament hams, tongues, pork, &c.; some confectioners cream the butter before using.

376. HOW TO ICE LARGE CAKES.

Brush all the crumbs off of the cake to be iced, then give a thin coat of well beat up whites of eggs icing, and set aside to dry, when dry give it a second coat, have the thickness of your icing that it will run *very* slow, if the icing is well prepared this will give a smooth, glossy surface. In very particular cases, when a level surface is needed, run a plain tube of icing around the edge of the cake and cover the cake with thin icing level with the rim and let it run smooth, and dry a little in the oven. But for wedding or bride cakes the icing ought to be as stiff as ornamenting icing, after you get your cake on the rotation stand, take spatula and cover the cake all over with icing, then take a large size pointed table knife, keep your right hand holding the knife steady, and use the left hand for rotation. The sides of a wedding cake ought to be piped and ornamented, but for any other kind of cakes you can put a printed or silver band around it; colored tissue paper looks very nice, and saves a good deal of work, wedding cakes must not be dried in the oven.

377. CONFECTIONERS PASTE.

1 lb flour, $\frac{1}{2}$ lb sugar, and whites enough to make a stiff moulding dough; this dough can be formed in any shape that is needed; let it dry, and bake in a cool oven.

PART VI.

378. JELLY.

For this recipe $500.00 was paid.

Boil 4 lbs gelatine with 11 qts water, put in 31 lbs white sugar, ¼ oz tartaric acid, and 2 oz fruit extract; boil 4 minutes, and it is ready to fill in your pails or tumblers, let it stand 12 hours, put a piece of paper, which is soaked in rum, on the top, and close them up tight; for coloring use colors which you will find on another page of this book. This jelly is nice, clear, cheap, and will keep for years.

COLORS.

379. COCHINEAL.

1 oz powdered cochineal, 2 oz cream of tartar, 1 oz burnt alum, 1 pt boiling rain water, 1 oz tartaric acid; strain it.

380. BLUE.

For sugar boiling take indigo, for icings take ultramarine or blue carmine.

381. ANALINE COLORS.

The beautiful analine colors, though much employed, are considered objectionable by many. The intensity of their color is so great however, that the quantity necessary to produce any injurious effect would not be likely to be introduced. For extracting the colors from these dyes, dissolve them with boiling water or alcohol; use with care, as one or two drops are sufficient to color a small boiling of sugar.

382. YELLOW.

Saffran, curcume, and yellow carmine.

383. BROWN.

Burnt sugar or sugar color you will find on another page.

384. GREEN.

Juice of spinach, all the rest of the colors you can get by mixing the above, as black and red makes brown, red and yellow makes orange, yellow and blue makes green, black and white makes gray, red and blue makes purple, yellow and white makes cream, red and white pink, etc.

385. HOW TO MAKE COLORED SUGAR.

Put some sugar in the oven, after it is warm take it out, and put a few drops of cochineal, analine or carmine solution into it, and rub and sift it until it is dry; do just the same with any other color. For such work have your color pretty thick.

386. ABOUT BREAD.

If bread be the staff of life it should be made so well and of such good material that it shall be healthful and strenght-giving.

From the first dawn of civilization to the present time some kind of bread has been made by mankind. One would think that, with a practice and experience of so many hundred years, perfection would now be reached and there would be no need of instructing the present or future generation. But although bread-making has reached perfection in the hands of thousands, there are still thousands, and there always will be, who must have the methods of good bread-making made plain to them.

Perfect bread will be light and sweet, and with a rich, nutty flavor of the wheat. To get this result good yeast and flour must be used; the dough, while rising, must be kept at a proper temperature, about 75^0 F., and the heat of the oven, when baking the dough, must be high enough to raise the inside of the loaf to about 220^0 F. This is necessary to cook the starch, expand the carbonic acid gas, air and steam, and drive off the alcohol.

A good way to test the heat is to put in a piece of white paper. If it turns a dark brown in five minutes the oven is of the right temperature, but if it burns, the oven is too hot and must be cooled a little before the loaf is put in; or, if the paper is only a light brown at the end of the five minutes the oven must be made hotter.

387. LONDON SNOW-FLAKE STOCK YEAST RECIPE

Prepare $2\frac{1}{4}$ oz hops and 4 oz malt, boiled in 12 qts of water 20 minutes.

Take 1 lb of corn meal, $1\frac{3}{4}$ lb wheat flour, $\frac{1}{2}$ lb rye flour, $\frac{1}{4}$ lb rice flour, $1\frac{1}{2}$ lb sugar, 4 oz ginger, $\frac{1}{2}$ oz soda, 2 oz salt, put in a jar or tub, and pour enough of the scalding hop and malt liquor on it to make a stiff batter. Beat it well, then pour the remainder of the liquor on, and dissolve all together. Let it stand until you can bear your hand in it,* then stock away with 1 qt of stock yeast. Let it work 24 hours before using. Make it every three days. To each 10 qts of ferment use 1 qt of this stock. For a 4 bucket batch, to stay your sponge, use 1 lb of salt in setting it. To bring it quicker use the same amount of sugar in place of salt. *In summer let stand until cool, then stock.

388. THE CELEBRATED DRY HOP YEAST.

This yeast when once made will keep for six months. Take 3 gallons of water and boil; when at the boiling point put in 3 oz of fresh hops; have ready in a jar or small yeast tub 1½ lb of wheat flour and 1 lb corn meal; now add sufficient boiling hop water to form a rather stiff paste; now, in order to keep 3 gallons of water in your boiler, you must make up for what you have taken out; keep on boiling hops until they sink to the bottom, then strain on top of your paste, stir well and set aside to cool; when cooled off ½ hour put in 4 oz malt and 1 lb A sugar; when cooled down to eighty-five or ninety degrees add 1 qt fresh stock yeast and let stand 24 hours; when ready strain through a hair sieve, and with this yeast you set a stiff sponge, (flour only); let this sponge ripen well, when ready add 1 oz soda and enough corn meal to form the whole into little stiff rivels or lumps, now put all in your flour sieve and sieve out all surplus corn meal; then spread out on boards covered with clean towels, and let them dry in the shade. This yeast is equal to Fleischmann & Co.'s compressed yeast, but will keep good for months and months in a dry place. You can either use it to stock away hop yeast or ferment.

DIRECTIONS FOR HOP OR MALT YEAST.—Boil the stock yeast as usual, and when ready to stock away add ¼ oz of dry yeast to every gallon of hop water; let stand until it works itself clear on top.

DIRECTIONS FOR FERMENT.—Boil and make as usual; to every gallon of ferment add ½ oz of dry yeast, stir well, cover up tight; in 10 or 12 hours it will be ready to use.

NOTICE.—Always dissolve your dry yeast in a little lukewarm water for storing away yeast or ferment. In managing this dry yeast the season of the year and weather has something to do with it

389. GLYCERINE BREAD.

Take a good mixture of flour, say 1 bbl, take 5 galls of ferment yeast, set a sponge very soft and let it stand 4 or 5 hours; when it bubbles on top, take 4 galls of luke-warm water dissolve 1½ lb salt in it, 4 lbs lard and about 4 or 5 lbs pulverized sugar, which makes a great improvement in the weight. Take 1 lb of the glycerine and melt it over the fire; after it is melted, pour it into the mixture, make a nice easy dough, and let proof; after it has proofed work it as much as you can, have a pair of rollers and break it through two or three times, and you will find it becomes white; mould in any shape desired. It is baked in box-shape, only a little narrower than the box and scroll on the sides, being round at the ends, same as Boston cream bread moulds. It can be baked in ordinary bread pans.

390. THE CROLL SYSTEM OF BREAD BAKING.

To make 250 lbs of flour into bread. I use three nine-quart pails of ferment and five pails of water, and a little over 4 lbs of salt. I have my flour sifted in one end of the trough, and mix the liquor, salt and ferment well together in the other end, and make the dough straight off. After the dough is made two hours, I throw it out on the table, and if it has slackened out, I stiffen it out a little with flour; then roll it up in liftable pieces and put it back in the trough for two hours more; it is then ready for the scales. Scale it off any weight to suit your trade, mould it up round, give it a little proof; now make it up into any shape you like, and give it sufficient proof and bake it in a good steady heat. I leave purchasers to figure up their own proportions of ferment, salt and water, to suit the extent of their business.

391. STOCK YEAST-LIQUID.

Prepare 3 oz hop and 8 oz malt, to which add $5\frac{1}{2}$ lbs of potatoes and 10 qts water. Boil until potatoes are thoroughly cooked.

Put in a jar or tub $1\frac{1}{2}$ lb corn meal, $1\frac{1}{2}$ lb flour, $\frac{1}{4}$ lb sugar, and pour on enough of the scalding liquor from the hops, potatoes, etc., to make a stiff batter, and then pour the remainder of the liquor, with the hops, potatoes, etc., into the tub, and then dissolve all together. Then add enough water to make 9 or 10 quarts of the whole. When sufficiently cool, stock away with 1 qt of good stock yeast. Let it work 24 hours. When ready add $\frac{3}{4}$ of a teaspoonful of ammonia, and same amount of salt.

392. STOCK YEAST-DRY.

Then make your dry stock yeast, using 1 flour to 2 corn meal. Having strained the yeast, pour on and work it as dry and stiff as you can conveniently, spreading it loosely and turning it frequently on table covered with cloths, drying as quickly as possible in cool, open air. When done put in sacks for a few days, and then in stone jars.

393. HOW TO MAKE THE FERMENT.

To make 20 quarts of ferment, put in a kettle 8 lbs potatoes, add water enough to cover them well, then take your tub and put 8 oz malt and 2 lbs good flour in it. When you have boiled your potatoes 30 minutes, then scald the flour and malt and beat well. Let stand for about 10 minu·es, then add 12 qts cold water, and then stock away with 8 oz of Dry Stock Yeast, or 1 qt of good ferment or Liquid Stock Yeast. Set in a cool place and the ferment will be ready for use in from 7 to 9 hours. In summer use one teaspoonful liquid ammonia to each pail of ferment.

394. HOW TO MAKE THE BREAD.

Sieve your flour and go to work in the ordinary way to set sponge. Use 30 qts of ferment to each barrel of flour, and 3 lbs salt dissolved in 40 qts of water. After having poured both water and yeast in the trough, draw the board, set aside and mix in the flour at once, and make a nice smooth dough, not too stiff, but *work it well*. Let it stand about two hours and work down again. Let it stand another hour and then cut it over, work in flour and lighten up well, leaving it smooth and nice. Let it stand another hour and get fully as light as other dough. Then work down and throw on table, cut, mould and put in the pans, and in the usual time your bread will be ready to go in the oven, and you will have nice, sweet bread, and can't very well help it. I expect and hope you will be well pleased, and write me a hearty recommendation of the same, which would be highly appreciated by me.

The above method is practiced in my bakeries, and is quite satisfactory to me, and also to my employes, being less laborious. Make a nice tough dough at once, let it stand about four hours, then lighten it up well, throw out on the table and mould and pan at once.

395. HOW TO GIVE EIGHTEEN OUNCES OF BREAD FOR THE SAME PRICE AS OTHERS SELL SIXTEEN FOR.

This is something not generally known by bakers, and yet it is correct, and no doubt it has been done by a few that have had the knowledge. Should you wish to accomplish the above result which I cannot disapprove of, as there is nothing to injure the health of anyone, but I do not advise anyone to adopt it. I give you the information, for perhaps you have been deceived by others that have the knowledge, and you have been compelled to give as big a loaf as they are and you being the loser thereby. Yet, as far as anyone can understand, they cannot do this, thinking they are not wronging the public, for selling that pure free gift of heaven's, water, is unjust. The following will show how it is done: Take four pounds of rice—common broken rice will suit—add to it as much water as it will soak; add the same when well soaked to one barrel flour. You will find that you will gain from twenty to twenty-five pounds of dough to the barrel than if you used flour alone; add the boiled rice to the dough; mix in well-made strong yeast; potatoes will suit if you have not the rice, as good boiled potatoes are nearly starch and can be used instead of rice. The bread is perfectly wholesome made; in this way more or less may be added. First try one pound of rice to the barrel; increase as you may desire.

396. BEST METHOD OF MAKING FERMENT.*

For the ferment take one pail of good patotoes, washed clean, boil in enough water so they will be covered when done; then empty them, water and all, into the yeast tub, and immediately pour in about six pounds of flour and stir well with the paddle, forming a thick paste; beat it well, then thin gradually by first adding a very little water at a time.

When finished there should be about four or five pails of ferment, leaving it the proper temperature, according to the weather.

For stocking this, use one pint of snow flake yeast, and in about ten hours, or as soon as it begins to fall, it is ready.

For setting the sponge, use about 4 pails of this ferment, ½ pound of salt, and 1 pound of sugar; make the sponge just thick enough so it will drop from the hand when held up, and so it will come up in 2 hours. As soon as it begins to fall it is ready.

To mix the dough add about 2 pails of water, 2 lbs of salt, 3 or 4 lbs of sugar, and 3½ lbs of melted lard. Mix into a medium dough; work well for ½ hour. This dough ought to come and be ready to scale in 1 hour, and the dough in the pans ought to come in the same time.

A baker must use his own judgement at what time to take the dough, as no definite rule can be given.

397. FINE BREAD WITHOUT FERMENT.*

For 1 lb of flour take 10 qts potatoes well done, pour off the water, work well, and run through a strainer in the trough, add 40 qts warm water, ½ lb salt, 1 lb sugar, 1 qt of the genuine snow flake yeast and set a medium stiff sponge, which will stand from 8 to 10 hours. When it begins to fall it is ready; to mix the dough add 20 qts water, 2 lbs salt, 3 lbs sugar and 3 lbs melted lard. This dough ought to come up in 1 hour, then knock it down and turn it over, let it come up again, now it is ready to scale, mould and bake.

398. MALT STOCK YEAST.

Take 12 qts soft water, 3 oz of hops, ¾ lb malt, put your malt in a sieve and shake the fine part through on a piece of paper and lay away, throw the coarse part into the kettle with the hops, let boil ½ hour, put 3 lbs best wheat flour in the tub and pour enough of your scalding liquid on to make a medium paste, beat well. When done, pour 3 pts hop water on top and set away to get cold, when cold put the fine malt on the paper into the paste, break up well with your hands, stock away with 1 pt of good stock, let work 10 or 12 hours, when you see it begin to fall strain in the rest of hop and malt liquid, stir well, set away to work. It will work from 36 to 40 hours. Put your paste together cold, so it does not work too fast. When done working set away in a cool, dry place. To make ferment take a reasonable amount of potatoes, 3 lbs flour to every bucket of water, do not scald the flour, (you can make bread without setting a sponge). Make a dough at once, let lay 3 hours, cut over, let lay 1½ hour, if light, pan at once, to start a Begin-Yeast put a hand full of paste and some hop-water in a glass jar, set in a warm place to let work, it will make you a new yeast in 2 or 3 days.

399. LONDON STOCK YEAST.

Boil ¾ lb hops with 20 qts water about 10 minutes, let it get milk-warm, put in 7 lbs of malt, stir and rub the malt with the hop-water, stock away with 1 qt of good yeast, set t in a dry place, in about 24 hours strain the yeast and it is ready for use; most of the London bakers are using the hops twice by adding new hops to every batch.

400. AMERICAN PLAIN YEAST.*

Boil ½ lb hops with 3 qts water 10 minutes, scald 3½ lbs spring flour with 4 qts of the hop water, beat well, strain the rest of your hop water on top of the paste, when lukewarm, add 3 pts of malt, stir and break it up good and stock away with 3 qts of yeast, keep in a dry place and it is ready for use in 24 hours.

401. GENUINE SNOW FLAKE YEAST.

Boil 10 qts nicely pared potatoes in enough water so they will be covered when done, at the same time boil ½ lb hops in 4 qts water. When the patotoes are done empty them, water and all, into a yeast tub, and immediately add 12 lbs flour, stir it briskly with the paddle. Also have the hop-water ready, boiling hot, and add enough of it to get the flour all well scalded, and to form a paste that will not run from the tub if turned bottom up, beat the paste about 20 minutes, reboil the hops in about 3 pts water, and set aside, then put the paste in a warm place for 9 hours, now it is ready to stock away, dissolve 14 cakes of yeast foam in the 3 pts hop-water and stir into the paste; in 4 hours it begins to work, stir down as soon as it comes up, stir it down again, always stir it down before it falls itself, in 10 hours it will be about done working, remove in a cool place until next day, it is now ready for use. This yeast will keep 6 weeks if kept in a large stone jar, stir it up from the bottom every time it is used. This recipe is worth a $100 to any baker on earth, it can be used with or without ferment.

402. COMPRESSED YEAST.

Set a upright sponge out of ½ lb compressed yeast and 20 qts of warm water, in 5 or 6 hours the sponge will be ready; let it go down only once, put 10 qts of warm water and 1½ lb salt on top, and make a nice smooth dough; have your trough greased, and let the dough come up twice, then it is ready for moulding; do not give it too much proof in the steam box, and bake in steady heat.

403. MILK ROLLS.

Take 20 lbs of the above sponge, 1 lb sugar, 1 lb butter and lard, little salt and flour.

404. BUNS AND RUSKS.

Take 12 lbs of the sponge, 1 lb sugar, 1 lb butter, salt.

405. DOUGH NUTS.

8 lbs sponge, 1 lb butter, ½ lb sugar, 4 eggs, salt, and flavor, and flour to make a nice soft dough.

408. CAESAR BUNS.

2 lbs flour, ½ lb butter, ½ lb sugar, ¼ lb currants, 1 oz cream of tartar, ½ oz carbonate of soda, 3 eggs, milk, essence lemon. Sieve the soda, cream of tartar, and flour well together upon the bench. Make a bay, put in butter, sugar, and currants, add few drops essence. Break in the eggs and work into a fine dough with milk. Lay out on to clean greased tins in thirty penny buns, dust over with sugar and bake in a warm oven. Sell at 1 cent each.

PART VIII.

407. EGG PRESERVING.*

This recipe has been thoroughly tested and proved to be the best yet discovered.—It has been brought into competition with most others at agricultural exhibitions abroad and in this country and has invariably triumphed.

To 30 gallons of soft water add 13 lbs unslacked white lime and 5 lbs salt. Stir it well each hour or two for one day. Then let it settle. Then dip off all that is clear. Now take 8 oz borax, 3 oz bi-carbonate soda, 8 oz cream of tartar and 8 oz salpetre. Pulverize these well, mix them thoroughly and dissolve in 2 gallons of *boiling water*, and pour it into the clear lime water you have dipped off. This will fill a coal oil barrel a little over half full. *Now be sure your eggs are fresh.* It does not *improve a bad egg one bit* to be preserved. Fill the barrels up within 4 inches of the top with eggs, and be sure that there is from 2 to 3 inches of the liquid above the eggs.

A coal oil barrel will hold about 150 dozen eggs. When you get the barrel full, spread an old cloth on top of the eggs, and cover the cloth an inch or more with lime settlings that were left in the barrel after dipping the water off. Do not have the cloth hung over the top of barrel or it will cause the pickle to run out. Do not use the pickle but once, but make a fresh pickle for each barrel of eggs. After the eggs have been in pickle for thirty days examine them. Keep them in a *dry, cool* place. Be particular to have *pure drugs* to make your pickle. Buy an egg tester (I will send you one for 50 cents), and examine every egg *particulary* before preserving. Any that are not *strictly fresh* mark immediately. You can sell them for at least as much as you paid for them. Then *preserve the fresh ones.* Do not put in any cracked eggs, as they will spoil. To clean coal oil barrels burn them out, fill with water and let soak several days.

The lime must be of the finest quality, free from sand and dirt—lime that will slack white, fine and clean. Have the salt clean, and the water pure and sweet, free from all vegetable or decomposed matter.

Slack the lime with a portion of the water, then add the balance of the water, the salt and other elements. Stir well three or four times at intervals, and then let it stand until well settled and cold. Either dip or draw off the the clear pickle into the cask or vat in which it is intended to preserve the eggs. When the cask or vat is filled to a depth of 15 to 18 inches, begin to put in the eggs, and when they lie, say about one foot deep, spread around over them some pickle that is a little milky in appearance, made so by stirring up some of the very light lime particles that settle last, and continue doing this as each lot of eggs is added. The object in doing this is to have the fine particles drawn into the pores of the shells, as they will be by a kind of inductive process, and thereby completely seal the eggs. Care should be taken not to get too much of the lime in; that is not enough to settle and stick to the shell of the eggs, and render them difficult to clean when taken out.

The chief cause of thin, watery whites in limed eggs is that they are not properly sealed in the manner described. Another case is the putting into the pickle old stale eggs that have thin, weak whites. When the eggs are within 4 inches of the top of the cask or vat, cover it with factory cloth, and spread on two or three inches of the lime that settles in making the pickle, and it is cf the greatest importance that the pickle be kept over this lime. A tin basin (holding about 6 or 8 dozen eggs) punched quite full of inch holes, edge muffled with leather, and a suitable handle about 3 feet long attached, will be found convenient for putting the eggs into the pickle. Fill the basin with eggs, put both under the pickle and turn the eggs out ; they go to the bottom without breaking.

When the time comes to market the eggs they must be taken out of the pickle, cleaned, dried and packed. To clean them, secure half of a molasses hogshead, or something like it, fill the same half full of water. Have a sufficient number of crates the right size (to hold 20 or 25 dozen eggs) made of lath or other slats, placed about a ¼ of an inch apart. Sink one of these crates into the half hogshead, take the basin used to put the eggs into the pickle, dip the eggs by raising it up and down in the water, and if necessary to properly clean them set the crate up and douse water over the eggs ; then if any egg are found, when packing, that the lime has not been fully removed from, they should be set out and all the lime cleaned before packing. When the eggs are carefully washed, they can be set out in a suitable place to dry, in the crates. They should dry quickly, and be packed as soon as dry. In packing the same rules should be observed as in packing fresh eggs.

408. EGG PRESERVING.

Germans take 1 lb of fresh slacked lime to 100 eggs, pile your eggs in a strong barrel broad side down, and pour only the clear lime water on top of the eggs so it will stand one inch above the eggs, then put a heavy piece of paper on top, and lay the thick lime that settled down on top of the paper; from time to time add fresh lime water, so that you always keep one inch above the eggs. These eggs will keep one year or more.

409. AMERICAN EGG PRESERVING.

To each patent pail full of water add 2 lbs of fresh slacked lime and 1 lb of salt, mix well. Fill your barrel half full with this fluid, put your eggs down in it any time; after June always keep the fluid one inch over the eggs.

410. MY OWN INVENTION.*

Put ¼ lb salycillic acid and 2 lbs powdered sulphur into an empty barrel, add 10 gallons of water, stir well, then deposit the eggs in the prepared water, and so continue to add eggs and water until the barrel is full, then cover the surface of the water with ½ inch depth of cotton seed oil; these eggs you can bake, boil or fry, and they taste like fresh ones.

PART IX.

411. FLAVORING EXTRACTS.

The following proportions of oils and alcohol make a better extract than can be obtained from most of the preparations manufactured for sale. Bakers, confectioners and families will find it to their interest to manufacture their own extracts from these recipes.

412. VANILLA EXTRACT.

2 oz vanilla beans, 6 oz alcohol, 4 oz water; cut and pound the beans, put the whole in a glass bottle, let it stand 2 or 3 weeks, shake it up once in a while, and it is ready for use.

413. CHEAP VANILLA EXTRACT.

4 oz vanilla, 1 lb tonka beans, 2 qt alcohol, 1 pt water.

414. EXTRACT OF ANISE.

1 oz anise oil, 1 pt alcohol.

415. EXTRACT OF CLOVES.

2 oz oil of cloves, 1 pt alcohol.

416. EXTRACT OF CINNAMON.

1 oz ceylon oil, 1 pt alcohol.

417. EXTRACT OF BITTER ALMONDS.

2 oz oil of bitter almonds, 1 pt alcohol.

418. EXTRACT OF CAPRISUM.

4 oz powdered cayenne pepper, 1 pt alcohol.

419. EXTRACT OF GINGER.

8 oz green Jamaica ginger, 1 pt alcohol; let stand one month, then filter and use.

420. EXTRACT OF SARSAPARILLA.

2 oz oil of sassafras, 2 oz oil of wintergreen, 1 pt alcohol.

421. EXTRACT OF LEMON.

2 oz oil of lemon, the best, 1 pt alcohol, mix and use.

422. EXTRACT OF PEPPERMINT.

2 oz oil of peppermint, 1 pt alcohol, mix and use.

423. EXTRACT OF WINTERGREEN.

1 oz oil of wintergreen, 1 qt alcohol, mix and use.

PART X.

ICE CREAM.

Put 2 lbs sugar, 4 eggs and vanilla in a clean kettle, stir together well with an egg beater, and add 4 qts of cream, place it on the fire, and stir constantly until it is about to boil, then take it from the fire and strain it through a hair sieve into an earthen crock, let it stand till cool and pour it into the freezing-can already imbedded in broken ice and salt, cover and turn the crank slow and steadily until it can not be turned any longer, open the can and remove the dasher. Scrape the hardened cream from the sides with a long handled spatula, then beat and work the cream until smooth. Close the can, draw off the water and repack with fresh ice and salt, and let rest for an hour or two to harden.

Ice cream is often made from fresh unscalded cream beaten with force during the entire freezing process, which makes it very light and snowy. It also increases considerably in quantity (recipes you will find below). Another kind of ice cream (called Hokey-Pokey) which you can buy on the New York streets from the sons of sunny Italy, I would like to mention: Dissolve 2 oz gelatine in $\frac{1}{2}$ pt milk or water, then 4 qts of milk and 8 eggs slightly beaten, add $1\frac{1}{2}$ lb sugar, little salt and the yellow rind of 2 lemons, put the ingredients into a clean kettle, set on the fire and stir till it begins to thicken, then remove quickly, and pour it into an earthen crock and continue to stir it till nearly cool. Then add your gelatine and pour the whole into the freezer, and freeze like other ices.

424. ICE CREAM.

6 qts cream, $1\frac{1}{2}$ lb sugar, vanilla flavor; no boiling.

425. ICE CREAM.

6 qts cream, $1\frac{1}{2}$ lb sugar, 1 pt glucose, flavor; no boiling.

426. CHOCOLATE ICE CREAM.

6 qts cream, 2 lbs sugar, $\frac{1}{2}$ lb chocolate; no boiling.

427. LEMON ICE CREAM.

6 qts cream, 2 lbs sugar, 4 lemons; no boiling.

428. RASPBERRY AND STRAWBERRY ICE CREAM.

6 qts cream, $1\frac{1}{2}$ lb sugar, 1 qt berries; no boiling. Put the ripe berries in a flannel bag, add a little sugar, and hang the bag on a nail; put a basin under to catch the juice.

429. CHEAP ICE CREAM.

5 qts milk, $1\frac{1}{2}$ lb sugar, $\frac{1}{2}$ lb corn starch; dissolve the starch in 1 qt milk, then mix altogether, stir it and let it come close to a boil; flavor to suit.

430. ICE CREAM.

Put 4 eggs, 8 yolks, $\frac{3}{4}$ lb sugar, 1 qt milk on the fire, beat it well, but do not let it come to a boil; strain and freeze, flavor to suit your taste.

PART II.

SYRUPS FOR SODA WATER.

13 lbs granulated sugar, 1 gallon water, boil about 5 minutes, the froth of the white of an egg mixed with it adds to its clearness, skim off, strain through a piece of flannel while hot and add 1 pt of glucose; keep it in a cool place.

431. RASPBERRY SYRUP.

The combination press will press the juice out of the berries very nicely and can be bought at any hardware store. To each gallon of juice add 13 lbs sugar, dissolve it by gentle heat, not to exceed 125 degrees, bottle while warm and cork for future use. Mix $\frac{1}{2}$ oz acetic acid in 3 oz water and add to each gallon of juice before bottling.

432. STRAWBERRY SYRUP.

Same as above.

433. PINEAPPLE SYRUP.

As above.

434. SARSAPARILLA SYRUP.

Add 20 drops of wintergreen and sassafras oils in a wineglass full of alcohol, color the syrup with burnt sugar or extract of licorice.

435. CREAM SYRUP

Reduce the condensed milk to the consistency of cream by adding a little water, then add an equal quantity of simple syrup.

436. CHOCOLATE SYRUP.

Melt $\frac{1}{2}$ lb chocolate and stir 2 qts of syrup through it, ready for use.

437. FOAM ON SODA WATER.

In order to create a foam that will stand on soda water when drawn from the fountain all you have to do is to incorporate with the syrup a certain proportion of dissolved gum arabic. 1 oz of gum dissolved and added to 1 gallon of syrup will be found amply sufficient for the purpose.

Bi-carbonate of soda is useful and harmless in preventing cream from souring for a day or two, especially if the cream is kept on ice or in cold spring water.

PART XII.

438. GUM PASTE

Gum paste or traganth is the stuff from wn.ch all beautiful cake ornaments are made, in this country it is a trade by itself, and we have quite a number of large factories in this kind of business, I will give you an idea how they make it:

Soak 2 oz of traganth gum in 1 pt of water for 36 hours, then press through a piece of cloth, put it into a large stone macaroon mortar, have everything very clean, then go to work and rub about ½ hour, put in 2 oz of xxxx sugar and rub again, then put in another 2 oz of xxxx sugar and rub until it feels dry and looks very white, then put it into a stone jar, and it is ready for future use.

This kind of work needs a little practice. The moulds you can buy in almost any baker tool supply house, but a good workman makes his own moulds, as the most of them are made of plaster-paris, sulphur or lead. After you have your moulds ready take a small piece of dough out of the jar, stiffen it with ⅓ oz corn starch and ⅔ oz xxxx sugar so as to have a nice easy working dough, out of this dough you can imitate most anything, then press your dough into your moulds, cut the dough even with the moulds, take a pinch of dough out of the jar, stick it in the back of the impression, take it out and lay on gauze, and let them dry, bent work is laid on rolling pins or different shapes of wood, or tins to suit.

439. HOW TO MAKE MOULDS.

Grease a pane of glass, lay your pattern on top of the glass; to make things plain we will say you want to make dollars. Put your new dollar on the glass, oil very light, put a paste-board ring around the dollar, which is a little larger in size, then mix some plaster-paris very thin and pour it into the ring, in less than an hour you can pick it up and by taking out the dollar you have got the mould.

If you want a mould of a dollar on both sides you will have to leave the dollar in the mould, scrape the mould down about half the thickness of a dollar, but do not move the dollar. Bore a little hole on each side; this is done so as to have the mould to fit, now oil the whole very lightly, put the same paste-board ring around it, and put some more plaster-paris on the top of the first mould, let it lay 6 hours and you can then take it apart, be very careful. These moulds must be soaked in cotton seed oil with a little terpentine for one week, take them out and dry them in the sun, and they are then ready for use. Illustrations of this kind of work you will find on other pages.

440. ORNAMENTS IN GUM PASTE, OR ALMOND PASTE.

Graduated stands, cups, tazzas, baskets, vases and a variety of other ornaments fitted for confectioners' use, may be advantageously imitated in gum paste or almond paste. The moulds used for making any of these are to be lined with either kind of paste, rolled out very thin and gently pressed into the mouldings or sunk portions of the moulds, so that when the objects moulded are delivered they may turn out perfect.

It is of the utmost importance that the different pieces comprising the whole edifice, whether this consists of what is generally called a piece montee (a term usually supposed to mean some representation of architecture in the form of a temple, pavilion, kiosk, fountain, castle, ruin, etc.), or of baskets, vases, stands, etc.—should be thoroughly dried before they are stuck together, otherwise the ornament would be liable to give way and fall to pieces. Almond and gum paste being usually colored for these purposes, it is useless to color them afterwards. When the body of the ornament is colored, the borders or other decorations should be white; when it happens that the vase, etc., is white, the ornamentation should be colored either brown, pink, blue or green, using in no case more than 3 colors; indeed it is admitted as a rule, that 2 colors only constitute the best taste. In some instances the whole ornament may be wrought in pure white; but this course requires the greatest precision and correctness in the execution of the whole work, as the absence of color tends to expose defects more distinctly to the eye.

441. ICING AND GUM PASTE ROSES.

Rose making is difficult, and it takes a good deal of practice and patience. I advise the beginner not to practice any longer than ½ hour at a time. 25 years ago we piped them on a half an egg shell, but they now have a certain kind of nail for it in the shape of an egg shell; the head of the nail is about 1 inch in diameter, arch like, the pin about 2 inches long. After all the nail heads have been greased lightly, place tnem in a flat box filled with sugar so that they stand up, the centre piece of a rose should be piped with a star tube. The trick of making roses lies in the turning of the nail; small roses can be finished at one operation, larger sizes get handled 2, 3 and 4 times, a good rose maker gives the nail 2 or 3 rotations without interruption. Gum paste roses are made with pincettes of different shapes, the leaves are flattened out on a piece of glass and put together on the nail.

442. GUM PASTE EGGS.

Wash 2 oz of traganth gum free from dirt, put it in a basin with water enough to cover it, let it stand a day to dissolve; squeeze it through a cloth, taking care that everything is perfectly clean, or it will spoil the color; put it in a marble mortar, adding gradually 12 to 16 ounces of XXXX sugar, sifted through a lawn sieve; work it well with the pestal until it is incorporated and becomes a very white, smooth paste; put it into a glazed pot, cover the paste with a damp cloth to exclude the air. When it is wanted, take a little of it and put it on a clean marble, and work some more sugar (which has been sifted through a lawn sieve) with the fingers until it is a firm paste, which will break when pulled. If it is not stiff enough it will roll under the knife when you cut it from the impression; if your paste works harsh and cracks it has too much gum in it, and will require a little water to work it down. For coloring the paste, use prepared cochineal or vegetable color. These require wooden moulds. If you have not got boxwood egg moulds, you can make some moulds from the following composition: mix one pound of Scotch glue, ½ pint of water, ¼ pound of white resin, ¼ pound of Burgundy pitch, ¼ pint of linseed oil; melt the glue, resin and pitch in a pan on a slow fire or in an ordinary glue pot; sift some powdered whiting through a fine sieve on a table; make a hole in the centre of the whiting and pour in the oil, which has been previously warmed, and then add other ingredients, and mix the whole into a smooth paste, which must be kept warm until used. Take a piece of the composition and knead it well; then roll it into a sheet about 2 inches thick; take the impression of half the egg lengthways, and cut away the superfluous composition. This will require 2 or 3 days' drying before the mould is ready for use. Now to make the sugar eggs: Roll out the gum paste into a thin sheet on a marble slab, and cut off pieces and form into the half egg shape, and with a knife cut away the paste outside the shape; now take them out of the mould and dry them for a few hours in the stove; when dry join the two halves together with piping or ribbon, If you require them to look like the natural egg, without any decoration, insert a strip of gum paste inside the edge of one of the halves, join the other half to, so that it fits like a boxlid, disguising the marks with a little gum paste softened down with water; trim them down with a knife.

ORNAMENTAL CONFECTIONERY.

The principal thing in making confectionery is to know how to boil the sugar, and its tendency to granulation while and after the boiling is done. Confectioners use two methods to determine the proper time, one is that of the common finger test, the other method is that of the thermometer; cream of tartar is generally used to prevent granulation.

443. LIST OF TOOLS.

1 furnace, 1 copper boiler, 1 thermometer, 1 marble and 4 iron rods ½ inch square to go around the marble and keep sugar from running off, also a candy shears and hook, a batch and a pallet knife; these tools are needed to run business on a small scale; for wholesalers there are very handy tools in the market, such as revolving steam pans, batch warmers, drop machines, rollers, etc., etc.

444. CLARIFYING.

The clarifying and boiling of sugar to the different degrees is the base or key to all sorts of candymaking.

15 lbs sugar, 3 qts water, 1 white of egg, which is beat up with 1 pt water, put the whole into the boiling pan, as soon as it comes to a boil add 1 pt water, when it rises again add another ½ pt water, this prevents the scum from boiling into the sugar and makes it rise to the top; now is the time to take all the scum off, when done dip in your finger, and if a drop hangs from it, it is the "I" degree, called "smooth".

445. FINGER TEST.

I. PEARLED.

Cover your preserving pan bottom two or three inches deep, boil it briskly over a clear fire for a short time, then dip in your finger and put it to your thumb, if on separating them a small string of sugar adheres to each it is boiled to the degree "pearled".

II. BLOWN.

After you have ascertained that the sugar is boiled to the degree called pearled put in the skimmer and let it boil a few minutes, then shake it out of the sugar and give it a blow. If sugar flies from the skimmer in small bladders it is boiled to the degree called "blown".

III. FEATHER.

Continue to boil the sugar from blown for a short time longer; take out the skimmer and give it a jerk over the pan, then over your head, and if sugar flies out like feathers it is boiled to the degree called "feather".

IV. BALL.

To know when the "ball" has been acquired, first dip your finger into a basin of cold water; then apply your finger to the syrup, taking up a little on the tip and dipping it into the water again; if upon rolling the sugar with the fingers and thumb you can make it into a small ball, that is what is termed the "small ball"; when you can make a larger and harder ball, which you could not bite without its sticking unpleasantly to the teeth, you may be satisfied that is the "large ball".

V. CRACK.

Boil the sugar from the degree called ball a little longer; dip your stick into water, then into the sugar and again into the water. If it cracks under your teeth it is boiled to the degree called "crack".

VI. CARAMEL.

Boil the sugar still further, dip a stick or your finger into water, then into the sugar, and again into the water. If it snaps like glass it is of the highest degree, called "caramel", and must be taken off the fire immediatety, for fear of burning.

446. THERMOMETER.

The pearl is to boil to 220 degrees; the small thread 228 degrees; the large thread 236 degrees; the blow 240 degrees; the feather 242 degrees; the small ball 244 degrees; the large ball 250 degrees; the small crack 261 degrees; the hard crack 281 degrees; the caramel 360 degrees.

447. ICE CREAM CANDY.

5 lbs sugar, 1 qt water, ¾ lb butter, ¼ oz cream of tartar, boiled to 280 degrees (add cream of tartar and butter when it starts boiling), pour on the marble, shove together when cool enough, put onto the hook, and flavor while pulling back and forth until it is white, put back on the table, and form to suit.

448. CHOCOLATE ICE CREAM CANDY.

As above, add ½ lb grated chocolate just before you start pulling.

449. STRAWBERRY ICE CREAM CANDY.

As above, add strawberry flavor and a little cochineal in place of chocolate.

450. VANILLA CARAMELS.

6 lbs sugar, 4 lbs glucose, 1¼ lb butter, 2 qts sweet cream, boil to 280 degrees (add the butter when it has boiled 10 minutes), pour on the marble and cut in small squares; while boiling it must be stirred constantly.

451. VANILLA CARAMELS.

10 lbs sugar, 2 lbs butter, 3 qts milk, ¼ oz cream of tartar, vanilla; stir while boiling as above.

452. IMITATION EGGS IN GRAINED SUGAR.

These can only be made with egg-shaped moulds of metal or wood. If made of the former material, the two halves must be slightly oiled before being used, and if of the latter, soaked in water and dried with a sponge afterwards, as they require to close perfectly air-tight. Only one-half of the mould must be filled with the sugar, while an assistant must be ready to instantly close the mould up and turn it round to distribute the contents equally all over the inside. To make the eggs lighter in weight some of the syrup may be drained from the interior of the eggs while they are warm by means of the small hole in the end. This opening may be stopped up with a patch of the grained sugar or the egg filled with yellow fondant cream in imitation of a yolk. The best or whitest refined sugar is used for these goods and boiled to a "soft ball", or about 240—245 degrees by the thermometer. It will be advisable for those who desire to manufacture this class of goods to use small boils in their first attempt, and only slightly grain the same, and well stir that in a drop-pan with a lip to it.

453. MALLOW CUPS.

They are made by placing the whites of 1 doz. eggs in a clean copper pan and beat them till they are quite stiff; then place 2 lbs of sugar and ½ lb of glucose in a copper pan and ½ pt water and cook to 225 degrees; then pour it on the beaten eggs in a fine stream, beating it through the eggs at the same time. Now place egg batch on a strong steam bath or on a fire covered with ashes and cook to a stiff paste, beating all the time; try the paste by placing a little in cold water, and when it is almost as stiff as caramels, it is about right to work well; then flavor with vanilla and let the batch set on the steam bath so as to keep it warm while you get the outside ready. For the outside take 6 lbs of sugar, ½ lb glucose and 1 qt of water and cook to 320 degrees; then pour on marble and when it is cool enough to handle color pink and flavor with oil of rose and pull on the hook rapidly till well pulled; then twist the air out of the batch and flatten it out on the table and scrape the egg batch on it; then wrap the pink batch around the egg batch and pull out like stick candy and cut with a butter cup cutter.

454. BUTTERINES.

1 lb of white sugar and 2 lbs glucose, 1 lb butter, ½ pint good rich cream, and five cocoanuts, grated fine, and placing all in a copper pan, and cook to a stiff paste, about as hard as caramels, stirring all the time; then add the grated rinds of 2 good oranges, and stir through the batch; then scrape the contents of the pan upon a marble and spread out in a sheet half-inch thick, and when cold, cut in pieces 1½ inches long, ½ inch wide, and cover in good chocolate coating, leaving a streak over the top of the coating, and when cold they are ready for the counter.

455. MAPLE CARAMELS.

Same as 450, use maple sugar, instead of A sugar; no flavor.

456. CHOCOLATE CARAMELS

6 lbs sugar, 4 lbs glucose, 1½ lb butter, 2 qts sweet cream, 1½ lb cocoa paste, vanilla, put on the fire, when it has boiled 10 minutes add the butter and cocao, stir while boiling it to 280 degrees.

457. CHOCOLATE CARAMELS.

10 lbs sugar, 2 qts milk, 1½ lb butter, 1½ lb chocolate, ¼ oz cream of tartar, when it starts boiling add the cream of tartar; rest as above.

458. PEANUT BARS.

2 lbs kernels to 1 lb sugar, take 3 lbs sugar and ½ oz cream of tartar, put dry in a kettle, set on the fire, stir quick until melted, throw in the nuts slowly, until there is enough sugar to cover them, when the nuts turn to a light brown, pour the batch on the marble, press down to an inch thickness and cut while warm.

459. PEANUT BARS.

Boil 5 lbs old candy, 1 qt water, 3 lbs glucose to 280 degrees, put in the nuts and work as above, roast the nuts on a light brown before using.

460. ALMOND BARS.

As above, use almonds in place of peanuts.

461. COCOANUT CAKES.

Boil 5 lbs sugar, 1 pt water to 275 degrees, remove the syrup from the fire and stir in 5 fresh grated cocoanuts, return it to the fire and boil until you can draw a thread between your finger and thumb, stir constantly from the time the nuts are put in, take a spoon and spread it with a fork to any size or shape.

462. COCOANUT CREAM BARS.

5 lbs sugar, 1 qt water, boil to 260 degrees, put in 5 grated cocoanuts, let boil 4 minutes, stir quick, pour on the marble, flatten it, cut into bars when cold.

463. CREAM FOR CHOCOLATE DROPS.

Boil 10 lbs sugar, 2½ qts water, ½ oz cream of tartar to 245 degrees, put it into a very cold place, when lukewarm stir the mass quick with a spatula until it turns white as snow (put in vanilla before stirring), it will keep a long time if kept in a covered stone jar.

464. WALNUT CANDY.

2 qts N. O. molasses, 2 lbs glucose, 1 qt water, boil to 280 degrees, put in your kernels slowly, turn it out and flatten it on the marble, cut before it gets cold, you can leave the glucose out if you like.

465. LEMON ACID DROPS.

Boil 10 lbs sugar, 2 qts water, ¼ oz cream of tartar to 305 degrees, put onto the marble ¼ inches thick, spread 20 drops oil of lemon and 1½ oz tartaric acid evenly over the hot sugar, knead the whole like dough, draw it out, cut or roll it into drops or sticks (always keep your marble oiled when in use.

466. OLD FASHIONED MOLASSES CANDY.

Stir and boil 1 gall. N. O. molasses, 1 qt water to a crack, take a small wet stick, dip in the syrup and in the cold water again, now take the little sugar there is on your stick between the teeth, if it sticks to them, it must be boiled a little longer, and if the sugar cracks or breaks between the teeth it is ready to use, when nearly done put in a $\frac{1}{4}$ lb butter, pull and flavor it on the hook.

467. MOLASSES CANDY.

$\frac{1}{2}$ gall. molasses, 1 qt water, 5 lbs brown sugar, 2 lbs white sugar, boil as above and flavor while pulling.

468. TAFFY CANDY.

As above, pouring it into trays and pans without pulling or flavoring it.

469. EVERTON TAFFY.

5 lbs C sugar, 1 qt water, $1\frac{1}{2}$ lb butter, $\frac{1}{2}$ oz cream of tartar, boiled to a crack, lemon flavor.

470. CHOCOLATE PASTE.

5 lbs sugar, 3 qts water, 1 lb chocolate, $\frac{1}{2}$ lb butter, $\frac{1}{2}$ oz cream of tartar, vanilla, boil to 230 degrees, then add the chocolate and butter, stir constantly, boil to soft ball and run it into greased pans, when cold it will cut like cheese.

471. CREAM CHOCOLATE.

5 lbs sugar, 1 lb glucose, 1 qt sweet cream, 1 lb chocolate, boil to a ball.

472. STARCH ROOM.

Models of bonbon, easter eggs, christmas goods, etc., etc., are generally made of plaster of paris glued one inch apart on a flat board, long enough to reach across the starch trays, size of trays 2 feet long and 18 inches wide, with sides about $1\frac{1}{2}$ inches high, these trays get filled with light starch and made even with the edges by a ruler. When starch is ready the impressions are made by gently pressing the moulds their full depth in the starch until all are full, the impressions get filled through a candy funnel.

473. CREAM BONBONS.

5 lbs sugar, 1 lb glucose, 1 qt sweet cream, 1 lb cocoa paste, mix sugar and cream, then add the glucose, when boiling put in the cocoa paste, boil to a ball degree and fill in starch trays, when hard enough take them out and put into a dry place for 2 or 3 days. They can also be crystalized.

474. CRYSTALIZATION.

The articles to be crystalized should be put in pans having sides $2\frac{1}{2}$ inches high. Then put in a copper or brass kettle as much water as will more than fill the pans. Then add 7 lbs of sugar to a gallon of water and boil by thermometer to 225 degrees, take it from the fire and let it cool until blood warm, then pour upon the goods sufficient to cover them, put them in a warm place for 10 hours, pour off the syrup aud let them dry well before turning them out. The principle upon which the above is conducted is readily comprehended. When water is cold it will dissolve but a certain quantity of sugar and no more. When heat is applied it will dissolve a much greater quantity. When taken from the fire and allowed to cool the superfluous sugar that was held in solution by the heat, now begins to form itself in crystals and is deposited on the sides and bottom of the vessel, or upon the goods. Cream figs, cream dates, cream nuts can easily and without trouble be crystalized in the above manner. No cream of tartar or alcohol must be used.

475. SUGAR SPINNING.

Boil 1 lb sugar, 1 gill water, little cream of tartar, 310 degrees. Any workman with ordinary ideas of symetry, designs and perspective can produce efforts in sugar spinning, which surprise themselves. All there is necessary for practice is a flat piece of glass well oiled, lay the glass onto the design you want to make. Dip your spoon in the above sugar and trace the designs, when cool put them together with caramel. Spun sugar is used for many decorative purposes, such as falling or running water, etc., this is made by dipping a docker or bunch of wires into the sugar, then hold an iron bar in your left hand, as high as you can reach, run the docker over the bar as quick as possible, letting it nearly touch the floor. Continue this until there is a skein of sugar that looks like a skein of silk, the threads can be made fine or coarse by moving the wires slow or fast.

476. SACCHAROMETER.

This instrument is an hydrometer for ascertaining the specific gravities of liquids. It is made in glass containing quicksilver, as the thermometer, divided into degrees or scales. When immersed in pure water it marks zero, which proves that the water contains no sugar. The advantages of the saccharometer are immense, not only as a matter of economy, but as a guide to the workman, who cannot work with certainty without knowing the degrees of boiling, which can only be learned by practice. For example, the pearl marks twenty-five degrees; the thread, large or small, thirty degrees; the blow thirty-four degrees; the feather, thirty-six degrees; the ball fifty degrees. After this last degree the sugar has become so dense and thick that the saccharometer can no longer be used. The remaining degrees, the crack and caramel, must be determined by the finger test.

In order to use the saccharometer you must have a narrow tin tube in which to dip up a quantity of the boiling sugar. This tube must be longer than the saccharometer, and have a handle. Wet the saccharometer and drop it into the tube containing the boiling sugar and it wil indicate the degree of the sugar. Both the saccharometer and the thermometer are most excellent instruments by which to ascertain the degrees of boiling sugar.

477. NOUGAT OR CROQUANT.

Weigh 2 lbs sugar in a sauce-pan and a few drops of lemon juice, set on the fire, as soon as it has dissolved add and stir in 1 lb of chopped almonds, turn it out on the oiled marble and roll it out in thin sheets and cut to suit; very nice looking ornaments can be made out of nougat, such as temples, fountains, churches, baskets, waterfalls, vases, etc., etc. It is also cut in strips and ribbons to be used for decorating large ornaments (see illustrations).

478. NEW ENGLAND TAFFY.

5 lbs of standard A sugar and $1\frac{1}{2}$ lb glucose; dissolve these in water and cook to 250 degrees, then add 3 pts New Orleans molasses and cook to 260 degrees, then add 2 lbs Spanish peanuts, and boil the whole batch to 270 degrees. Take off the fire, and add 3 oz butter and $\frac{3}{4}$ oz soda. Pour on a greased marble and form to suit,

479. SOFT FONDANT.

5 lbs sugar and 3 pts of water; place it on the fire and stir until the sugar is dissolved; remove the scum, boil it to the "feather," then pour it on a cold marble slab. The space on the marble on which the fondant is poured should be inclosed with iron bars, in order to prevent the fondant in its hot fluid state from running off the marble. Let it remain undisturbed until it becoms quite cold, then remove the bars, sprinkle a teaspoonful of cream of tartar over the top, and by means of a

short pallet knife you scrape in the outer edges; then, with a large wooden spatula, you work the sugar to and fro continually, without rest, until the whole mass granulates into a smooth white paste, which you can no longer work with the spatula; then with your knife immediately scrape off that which has adhered to the spatula, and scrape all together on the marble and knead it together with the hands into one compact mass; then place it in an earthen tureen and it is ready for use.

480. PARAFFINE.

Paraffine is a harmless substance obtained from the tar of coal oil; also from the distillation of the tar of beechwood. It is a tasteless, inodorous, fatty matter, fusible at 112^0, and resisting the action of acids and alkalies. It is so named from its little affinity for other substances. The object of its use by the confectioner in caramels and other candies, is to firm them and hold them in shape. The paraffine introduced into the boiling sugar dissolves and mixes with the boiling mass, and on cooling concretes and holds in shape, when it is cut into cubes; the cubes are then wrapped or folded in neatly small squares of waxed or paraffine paper; this is done in order to protect it from the atmosphere, and thereby prevent them from becoming sticky. The quantity of paraffine required is about one ounce to each two pounds of sugar.

481. CARAMEL ORNAMENTS.

They generally require moulds out of lead or copper in which you pour your boiling sugar, but there is a way to make these kind of ornaments without moulds, which I would like to explain.

Cut out the different parts of the ornament into pasteboard, put them onto the oiled marble, and run a plain tube of icing around the edge of the patterns, when done take out your pattern and continue until all the parts of the ornaments are done, when dry pour in your sugar, boiled to 280 degrees, when cool pick them up and put together with caramel or icing. These ornaments can be crystallized or decorated with icing gum leaves, roses, flowers, paper leaves; you can also cast the different parts into different colors.

482. VANILLA SUGAR.

Cut and split $\frac{1}{2}$ dozen vanilla beans, and pound them with $\frac{1}{4}$ lb loaf sugar in a stone mortar, sift it, and it is ready for use; this is a very nice flavor for charlottes, meringue, creams and other light mixtures.

483. PAPIER MACHEE.

Soak any amount of white paper in scalding water for 1½ hour, then press all the water out of it, and pound into a smooth pulp. Now add 4 oz of glue dissolved, and ¾ lb powdered chalk and make a stiff paste; this paste can be used in place of gum paste.

484. PASTILLAGE.

1 qt water, 2 oz of gum traganth, soak for 36 hours, now press it through a cloth, then add a few drops glycerine and equal parts of icing sugar and corn starch, and make a nice paste by working it well; this paste may be used instead of gum paste.

485. ROCK SUGAR.

Boil 2 lbs sugar to a crack, and stir in ¼ lb ornamenting icing, let it cool off, turn it out, and break into suitable pieces for the construction of rocks.

486. ALMOND PASTE FOR STANDS AND ORNAMENTS.

1 lb macaroon paste, 1½ lb sugar, ¼ oz traganth, soaked and pressed through a cloth, and a little rose water; put all the ingredients in a kettle and set on a slow fire, keep stiring for 20 minutes, take off, add the juice of a lemon, and work it until cool, it is now ready for use; if not used directly place the paste under a basin, and it will keep for months. This paste can be used in place of gum paste, and is very handy to make cake stands, pedestals, etc., etc.

487. PANORAMA EGGS.

These require a special mould, extra dry starch powder, and deep starch coffers or boxes. You must make a mould of plaster of Paris, as follows : Form a wall of potters' clay about 2½ inches deep, into which run some soft plaster, and while it is yet soft press into it, exactly half way, an egg that has been well greased. As soon as the plaster sets remove the egg and the clay, and you have a mould with the impression of half an egg in it. Drill a small hole through the mould at the bottom of the egg impression in order to facilitate the escape of the air when the mould is in use; trim the mould nicely and smoothly on the outside. When the mould is perfectly dried fasten on the flat surface a piece of cork or wood, to serve as a handle. Now have coffers or shallow boxes, say three or four inches deep; fill these with fine dry starch powder, smooth off the top of the starch with a ruler, and with your mould print the starch; then boil your sugar to the "feather" degree, and by means of a confectioner's funnel or a small lip pan, fill your starch prints with it; sieve some starch powder lightly over the top and set it away in a moderately warm place until next day. Then gently remove the castings from the boxes, and with a soft brush carefully brush off any adhering starch. Now make a little hole in the top of the casting, drain off the syrup contained in them, after which set them for one moment on a wetted towel and then gently break away the surrounding sugar and you have half an egg—the outside crystal and the inside smooth. Now, in the pointed end of the egg, make a small hole, and in one of the half eggs construct your panorama. Place a small round piece of glass in the hole at the end and fasten it with a little icing; join, also, another half egg to it with icing, thus forming a whole egg; conceal the joints by means of a narrow strip of gold paper and you have a panorama egg.

A much easier way of making egg moulds is as follows: Take a sharp scissors and cut and trim the edges of a half an egg shell lenghtways, grease the shell very light, and fill it up with thin plaster of Paris, when set take off the shell, put a handle onto it, and it is ready for use. If you like to have the outside mould of an egg turn the shell over, grease them, put a paste board ring around it, and fill up with plaster of Paris. Very nice moulds are made by not greasing at all and keeping the shells onto the moulds

488. CONSERVE SUGAR.

The proper moulds to use for casting this sugar are composed of plaster of Paris, and are usually made in several pieces, so as to facilitate the delivery of the objects cast in them. When about to use them the mould should be taken to pieces, washed clean, and put to soak for an hour or two in a tub of lukewarm water; then let the pieces composing the mould be put together and tied securely with a string and placed in proper position for casting the sugar. The sugar must be boiled to the "soft ball" degree; add a few drops of acetic acid, and work a small portion of the sugar with a small wooden spatula up against the side of the pan till granulated; stir this into the body of the sugar till it acquires an opalized or whitish appearance; as soon as the sugar assumes this states, which constitutes "graining," pour it immediately into the ready prepared mould, and when the sugar has become perfectly set to the depth of about one quarter of an inch on the sides of the mould reserve it, so that the still fluid centre of sugar may run off, thus you will have the casting hollow in the centre; then take it out of its mould and stand it up to drain and dry. In this manner vases, baskets, eggs, fruits, birds, animals, fish, flowers, &c., may be made; they may also be painted in colors so as to imitate nature as nearly as may be. The finish and style and the degree of perfection to be obtained in the production of these beautiful objects must greatly depend upon the amount of knowledge and experience possessed by the practitioner; yet it is to be remembered that an indomitable determination to succeed will accomplish wonders

489. APPLE SUGAR.

This is an old confection, and has for many years been much used in France as a healthful and nutritious confection for children. The following is the recipe: Cut a dozen or more pippins, or any other full-flavored, juicy apples into slices; skin, core and all; add water sufficient to cover them, and boil until very soft; then strain the liquid from them through a fine sieve or a flannel filtering-bag; add to this strained liquor 4 lbs of white sugar to each quart, and half a teaspoonful of cream of tartar; boil to the "crack" degree and pour on a greased marble slab; fold in the edges and then into a mass, and pull it out into rather thick sticks; when these are cold cut them into suitable lenghts, and wrap a fringed paper round them, and tie with bright colored test ribbons.

490. CREAM MINT DROPS.

Put the powdered sugar in a bowl or basin, and mix it with sufficient glucose to form it into a paste or dough, not too stiff to roll out into sheets. Flavor the mass to your taste with a few drops of the best and freshest oil of peppermint, work well together, dust a perfectly clean marble slab with powdered sugar, and roll out your mixture in a sheet to about a quarter of an inch in thickness, dust the top over with powdered sugar and cut out the drops with a tin cutter; lay them out so as not to touch each other upon powdered trays or smooth flat boards until they become dry enough to handle, which will be in a couple of hours. Then arrange them in your pans and crystallize them in syrup boiled to the "blow." This will give you a light and fine crystal.

491. PINK BURNT ALMONDS.

Put 1 pt of clarified sugar in a round-bottomed pan on a clear fire, boil it to the degree called "blown," mix in as much prepared cochineal as will make it a good color, boil it again to the degree called "blown," throw in the brown burnt almonds free from shell; take the pan off the fire and stir the almonds well about in the sugar with the spatula until it is all upon them, which is very easily done if you are careful. You may repeat this two or three times, which will make the almonds very handsome

492. PRALINE CUPS.

Take 1 lb of Valencia almonds and roast to a light brown co.or (being careful not to burn them, as they will color up more after they have been taken from the fire before they cool off), then grind to a smooth paste through a sausage cutter or a Universal grater; then take 2 lbs of cream that has been cooked to 238 degrees, and place it in a steam bath, warm it, and then add to the almond paste $\frac{1}{2}$ lb of melted chocolate No. 1, and boil all well together. Your assistant can have 4 lbs of white sugar, 2 lbs of glucose, and 3 pts of water cooked to 310 degrees; then add $\frac{1}{2}$ lb of butter, and stir till the butter is well cooked through the batch, then take from the fire and add 1 lb of melted chocolate, stir through the batch well and pour on the marble, and when it is cool enough to handle, turn it up into a heap and cool it off, so it can be handled nicely, then place it on the table and wrap the almond paste batch in the chocolate batch, and pull out like stick candy and cut like buttercups, and when cold they are ready for the counter.

There can also be a nice candy made by shaping the same batch three-cornered, or triangular shaped, and pull out like stick candy, twist in auger shape, and cut in sticks five inches long, and when cold stack up in silver trays and place on the counter.

493. TO SPIN A SILVER WEB.

Take 1 pt of clarified sugar and 1 teaspoonful of lemon juice, boil in a small pan to the degree called "caramel;" the moment the sugar is ready take it off and put the bottom of the pan in cold water. As soon as the water is warmed take the pan out. Tnis precaution will keep the sugar from discoloring. As this sugar is to represent silver you must be particularly careful not to boil it too high. Have ready a crocanth mould neatly oiled with sweet oil, then take a teaspoon and dip the shank of it into the sugar on one side of the pan, take up a little sugar and throw the spoon backwards and forwards in the mould, leaving as fine a thread as possible. Continue to do so until the mould is quite full. You must observe that there be no blotches and that the threads be as fine as hair; you may then take it out and cover it over a custard or any other sweet, and may, if you please, raise it by spinning light threads of sugar on the top.

TO SPIN A GOLD WEB.

Proceed with a gold web exactly the same as with the silver web, only boil the sugar a moment longer.

494. BLOW CANDY.

Place 5 lbs sugar in a copper pan and 4 oz glucose, small pinch of cream of tartar, and 1 qt water; cook to 330 degrees, and add a little color; pour on the marble, and when it is cool enough to handle, flavor with rose or teaberry, place it on the table and pull it out a little; double it up again and pull it out the same way, and continue in this way so as to slightly pull the batch, and when it is partly cool shape it in one strip about 3 feet long and 3 inches wide, and lay a tin pipe (3 feet long and $\frac{1}{2}$ inch in diameter) on the batch; now press the pipe down in the batch and bring the candy up over the pipe so as to cover it; then roll the batch round, (moving the pipe so as to keep the pipe from sticking to the batch); then pull the pipe out and at the same time blow the hole full of air, closing the end as soon as possible, so as to keep the air in the batch; then pull the batch out in a stick 12 feet long and put it in 4 lengths 3 feet long, and place the four sticks together and place a tin pipe 1 inch in diameter and 3 feet long on the sticks and bring them up over the pipe so as to cover it; now pull the pipe out, blow the hole full of air, close the ends, and stretch it out 12 feet long and cut it in 3 feet lenghts and place it together once more, placing the inch pipe again in the strips, bring them up over the pipe, pull the pipe out and close the ends, stretch the batch out in strips $1\frac{1}{2}$ inches thick and let lay till they are cold; then mark them with a knife in 3-inch sticks and break them off, when it is ready for the counter. This candy ought to be well perforated, with a large hole in the centre. When you cut the lengths off be sure and keep the air in the batch. Have a warm table. It can be made in different colors and flavors.

495. CREAM CANDY.

Take 15 lbs of white sugar and place it in a copper pan with 3 qts of water and one teaspoonful of cream of tartar and 8 oz glucose, and cook to 280 degrees; then pour on a greased cool marble, and when partly cold turn it up into a heap and flavor with floral extract of rose and vanilla, color a light tea color like tea satin; then place it on the hook and pull rapidly till it is well pulled, then add to the batch while on the hook 1 lb of glucose, pulling the batch well so as to mix the glucose through the batch to soften it, continue to pull it till quite cold, then shape it up on the table and pull out in long strips 3 inches wide and 1 inch thick, then let it lay till it turns to a cream (which will soon take place if you have pulled the batch well); then cut in bars and wrap in wax paper and it is ready for the counter.

496. SACCHARINE.

An article called "saccharine", so pungent that its sweetening properties are stated to be three hundred times stronger than sugar, is offered to the trade. An article of this strength must be of great value in sweetening fruits, jellies, etc., especially when the proprietors say it is not in any way injurious, and improves the flavor of what it is used in.

497. BEE HIVES AND PYRAMIDS IN MERINGUE, MACAROONS AND MASSEPAIN.

The frame of each may be composed of ten or a dozen rings of meringue, laid on paper and baked in the usual manner: Or, rings of macaroon or massepain paste may be substituted. When the rings are detached from the paper, and well dried, but still retaining their thickness, they are ranged in shape, one on top of the other.

498. CHOCOLATE CARAMELS.

One pound "A" white sugar, 12 oz glucose, 1½ gallon cream, and 4 oz chocolate. Take cream and sugar and let it come to a boil, stirring slowly; when about to boil try by dipping your finger in cold water, then into the boiling sugar, then again into the cold water; if it adheres to your finger try and make a ball of it, and if you can it is ready for the glucose and chocolate. Cut the chocolate fine before adding, as it will dissolve more readily; then stir and continue until all boils to a crack, but don't let it boil longer than to the crack.

499. EASTER CARDS.

Soak ½ lb gelatine, weighed dry, take 2 lbs of glucose and put in a clean pan, and bring it to a boil; remove it from the fire, and put in the soaked gelatine, stirring it well until quite dissolved ; then mix in a little cachou flavor. Now take 28 lbs of fine pulverized sugar, which has been sifted free from lumps, and make a bay with the sugar on your slab, into which you pour your liquid, mix well up into a nice smooth paste, at the same time working in the color that is desired. When it is well mixed, cut a small portion off the bulk, and roll it out with the rolling pin, dust lightly with farina, and then cut them out with a large cutter about the size of a medium-sized envelope. As they are cut, place them on trays which have been lightly dusted with farina, and put them into the stove to dry. When dry, take them out and decorate them by piping a fancy edge right round them with icing ; then in the centre write various mottos— one motto for each card. The icing may be colored according to fancy, so as to make a variety, and will give a very nice effect if 2 or 3 colors are used on each card; if nicely decorated, these will sell well.

500. SPUN SUGAR BEE-HIVE.

Mould 20 or 30 bees in gum paste, as near the color and shape as possible, make a hole with a pin on each side of the mouth and let them dry ; make some of the wings extend as if flying. Provide a large round crocanth mould as near the shape of a bee-hive as possible, then boil the sugar as formerly instructed. Spin the sugar hot close to the inside of the mould. It must be regularly spun and very strong, the threads very fine, and no blotches. When it is so, let it stand until quite cold, then turn it out of the mould on to a large dish and ornament.

501. LOZENGES.

The proportion of gum and water in general use is 1 lb gum arabic dissolved 1 pt of water.

502. PEPPERMINT LOZENGES.

Take some finely powdered loaf sugar, put it on a marble slab, make a bay in the centre, pour in some dissolved gum, and mix into a paste, flavor with the essence cf peppermint, roll the paste on the marble until it is about ¼ inch thick. Use starch-powder to dust it with ; this keeps it from sticking. Dust the surface with a little starch-powder and sugar, and rub it over with the palm of your hand. Cut out the lozenges and place them on wooden trays, and place them in the stove to dry. All lozenges are finished in the same way.

503. FRUIT JUICES.

The combination press is about the handiest instrument to separate the juice from the different fruits. Now fill your juice into clean bottles and cork well, and boil it ¾ of an hour; the boiling is done as follows: Put a little hay or straw on the bottom of your cruller-pot, place your bottles on top, and put a little hay between and around the bottles, fill the pot with water and boil ¾ of an hour, then take off the fire, pour off the water, when cool dip the tops of the bottles in hot wax, now keep in a cool place by laying them on their sides for future use. Do not use any sugar or salicylic-acid as they will spoil the flavor of the juice.

504. FRUIT PRESERVING.

Place your prepared fruits in bottles, jars or tincans and fill them with clarified sugar, now cork or solder so they will be perfectly air-tight, the corks of the bottles or jars ought to be covered and tied over with wet bladders; now place them in your cruller pot and boil them for 20 minutes in the same manner as mentioned above, and keep in a cool place for future use.

505. THE THERMOMETER.

Their are three different thermometers in use, the one of Fahrenheit (in America and England), the one of Reaumur (in Germany and Austria), and the one of Celsius (in France and Switzerland). Fahrenheit sets his freezing point at No. 32, the boiling point at 212. Reaumur has the freezing point marked 0, and boiling point 80. Celsius sets die freezing point at 0, and the boiling point at 100.

In this book we use the one of Fahrenheit graded up to 400 degrees. If you buy a new thermometer you will have to be careful, as thermometers vary some, which you can very easy find out by boiling a batch or two.

Behandlung der I. Abtheilung.
506. RUBBING.

Sämmtliche Recepte in dieser Abtheilung werden aufgerieben und behandelt wie folgt: Zuerst wiege und löse das Ammonia, dann reibe man den Zucker und die Butter mit der flachen Hand recht schaumig, jetzt werden die Eier nach und nach dazu gerührt, d. h. jede halbe Minute 2 Eier. Sobald die Eier alle darunter sind, thue man Milch, Ammonia, Soda und Gewürz dazu, schabe mit dem bowlknife von den Seiten und dem Boden, rühre es nochmals durch und mische das Mehl und cream of tartar behutsam unter die Masse; alsdann tressire oder fülle man die Formen und backe. Enthält das Recept kein Ammonia, so fängt man natürlich mit Zucker und Butter an und fährt fort wie schon erwähnt. Bei pound cake oder allen anderen Massen, welche keine Flüssigkeiten enthalten, mische man das Mehl recht vorsichtig unter die Masse, sobald die Eier darunter sind. Raisins, Currants und Citron setzt man gerne dann zu, wenn das Mehl halb durch gemischt ist.

Behandlung der II. Abtheilung.
507. MIXING.

Alle Recepte in dieser Abtheilung werden der Reihenfolge nach gemischt, ohne schaumig zu rühren. Man verfahre wie folgt:

Wiege und löse das Ammonia, dann mische Zucker und Butter gut durch; wenn dieses geschehen, rühre die ganzen Eier mit einem Mal darunter und thue Milch, Soda, Ammonia und Gewürz dazu, schabe mit dem pallet knife vom Boden und den Seiten, rühre die Masse gut durch einander und mische das Mehl und cream of tartar behutsam darunter. Alle Massen sollten, sobald das Mehl darunter ist, so wenig wie möglich gearbeitet werden. Auch bei dem Ausstechen verhüte das Mehl und Arbeiten des Teiges soviel wie möglich, und steche stets so dicht wie irgend thunlich, um nicht zu viel Abfall zu bekommen. Bei Molasses-Massen fange mit Molasses und Lard an zu mischen, statt Zucker und Butter. Im Uebrigen verfahre wie schon erwähnt.

Behandlung der III. Abtheilung.
508. BEATING.

In dieser Abtheilung werden sämmtliche Recepte vermittelst Schneebesen oder Schaumruthe aufgeschlagen.

Sauber, reinlich und trocken ist das Loosungswort. Nachdem man den Kessel und die Schaumruthe recht sauber und trocken hat, wiege und siebe man den XXXX Zucker, alsdann lasse man das Eiweiss recht vorsichtig ab, damit nichts Gelbes hinein kommt, thue es in den Kessel und fange langsam an zu schlagen, schlage immer etwas schneller, bis der Schnee recht steif ist; dann setze man einen Esslöffel voll XXXX Zucker dazu und schlage es nochmals steif; man wiederhole dieses letztere noch einmal, nehme dann die Schaumruthe heraus und mische den Rest des Zuckers mit einem Spatel recht vorsichtig darunter, tressire so schnell wie möglich. Ununterbrochenes, immer schneller werdendes Schlagen und Händewechsel ist sehr zu empfehlen. Im Falle sich das Eiweiss schlecht schlägt, kann man einige Tropfen Essigsäure dazu setzen. Bei Cream lässt man natürlich die Säure fort, im Uebrigen verfährt man wie beim Eiweiss.

Miscellaneous Recipes

WITH INSTRUCTIONS.

FRITTERS.

1½ lb flour, 1½ qt milk, 10 eggs, ½ oz soda, ½ oz salt.
Let the milk come to a boil, stir in the flour, remove it from the fire and mix in the eggs, also the dissolved soda and salt; then drop them in pieces the size of a walnut into hot grease and bake like crullers or doughnuts.

APPLE FRITTERS.

Peel carefully and slice your apples, soak them a little in a mixture of powdered sugar, lemon juice and brandy. Then dip them in the following batter, fry them in hot lard and dust with sugar.

BATTER.

1 lb flour, 2 eggs, ½ pt salad oil, little salt and milk enough to make a thick batter; almost any kind of fruit can be used in place of apples.

CRUMPETS.

Make a thin batter out of 2 lbs flour, 1½ oz compressed yeast, 1 oz salt and 2½ qts milk at 100^0 Fahr., let it stand one hour and give it a good beat up, let stand another hour, and it will be ready to bake; then have your rings and hot plate greased, set the rings onto the hot plate and fill and level them with the bowl knife, as soon as they are baked on one side turn them over, ring and all. Bake to a nice yellow color (rings must be ½ inch in height).

BUTTER CAKES.

4 lbs flour, 4 oz butter, 4 oz sugar, 1 oz soda, 2 oz cream of tartar, and milk enough to make a nice working dough; roll it out to ½ inch thickness, cut out with tea biscuit cutter, dock and bake on hot plate by turning them over.

SAUSAGE ROLLS.

Roll pie paste ¼ inch thick and cut 3 inches square, put a little sausage meat in centre lenghtways, form a roll, wash with eggs and cut them 2 or 3 times slantways; bake in medium oven.

BUTTER CAKES.

Make a nice dough out of 2 lbs flour, $\frac{1}{2}$ oz soda, 1 oz cream of tartar, little salt and milk to suit, roll out $\frac{1}{2}$ inch thick and 3 inches diameter, and bake on hot plate by turning them over.

JOHNNY CAKE.

1 qt milk, 3 eggs, $\frac{1}{2}$ oz soda, $\frac{1}{4}$ lb flour, little corn meal and salt. Bake in greased square tins.

BUCKWHEAT CAKES.

1 qt warm water, 1 oz compressed yeast, and buckwheat flour enough to make a thin batter; let it rise, add $\frac{1}{8}$ oz soda, dissolved, and fry or bake.

BATH BUNS.

2 lbs flour. 1 lb butter, 20 yolks, $2\frac{1}{2}$ oz compressed yeast, and warm milk enough to make a nice sponge; when ready work in 1 lb of coarse sugar, let lay a little, then break into 2 oz pieces and set on greased tins rather rough, in shape of rocks; then wash them with eggs, let them prove a little, and bake in hot oven.

DOMESTIC BREAD.

No more dry bakers bread.

1 barrel Pillsbury's flour, 12 lbs 8 oz cottolene, 2 lbs 13 oz compressed yeast, 1 lb $6\frac{1}{2}$ oz granulated sugar, 5 lbs 10 cz glucose, 1 lb 4 oz salt, 6 qts potato yeast made without hops.

Sift the flour into the mixer or trough, make a hole in it and put in the cottolene.

To the glucose add 2 qts of hot water and stir them together (on the stove if necessary) to dissolve the glucose. Put it into some milk and bring it to 80 degrees by the thermometer (a little higher in winter). Measure it and add to the batch in the mixer or trough enough milk at the same temperature to make the whole wetting measure 41 q's. Then in the mixture of glucose, water and milk dissolve the yeast, sugar and salt. Pour this into the batch. Then put in the potato yeast. Stir in enough of the flour to make the sponge about as thick as very thick cream. Let it stand $\frac{3}{4}$ of an hour and then start the mixer or mix in the trough in the usual way. Passing it two or three times through the brake is a great improvement. In the absence of a brake it wants a thorough kneading.

I would advise a person beginning to make the domestic bread to make two or three very small batches to learn about proving it as that is something that cannot be exactly described and must be learned by observation. For this purpose I give the formula figured down to a very small quantity.

WHITE BREAD.

13 lbs flour, 13½ oz cottolene, 3 oz compressed yeast, 1½ oz sugar, 1½ oz salt, ¾ pt potato yeast, 6 oz glucose.

GRAHAM BREAD.

6 lbs 8 oz flour, 3 lbs 14 oz graham, 15 oz lard, 9 oz sugar, 1¼ oz salt, 6 oz glucose, ¾ pt potato yeast.

Dissolve the 6 oz glucose in a gill of hot water and add to it enough milk to make 2 qts 1¼ pt, warm it to 80 degrees (85 or 90 in cold weather), dissolve in it the compressed yeast, sugar and salt. Then add the potato yeast. Pour this into a hole in the flour, mix in enough flour to make a sponge as thick as cream. Let it stand ¾ of an honr. It does not fall. Then knead it thoroughly and let it stand till light enough to scale (an hour, more or less). Scale it, round it up into loaves, put it into proving boxes, cover with wax paper and prove about an hour, but don't let it stand long enough to run together. When proved enough, mould it into the pans, let it prove and bake in hot oven.

POTATO YEAST.

To make the yeast, boil one bushel potatoes, peel them and pass through a masher. Do not let the mashed potatoes stand warm but stir in enough ice water immediately to cool them. Dissolve 1 lb compressed yeast in some cold water and stir it in. Then add 16 lbs of sifted flour, and ice water to make it thin enough. Set away in the refrigerator. Ready to use in twelve hours. This yeast is not so strong as that made with hops, but it gives the bread a nicer flavor. It is better not to make more than two days supply at a time.

GOLDEN COTTOLENE.

The edible fat "Golden Cottolene" justly deserves the appellation "Golden", as it is among all edible or cooking fats the best that ever has been brought in the market.

Not alone is its solidity as fat a very considerable one, but the flavor of the cakes prepared with it must be termed quite superior. I am firmly convinced that ⅔ lb of cottolene contains exactly as much fat substance as 1 lb of either butter, lard, or any other cooking fat.

Furthermore considering the enormous economy to the baker through its use, cottolene will certainly command the markets of the world.

In using cottolene for all cooking purposes, as shortening, but ⅔ as much as of lard or butter should be used, as it is so much richer in shortening properties; if more than ⅔ be used the food is made too rich. In frying with cottolene it should be put in a cold kettle or pan and allowed to heat gradually. It should be borne in mind that cottolene reaches a cooking temperature without any sputtering or smoking and quicker than lard with the same heat. Drop a piece of bread in the kettle in deep frying and if it browns in half a minute, or while you count sixty, it is ready for use. For all kinds of common bread, rolls, etc., it is the best shortening, and for frying doughnuts, croquettes, fritters, vegetables, fish, oysters, etc., it is unequaled.

NOTE.

In making up goods always get the ingredients ready. Before beginning the preparatory beating, etc., see that the cake-tins, pans, or baking-tins, are ready; currants, etc., washed, picked and weighed; peel cut; flour, butter, sugar, eggs, all weighed; and then the mind will be left clear to work out the necessary formula and directions. Also be sure and watch the process in every stage; be most careful about small details, such as the flavoring, baking, sending up or displaying; and above all, beware of dirty pans or cooking utensils, and grit in the fruit.

COMPOSITION CAKE.

20 eggs, 2 lbs sugar, 2 lbs butter, 4 lbs flour, 2 lbs currants, 3 lbs sultanas, 1 lb peel, ½ oz cream of tartar, ¼ oz soda. Cream the butter and sugar and mix as usual, place in 1 or 2 square tins, with edges about 3 inches deep, chopped almonds thickly sprinkled on top. This cake must be baked in a cool oven, and if baked in one piece will take two hours or more. The tins must be prepared with white stiff paper. It is usual in lieu of square pound cake tins to cut pieces of wood of the required height, and fasten them on a flat baking-tin, prop them up with pieces of brick.

SILVER CAKE.

1¼ lb butter, ½ lb sugar, 1 pint egg whites, 1½ lb flour, 12 drops of rose-flower water, and 1 glass of sherry ; cream the butter and sugar, and thoroughly beat with them the pint of whites, adding a few at the time ; having beaten these very light, put in the rose water and stir the flour in lightly ; put this into a buttered and prepared tin, and bake carefully. This cake is usually iced and ornamented in white, but it is very good indeed without icing.

BAKING HEAT.

Bread, rolls, buns, scones, tea biscuits, drop cakes, fancy cakes, New Years cakes, muffins, puff-paste, etc., needs a hot oven, or better, 450^0 Fahrenheit.

An expert can tell the heat of his oven by simply looking or touching the handle of the oven door, but the more common test is by throwing a little corn meal or flour in the centre of the oven, if the flour smokes before you can count 10 the oven is too hot, if it smokes at 10, the oven has the proper heat for the above goods.

As soon as these goods are baked and the heat reduced to 400^0 Fahrenheit the oven is ready to bake the following cakes :

Cream puffs, sugar cakes, queen cakes, rock cakes, jumbles, lady fingers, rough and ready, jelly rolls, etc.; after these cakes are baked the heat will be reduced to 350^0 Fahrh. and just right to bake wine cakes, cup cakes, sugar cakes, ginger nuts, and snaps, pies, ginger bread, spice cakes, madeira cakes, etc. Now your oven is ready to bake large cakes, such as raisin, currant, pound, citron, bride, white, marble cakes, and macaroons, etc.

After all these cakes are baked we have got the proper heat for : Wedding cakes, kisses, anise, drops, Auflauf, Windmassen, Zwiebackrösten, Zimmetstangen, etc.

Advice and Instructions.

1. It will pay to use the best Materials.
2. For Pastry, Pound and Lady Cake; have butter washed.
3. For common cake, knead the butter before using.
4. Always put your Soda, Ammonia in the milk or water.
5. Cream of Tartar, Baking Powder, Tartaric Acid in the flour.
6. Never stop when beating, rubbing or mixing.
7. Never bake anything in flash heat.
8. Always remove the contents of tin cans as soon as they are opened.
9. Keep your yeast cool and in a dry place.
10. Set your sponge warm and away from draft.
11. Have your dough cool and the trough greased.
12. Keep your peels clean and yeast tubes dry and clean.
13. Take ½ lb salt to 10 qts. water, summer time a little more.
14. Put a little lard into your bread, it will improve it very much.
15. 1 barrel of flour on an average will make 260 lbs of bread.
16. White-wash with plenty of carbolic acid into it, will kill all the cockroaches in the bakery.
17. The little brown spots on drop or fancy cakes shows that your Ammonia was not fine enough.
18. Soda, if not dissolved proper, will make brown spots on the inside of the cakes, which tastes bitter
19. Too much soda gives cakes and biscuits a bad green color.
20. All kinds of cakes or biscuits ought to be baked up in their own steam, that means, keep door and damper shut until they are done spreading, than if the oven is hot enough open door and damper and give the cakes a light bright color, Kisses meringue or large cake are not included.
21. 10 eggs are counted for a pint.
22. Never put flavoring extract or oil in the flour, as it will form lumps, always put them into the wet part of your mixture.
23. Cruller grease ought to be cleaned by every batch, the best and easiest way is as follows: As soon as you are done frying, pour your grease red hot in a tin pail, dirt and all, let it stand 2 or 3 hours and pour it back into the clean cruller pot and it is ready for use again.

Illustrirtes Cake- & Conditor-Buch

enthaltend

Ein Tausend werthvolle Recepte und Illustrationen für Cakes, Crackers, Custards, Pastry, Pies, Ice Creams, Traganth, Torten, Thee-, Tafel-, Mandel-, Leb- und Honig-Kuchen-Bäckerei.

Herausgegeben von

HERMAN HUEG,

Praktischer Conditor.

~~~Gedruckt in Englisch und Deutsch.~~~

PREIS $1.00.

1892.

VORWORT.

Das über Erwarten schnelle Bedürfniss nach erneuerter Auflage dieses Buches lieferte den Beweis seiner Nützlichkeit und Brauchbarkeit in hinlänglichem Maasse.

Die mir von mancher Seite gewordenen practischen Winke zur Verbesserung fanden in dieser Auflage ihre Anwendung, und es ist dem Collegen, dem jüngeren wie dem älteren, hiermit ein Hülfsbuch geworden, wie es an Reichthum und Vollkommenheit bisher auch nur annähernd niemals erreicht wurde.

Bei jeder einzelnen Sache sind die Verhältnisse genau angegeben, ebenso die Reihenfolge der Zumischung und das Verfahren bei der Bereitung. Ich bitte diesen Punkten die nothwendige Aufmerksamkeit zu schenken und versichere, dass denjenigen, die sich genau darnach richten, nichts misslingen dürfte; aber aus eben dem Grunde, ist die Art der Ausdrucksweise und die Kürze der Fassung entstanden.

Da es mir wohl bekannt ist, dass letzterem Umstande zufolge mancher Verstoss gegen Satzbildung und die Regeln der Grammatik sich eingeschlichen hat, dies aber nur durch ein nochmaliges Umschreiben verhindert werden konnte, so tröste ich mich damit, dass dieses Buch nur für praktische Fachgenossen, Hausfrauen und Mädchen bestimmt ist, aber nicht für Gelehrte ; ich bitte also diesen Punkt in Beziehung auf Kritik mild auffassen zu wollen.

Alle auch in Zukunft mir wieder werdenden Winke auf Verbesserung und Bereicherung von practischer Seite werden auch fernerhin dankbar entgegen genommen.

CONDITOREI.

I. Theil.

1. Das Läutern und die Proben des Zuckers.

Wenn der Zucker noch so schön und rein aussieht, so ist derselbe doch in der Auflösung nicht ganz klar, was man bei jedem Glas Zuckerwasser bemerken kann. Es ist jedoch bei vielen Arbeiten eine Hauptsache, den Zucker recht klar zu haben, deshalb unterwirft man den Zucker noch einer Reinigung, oder, wie die Conditoren sagen, man läutert denselben. Dies geschieht nun auf folgende Weise: Man nimmt je nach der Grösse des Kessels eine Quantität Zucker, meistens nimmt man dazu Brod-Melis oder A Sugar, rechnet auf 10 Pfund Zucker 4 Quart Wasser, welches man darüber giesst, quirlt auch noch ein Eiweiss mit etwas Wasser durch, giesst es ebenfalls über den Zucker und setzt den Kessel über Kohlenfeuer. Bevor der Zucker an das Kochen kommt, muss er ganz aufgelöst sein. Sobald der Zucker kocht, steigt er sehr stark, und man muss sich hüten, einen zu kleinen Kessel zu nehmen, da er leicht überlaufen kann. Sobald der Zucker also steigt, muss man etwas Wasser zur Hand haben; man giesst etwa $\frac{1}{4}$ Quart hinein und der Zucker fällt dadurch sofort. Dieses Experiment, Abschrecken genannt, wird dreimal wiederholt, alsdann nimmt man den Zucker vom Feuer und lässt ihn eine halbe Stunde stehen. Darauf hebt man den Schaum recht vorsichtig mit einem Schaumlöffel ab und setzt den Zucker wieder über das Feuer, um ihn bis zu der Probe zu kochen, als man denselben zur Verwendung bringen will. Oder man setzt auch den Zucker zurück, um bei vorkommenden Fällen Läuterzucker zur Hand zu haben.

2. Breitlauf.

Nachdem man obigen Läuterzucker auf starkem Kohlenfeuer mehrere Minuten gekocht hat, wird man finden, dass der Zucker von dem Schaumlöffel etwas breit abläuft. Dies wird der Breitlauf genannt.

3. Kleiner Faden.

Hat der Zucker wieder eine kleine Weile gekocht, so wird man finden, dass, wenn man etwas zwischen Daumen und Zeigefinger nimmt, man einen kleinen Faden ziehen kann.

4. Grosser Faden.

Wieder nach einer Weile wird man einen grossen Faden ziehen können.

5. Kleiner Flug.

Diese Probe lässt sich erkennen, wenn man den Schaumlöffel heraushebt, durch diesen bläst und kleine Blasen davon fliegen.

6. Grosser Flug.

Wie vorhergehend, nur müssen grosse Blasen davon fliegen.

7. Der Bruch.

Nun kommt ein Grad des Zuckers, der ziemlich schwer zu beschreiben ist und mehr Kenntniss erfordert, als bei den vorhergehenden Proben erforderlich ist; es ist dies der Bruch, diejenige Probe, welche der Zucker haben muss, um Bonbons davon anzufertigen. Diese Probe erkennt man am leichtesten, wenn man einen kleinen Stab in den Zucker taucht und schnell mit dem Stab in's kalte Wasser fährt; der dann am Stab befindliche Zucker muss recht hart sein und unter den Zähnen brechen. Wird dann der Zucker noch länger gekocht, so geht er dem Verbrennen entgegen.

In grösseren Ceschäften bedient man sich des Fahrenheit Thermometers. Der Bruch steht auf 280 Grad.

8. Conserven oder Morsellen.

Hierzu gebraucht man kleine Bretter, ungefähr 1 Fuss lang und 2 Zoll breit, welche man kurz vor dem Gebrauch in's Wasser legt, stellt dann eins auf die Kante legt dann eins flach, darauf wieder eins auf die Kante, und so fort. Man befestige sie mit Klammern.

9. Zweifarbige Conserven.

Hierzu nimmt man ein Pfund Zucker, den man zum Flug kocht, und dann einen Theelöffel voll Orangeblüthenwasser zusetzt, tablirt, und dann ausgiesst auf die Brettchen. Dann nimmt man abermals 1 Pfund Zucker, färbt ihn roth, kocht ihn zur Probe, giesst 3 Tropfen Rosenöl zu und tablirt ihn. Diesen Zucker giesst man nun genau auf den vorher ausgegossenen und hat dann zwei Farben auf einander, was sehr gut aussieht.

Auf dieselbe Weise kann man auch noch die dritte Farbe darauf bringen, indem man noch Chocoladen-Conserve darauf giesst.

10. Conserven in Puder.

Dieselbe Conserve, die in den vorher beschriebenen Paragraphen in Formen oder Holz gegossen ist, kann nun auch in Puder gegossen werden.

Hierzu hat man flache, etwa 1 bis 2 Zoll hohe Kästen, 1½ Fuss breit und 2½ Fuss lang, und füllt dieselben mit feinem Puder, den man recht ausgetrocknet hat. Diesen Puder streicht man nun recht glatt und drückt aus Gyps geschnittene Formen oder Figuren hinein. In diese Eindrücke giesst man nun die Conserve ein; dazu bedient man sich eines Trichters, der wie eine Düte geformt ist und unten eine Oeffnung, so gross wie eine Erbse, hat, welche durch einen Stock verschlossen ist, den man oben mit der einen Hand hält, während die andere den Trichter hat. Nun lässt man von einer zweiten Person sich von dem etwas schwächer tablirten Zucker in den Trichter giessen, hält ihn über die Eindrücke, hebt den Stock und lässt dieselben voll laufen. Diese Figuren kehrt man nach dem Erkalten mit einem feinen Handfeger oder Pinsel ab, gummirt sie, indem man sie mit aufgelöstem Gummi Arabicum, der so dick ist wie Zuckersyrup, bestreicht. Nun kann man die Figuren bemalen und sonst geschmackvoll decoriren.

11. Conserve-Figuren und Früchte.

Hierzu bedarf man Formen von Gyps oder Holz, die sich tüchtige Conditoren wohl selbst anfertigen können, sonst aber von Formenstechern gemacht werden. Diese Formen legt man in reines Wasser; wenn sie von Holz sind, müssen sie mehrere Stunden darin liegen, von Gyps ist es nicht so lange nothwendig. Hat man den Zucker nun wie oben zubereitet, so muss man einige Minuten vorher die Formen aus dem Wasser genommen haben und sie gehörig ablaufen lassen. Dann giesst man die Conserve in die Formen und nach einigen Minuten kann man die gegossenen Gegenstände schon herausnehmen, schneidet die Ränder, die sich durch die Formenkanten bilden, ab und legt sie zum Trocknen auf Siebe.

Sind die Formen zu den Figuren gross, so würde viel Zucker hinein gehen und dieselben sehr schwer werden; deshalb giesst man grössere Figuren und Früchte hohl, um sie dadurch leichter und auch besser aussehend zu machen, weil sie dadurch transparent werden. Um die Figuren nun hohl zu giessen, verfährt man so: man giesst die Formen erst ganz voll und nach einer Minute macht man mit einem Stöckchen oben an der Oeffnung der Form den erstarrten Zucker weg und giesst Alles, was herauslaufen will, wieder zurück in die Kasserolle, wendet dann die Form öfter um, damit, was etwa noch flüssig ist, egal in der Form sich vertheilt. Die offene Lücke, die sich nun gebildet hat, verschliesst man, wenn die Figur aus der Form heraus genommen ist, indem man ein wenig Conserve auf die Bonbonplatte giesst und die Figur darauf legt. Sind es indess Figuren, die unten einen Fuss haben, so ist dieser Verschluss nicht nothwendig. Wenn ich hier das Verfahren, Figuren und Früchte anzufertigen, zu erklären versuchte, so geschah es weniger, um es Denen klar zu machen, die es versuchen wollen, sondern um Denen einen Begriff davon zu geben, die gern wissen wollen, wie es gemacht wird. Es gehört jedenfalls zu solchen Arbeiten mehr Erfahrung und etwas Geschicklichkeit, um Früchte und Figuren natürlich und hübsch herstellen zu können.

12. Zucker-Coleur.

Wie schon erwähnt, geht der Zucker, wenn er den Bruch erreicht hat, dem Verbrennen entgegen, d. h. der Zucker bekommt zunächst eine gelbe Farbe, dann wird er braun und immer dunkler. Man kann mit diesem Zucker die schönsten Farben von Gelb bis zum tiefsten Braun erzielen, nur muss man den Zucker, wenn er dunkel genug ist, mit etwas Wasser verdünnen. Auf folgendem Wege lässt sich diese Coleur schneller anfertigen: Man thue $\frac{1}{2}$ lb Zucker in einen Kessel und rühre diesen Zucker über einem Feuer bis er sich gelöst und die erwünschte Farbe erreicht hat, alsdann schütte man etwas Wasser dazu und hebe diese Farbe zum Gebrauch auf.

Die Bonbon-Recepte findet man in einem andern Theile.

13. Nougat oder Croquant.

$\frac{1}{2}$ lb weisse Mandeln werden länglich geschnitten und geröstet, dann schmelze $\frac{1}{2}$ lb Zucker über Feuer, schütte die Mandeln hinein, rühre es mit $\frac{1}{4}$ lb Zimmet gut durch und schütte die Masse auf die gestrichene Bonbon-Platte und formire nach der Zeichnung.

14. Candiren.

Candiren heisst, verschiedenen Gegenständen einen Ueberzug von kleinen Zuckercrystallen zu geben, welcher diesen Gegenständen einen glitzernden Glanz verleiht, was besonders bei Licht einen hübschen Effect macht, wenn sich die Strahlen in den kleinen Crystallen brechen.—Man kann fast alle Gegenstände, die in der Conditorei gefertigt werden, candiren, wenn sie sonst einigermassen fest sind, sogar Auflauf, auch Chocolate und Tragantsachen. — Zum Candiren gehört nun eine Einrichtung, die besonders rein gehalten werden muss. Man lasse sich vom Klempner einen Blechkasten machen, ungefähr 1 Fuss breit, $1\frac{1}{2}$ Fuss lang und

4—6 Zoll hoch, oben etwas breiter als unten. Unten über dem Boden hat der Kasten ein kleines Abzugsrohr, welches mit einem Kork verschlossen wird. Im Innern des Kastens sind kleine Haken angebracht, worauf man Drahtgitter legen kann, die die Grösse des Kastens haben. Auf diese Gitter legt man nun die zum Candiren bestimmten Sachen nicht gar zu eng, auch der Boden wird damit belegt. Die Anzahl der Gitter zu dem beschriebenen Kasten richtet sich natürlich nach der Höhe der zu candirenden Sachen und dürfte von $\frac{1}{2}$ Zoll als niedrigste Entfernung ausgegangen werden.

Das Candiren bedarf jedenfalls einiger Erfahrung, wie die meisten Laborator- oder Kesselarbeiten, die auch in den Conditoreien von den älteren und erfahreneren Gehilfen besorgt werden und so gehört besonders zum Candiren Erfahrung und viel Sorgfalt. Der Zucker, der zum Candiren verwendet werden soll, muss sehr gut gereinigt sein; man nimmt auch nur den feinsten Raffinat dazu und kocht denselben zum Faden. Man richtet sich auch hier nach den zu candirenden Sachen, einigen giebt man gern grössere Crystalle, deshalb muss man wissen, ob der Faden stärker oder schwächer zu nehmen ist. Ist der Candirkasten gefüllt und man hat eine angemessene Menge Zucker zur Fadenprobe gekocht, so lässt man denselben so viel abkühlen, dass er nur noch lauwarm ist und giesse ihn nun über die zu candirenden Gegenstände in den Kasten hinein. Der Zucker muss einen Finger hoch über die zu candirenden Gegenstände stehen. Oben auf den Zucker legt man nun ein Papier, so gross wie der Kasten und setzt denselben in einen mässig warmen Raum. Nach circa 6 Stunden hebe man das Papier etwas in die Höhe, um einen der hineingelegten Gegenstände herauszunehmen und zu untersuchen. Findet man, dass sich schon Crystalle genug angesetzt haben, so zieht man den Kork aus der kleinen Röhre heraus und fängt den herauslaufenden Zucker in einer Schüssel auf, setzt den Kasten etwas schief, damit alles ablaufen kann und darauf in einen Trockenschrank, wo die Gegenstände bald getrocknet sein werden, um sie dann herauszunehmen, auf Siebe zu legen und sie noch weiter abzutrocknen.

15. Das Carmeliren.

Wenn in der vorhergehenden Nummer vom Candiren gesprochen ist, so soll diese Nummer von dem Carmeliren sprechen. Man karmelirt gern solche Sachen, die dadurch einmal an Geschmack und dann an Aussehen gewinnen. Zuerst wollen wir von den Sachen reden, die an kleine Stöckchen oder Drähte gesteckt werden. Das sind Nusskerne von Wallnüssen, geröstete Maronen, auch wohl Mandeln. Man kocht, nachdem die zu überziehenden Sachen alle an Stöckchen gesteckt sind, den Zucker, dem man einen Löffelvoll Essigsprit zugesetzt hat, zum Bruch und taucht die Nüsse etc. so tief in den Zucker, dass sie ganz davon überzogen sind und reicht dieselben einer zweiten Person, die dieselben noch mehrmals umwendet und dann auf die gestrichene Bonbonplatte legt, während die erste Person fortfährt, in den Zucker einzutauchen. Nach dem Erkalten der Sachen zieht man behutsam die Stöckchen heraus und verwendet die überzogenen Gegenstände entweder zum Garniren oder giebt sie als Dessert.

II. Theil.

16. Torten-Bäckerei.

Leider muss ich erwähnen, dass der vielgeliebte Mandelstein dem Almond-Paste das Feld räumt, somit bin auch ich gezwungen, die nachfolgenden Recepte für den Almond-Paste zu bearbeiten.

Sehr wesentlich ist es beim Tortenbacken, dass die Massen gut gerührt, die Eier nach und nach dazu gerührt und dann recht vorsichtig gebacken werden.

17. Mandeltorte.

$\frac{1}{2}$ lb Almond-Paste verreibe mit 4 Eier, thue $\frac{3}{4}$ lb Zucker dazu und rühre nach und nach 8 Eigelb darunter, das Weisse der Eier schlägt man zu Schnee und rührt denselben mit $\frac{3}{4}$ lb Mehl behutsam unter die Masse, fülle in eine mit Papier ausgelegte Form und backe. Backzeit ungefähr $\frac{3}{4}$ Stunden. Bei gefüllten Mandeltorten bäckt man die Masse in Böden und füllt sie Marmalade.

18. Nuss-Torte.

Wie oben, nur nimmt man $\frac{1}{4}$ lb Nusskerne statt Mandeln.

Bemerkung.

Erwähnen möchte ich, dass die Conditoren ihre Massen nicht mit der blossen Hand rühren, wie es der Fall bei Cake-Bäckern ist, sondern mit einem Spatel. Nach dieser Methode werden auch die folgenden Recepte bearbeitet:

19. Apfelsinentorte.

Backe 3 oder 4 Böden aus Mandelmasse und fülle sie mit folgendem Crême, thue ¼ lb Zucker und die abgeriebene Schale und Saft einer Apfelsine, 3 ganze und 4 gelbe Eier in einen Kessel, giesse ein Glas Weisswein und den Saft einer Citrone dazu und schlage es auf Kohlenfeuer schaumig, ohne es jedoch kochen zu lassen, fülle die Torte und belege sie mit Apfelsinen-Scheiben.

20. Wiener-Torte.

Rühre ½ lb Zucker mit 12 Eigelb schaumig, inzwischen hat man ½ lb Mehl gewogen und ½ lb Butter in einer Pfanne heiss gemacht, das Weisse der Eier schlägt man zu Schnee, alsdann rührt man die heisse Butter mit etwas Schnee unter die Masse, und mischt das Mehl und Schnee behutsam darunter, bäckt die Masse in Böden, füllt sie mit Marmalade, glasire und garnire. Erwähnen will ich, dass dieses das Original-Recept für Jellyroll ist, welcher jetzt überall aus Biscuit-Masse gemacht wird, aber ein Jellyroll aus obiger Masse ist eine Delicatesse.

21. Punsch-Torte.

Backe 2 bis 3 Böden aus Wiener Masse, fülle sie mit Apfelmarmalade, welcher man etwas Rum zugesetzt hat, thue auch etwas Rum in die Glasur.

22. Brod-Torte.

Verreibe ½ lb Almond-Paste mit 4 Eier, rühre diese Masse mit 10 oz Zucker und 10 Eigelb schaumig. Inzwischen sind 3 oz geröstetes und gestossenes Brod in etwas Rum aufgeweicht und 2 oz Chocolade gerieben, dann schlägt man 6 Eiweiss zu Schnee, rühre denselben mit Brod, Chocolade und 2 lb Mehl unter die Masse, mittlere Hitze, glasirt und garnirt.

23. Torte-Imperial.

Wie oben, nur setzt man ein Gläschen Kirschwasser und etwas Zimmet und Nelken zu, und lässt das Brod fort.

24. Chocoladen-Torte.

Wie oben, und mit Chocoladen Glasur glasirt und weiss garnirt.

25. Biscuit-Torte.

Schlage ½ lb Zucker, 8 Eier über schwachem Feuer schaumig, schlage es wieder kalt und rühre ½ lb Mehl mit etwas Gewürz behutsam darunter; mehr wie Milchwarm darf die Masse nicht werden.

Biscuit-Torte, kalt.

Rühre ½ lb Zucker mit 10 Eigelb schaumig und rühre den Schnee von 10 Eiweiss mit ½ lb Mehl und etwas Gewürz darunter.

27. Aleanca-Torte.

Theile die fertige Mandelmasse in 3 Theile, fàrbe ein Theil braun mit Chocolade, den anderen Theil roth mit Cochenille, und fülle. Diese 3 Farben mischt man nun so in der Form, dass, wenn die Torte geschnitten wird, alle 3 Farben zu sehen sind.

28. Gefüllte Aleanca-Torte.

Wie oben, nur bäckt man die Masse in Böden.

29. Eisenbahn-Torte.

Setze der Mandelmasse etwas Chocolade, Zimmet und Nelken zu, backe 2 Böden, fülle mit Marmalade und glasire. Bei dem Garniren ziehe man Streifen von Chocoladen-Glasur rings um die Torte, die die Eisenbahn versinnbildlichen soll.

30. Berliner Torte.

Backe 2 Böden von Mandel-Masse und fülle sie mit folgendem crême: Schlage über Feuer einen crême von 3 oz Zucker, 6 Eigelb, ½ pt Sahne oder Milch, ½ oz corn starch und etwas Vanilla.

31. Sand-Torte.

Rühre ¾ lb Butter recht schaumig, setze ¾ lb Zucker zu und rühre fort. Inzwischen hat man ¾ lb Mehl gewogen und rührt davon je 1 Löffel voll und 1 Eigelb in die Masse, bis man 9 Eigelb darunter hat; alsdann rühre den Schnee von 9 Eiweiss, 1 Gläschen Rum und etwas Gewürz darunter. Diese Masse wird in einer Form, welche eine Tülle hat, gebacken, dann glasirt und garnirt.

32. Macronen-Torte.

Mache eine Macronen-Masse von 1 lb almond paste, 12 Eiweiss, 1½ lb Zucker, bestreiche hiermit einen Oblaten-Bogen und tressire mit einer Spritze Streifen darüber, setze Tupfen rings um die Kante, backe, glasire und belege die tiefen Stellen mit eingemachten Früchten und garnire mit Spritz-Glasur.

33. Baiser-Torte.

Von 10 Eiweiss schlägt man einen recht festen Schnee und rührt 1 lb Zucker darunter; dann nimmt man 2 Bogen Papier, zeichnet mit einer Bleifeder auf jeden einen runden Kreis von etwa 10 Zoll Durchmesser, bestreicht beide Kreise mit der Baiser-Masse recht glatt, etwa $\frac{1}{4}$ Zoll hoch, macht dann eine Tüte, füllt von derselben Masse hinein und spritzt nun auf den einen Boden eine hübsche Verzierung und setzt eine Perlkante auf den Rand. Nun bestäubt man beide Boden mit Zucker und backt sie recht langsam ab. Es ist gut, wenn man die Torte auf ein heiss gemachtes Blech setzt, weil sich dann das Papier ablösen lässt. Sobald die Torte trocken genug ist, zieht man das Papier davon ab und trocknet sie noch weiter ab.

Den verzierten Boden, der als Deckel gebraucht wird, kann man auch so machen, dass man die Verzierung gleich auf das Papier spritzt und dann einen Rand darum macht, man muss aber dabei beobachten, dass guter Verband darin ist, weil sonst die Arbeit leicht zerbrechlich ist.

Diese beschriebene Torte füllt man nun mit geschlagener Sahne, die mit Zucker und gestossener Vanille versetzt ist. Die Torte darf jedoch erst kurz vor dem Gebrauch gefüllt werden.

34. Eis-Torte.

Um eine Eis-Torte herzustellen, muss man auch erst eine Baiser-Torte backen und füllt statt der Sahne Vanille-Eis hinein, wenigstens ist dieses das dazu passendste und beliebteste.

35. Baiser-Berg.

Hierzu bereitet man, je nach der Grösse, die man gebraucht, von Baiser-Masse einen Boden mit Tupfen auf dem Rande, wie bei der Baiser-Torte, dann einen zweiten einen Zoll kleiner, und so fort jeden Boden einen Zoll kleiner, die, wenn man dieselben auf einander legt, eine Pyramide bilden. Diese einzelnen Böden werden nun alle mit geschlagener Sahne, die mit Zucker und Vanille versetzt ist, gefüllt, auch nach Belieben noch mit Sahne bespritzt.

36. Baiser-Berg auf andere Art.

Da der vorhin beschriebene Baiser-Berg sich sehr schlecht trangiren lässt, so hat man es dahin geändert, nur einen Boden zu backen und darauf die Sahne pyramidenförmig aufzustreichen und die Sahne dann mit kleinen Baiser-Tupfen zu belegen, die man von derselben Baiser-Masse gebacken hat.

37. Schaum-Torte.

Backe 2 Böden von Wiener Biscuit-Masse, fülle sie mit Gelee oder Marmelade zusammen, bestreiche auch den oberen Boden damit und bestreiche dann das Ganze mit einem Baiser von 8 Eiweiss und $\frac{1}{2}$ lb Zucker, verziere auch damit die Torte und backe sie flüchtig etwas gelblich ab. Verziert wird diese Torte, wie schon früher beschrieben, mit Gelée.

38. Elisen-Torte.

Ein Boden von Mürbeteich, eine Federspule stark ausgerollt, rund geschnitten, ein Rand darauf gelegt, den man etwas kneift und halb ausbäckt, wird mit Marmelade gefüllt, dann eine Wiener oder Mandelmasse $\frac{1}{2}$ Zoll hoch hineingefüllt und flüchtig gebacken. Auf diese Torte spritzt man von Macronen-Masse lauter Kränze, zwischen denen man etwas Raum lässt, und noch einen Rand von Tupfen, bäckt diese wieder flüchtig aus, glasirt sie dann sofort und garnirt die Torte noch mit Gelée und Früchten.

39. Marschall-Torte.

Backe eine Wiener Torte, bestreiche dieselbe mit Gelée, schlage eine Windmasse von 6 Eiweiss und $\frac{1}{2}$ lb Zucker, bespritze die Torte gitterartig, bestaube sie mit Zucker und backe sie hellgelb im heissen Ofen, dann verziere sie mit Gelée und Früchten.

III. Theil.

Von den Tafel-Aufsätzen.

Tafel-Aufsätze nennt man solche Torten oder Kuchen, die eine hohe Form haben, die entweder durch Zusammensetzung von mehreren Torten, Ringen oder Blättern erreicht wird. Auch bereitet man aus verschiedenen Massen, als Croquant, Marzipan, Caramel etc., noch Aufsätze, die schwieriger herzustellen sind, zu denen sich aber nicht gut eine Anweisung geben lässt, weil dabei der Geschmack und die Phantasie des Anfertigers sich nicht gut an eine Anweisung binden lässt. Soweit dies jedoch geschehen kann, sollen hier einige Beispiele folgen.

40. Fruchtkorb aus Macronen-Masse.

Der Korb lässt sich rund oder auch oval herstellen. Mit der Blechspritze und Sterntülle dressirt man aus fester Macronenmasse Ringe auf Bleche, die man mit Butter und Mehl bestrichen hat. Hat man den ersten, unteren Ring gespritzt, so macht man den zweiten, dritten und vierten, je um einen halben Finger breit schmäler, als den vorhergehenden. Diese bilden den Fuss des Korbes. Von da ab macht man jeden Ring wieder etwas grösser, bis der Korb, nachdem die Ringe mit Glasur zusammengesetzt sind, eine angenehme Form erhalten hat. Auf eine Marmorplatte spritzt man einen längeren und entsprechend breiten Streifen, der als Henkel dienen soll. Zucker, den man etwas roth färbt, kocht man zu Caramel. Mit diesem Caramelzucker wird jener Streifen, den man zu einem halbrunden Bogen zusammenbiegt, als Henkel an den Korb befestigt. Von gewöhnlicher Macronenmasse backt man eine Platte, so gross als die obere Weite des Korbes, setzt sie hinein, befestigt sie und belegt sie mit carmelirten Früchten und Blättern. Der Korb wird sodann noch passend verziert.

41. Baumkuchen.

Zur Anfertigung von Baumkuchen bedarf es vor Allem einer Backanstalt. In grösseren Conditoreien ist eine solche stets feststehend aufgestellt, in kleineren Geschäften jedoch stellt man eine solche auf einem Queerherd auf, der eine massive Rückwand hat. Man hat dazu zwei Böcke nöthig, etwa wie beim Kaffeebrennen, jedoch müssen dieselben fester und so eingerichtet sein, dass die Baumkuchenwalze etwa 10 Zoll hoch zu liegen kommt und ebenso weit von der Wand absteht. Das Feuer kommt unmittelbar an die Wand und man stellt Steine in der Höhe von 3 Zoll und 3 Zoll von der Wand davor und bildet auch von Steinen Seitenwände, die so weit von einander stehen, als die Baumkuchen-Walze lang ist. Die schon genannte Baumkuchen-Walze ist aus sehr trockenem, festem Holze gedreht, etwa 2 bis $2\frac{1}{2}$ Fuss lang, an der Spitze 6 Zoll, unten 8 bis 10 Zoll dick und mit eisernen Ringen beschlagen. Genau durch die Mitte geht ein eiserner Spiess, der $1\frac{1}{2}$ Fuss länger als die Walze ist und an der einen Seite einen Griff mit Bogen hat, womit man drehen kann. Der Spiess muss fest in der Walze stecken. Die Walze wird mit festem Papier umwickelt und ausserdem mit Bindfaden umwunden, dessen Faden oben und unten an der Walze an einem kleinen Nagel befestigt ist.

Ausser diesen Vorrichtungen bedarf man noch eines kupfernen oder eisernen flachen Kastens, so lang als die Walze und 10 Zoll breit und 2 Zoll hoch, um die Masse aufzutragen und auch die abfliessende Masse wieder aufzufangen. Das Auftragen der Masse geschieht mit einem grossen Löffel von Blech mit hölzernem Stiel.

Zum Backen der Baumkuchen muss man recht trockenes, fein gespaltenes Holz haben und ist ellernes oder buchenes

Holz das geeignetste dazu, weil dasselbe keine Funken abwirft.

Nachdem man alle Vorbereitungen getroffen hat, fertigt man die Masse an, und will ich nun beschreiben, wie man beim Backen verfährt.

Zuerst macht man Feuer und stellt dabei das Holz meist hoch auf, damit die Flamme recht nach oben schlägt, auch legt man Holzstücke quer, doch muss man immer darauf achten, dass der Rauch nach hinten schlägt und nicht an den zu backenden Kuchen, weil das nicht allein den Geschmack beeinträchtigt, sondern auch schlecht aussieht. Man legt nun die Baumkuchen-Walze auf und lässt sie recht heiss werden, nimmt dann 2 Löffel voll von der Masse in die Baumkuchen-Pfanne, die unter der Walze steht, und trägt davon mit dem Löffel auf die Walze, die von einer zweiten Person fortwährend gedreht wird. In der Regel bildet man zuerst lauter Ringe aus der Masse, etwa 4 Zoll von einander, und muss dabei fortwährend das Feuer gut unterhalten. Hat man den ersten Theil der Masse verbraucht, so nimmt man wieder ebensoviel in die Pfanne und trägt sie ebenso auf wie die erste, jedoch muss die zuerst aufgetragene Masse schon etwas gelblich gebacken sein, was nur die Zeit weniger Minuten bedarf. Man fährt nun fort, in der beschriebenen Weise die Masse in kleineren Theilen aufzutragen und achte dabei darauf, die schon gelblich gebackene Masse möglichst zu decken, weil, wenn nicht frische Masse darüber kommt, sich dunkelbraune Stellen bilden, die den Geschmack und das Aussehen des Kuchens beeinträchtigen. Nachdem nun die Ringe durch 6- bis 8maliges Auftragen sich hoch genug gebildet haben und Zacken angesetzt, so nimmt man etwas mehr Masse und füllt dann, nachdem erst wieder die Ringe übergossen sind, die Lücken zwischen denselben aus. Beim nächsten Auftragen richtet man sich wieder so ein, dass die Masse für die Ringe und dazwischen ausreicht, und um das Uebergiessen zu erleichtern und die Masse deckender zu haben, giesst man wohl $\frac{1}{2}$ Tasse Milch dazwischen, besonders beim letzten Auftragen. Nachdem die Masse nun alle aufgetragen, was etwa auf eine Masse von 1 Pfund Zucker eine Stunde dauert, lässt man den Kuchen über den Kohlen, die man etwas ausbreitet, hübsch goldgelb ausbacken und glasirt ihn dann mit Wasserglasur vermittelst eines Pinsels, schneidet dann unten und oben den Bindfaden ab und hebt den Kuchen mit dem Papier ab.

42. Kranz-Kuchen.

Man reibe 1 lb geschälte und getrocknete Mandeln, recht fein, mit etwa 16 Eiweiss und reibe dann 1½ lb feinen Zucker dazu, auch nimmt man etwas Citronenschaale und fein gehackten Citronat hinein. Nun klebt man ein Paar Tafeln Oblaten zusammen und schneidet mit dem Cirkel zwei runde Böden, die einen etwa 10 Zoll im Durchmesser, den zweiten einen halben Finger breit kleiner. Aus diesen Oblatenböden schneidet man nun lauter einen Finger breite Ringe vermittelst des Cirkels aus und erhält dadurch eine regelmässige Pyramide. Nun legt man diese Ringe auf Papier auseinander, füllt die Macronenmasse, die nicht zu fest sein darf, in eine Spritze, die eine Tülle in der Stärke eines kleinen Fingers hat und bespritzt damit die Oblatenringe, dann streuet man etwas geschnittene oder gehackte Mandeln darüber und bäckt sie recht saftig aus. Nachdem sie aus dem Ofen kommen, glasirt man die Ringe mit Vanille-Glasur. — Man wird nun noch Macronenmasse übrig haben und verwendet dieselbe, indem man auf Papier kleine Ringe oder Macronen spritzt, die man auch mit gehackten Mandeln bestreut und die nachher zwischen die Ringe gesetzt werden.

43. Aufsatz auf Baumkuchen.

Werden aus obiger Masse gemacht, indem man dieselben durch eine Stern-Scheibe spritzt, zuerst einen Ring so gross wie der Baumkuchen, dann 6 Stück Schnörkel in C- oder S-Form, setzt dieselben zusammen auf den Ring zu einer Krone, dazwischen setzt man Mandelblätter, Blumen u. dgl., oben darauf eine Figur. Auch kann man die Seiten des Baumkuchens mit Schnörkel, Mandelblätter, Blumen u. dgl. schmücken.

44. Caramel-Figuren und Blumen.

Der zum Bruch gekochte Zucker wird in leicht geschmierte Zinnforme gegossen. Blumenstempel taucht man in Caramel und lässt sie bei öfterem Umdrehen erkalten.

45. Mandel-Spähne.

Man schneide aus fester, doch nicht zu starker Pappe Schablonen, wie etwa ein Eichenblatt, in verschiedene Grössen, oder wählt eine andere Form, etwa ein oval, oder wie sonst der Geschmack es liebt. Dann bestreicht man Bleche mit Butter, legt die Schablone darauf und streicht mit einem biegsamen Messer (Bowl-knife) von der beschriebenen Masse über die Schablone weg, hebt dieselbe dann fort und wird dann ein Blatt, oder was die Schablone vorstellt, auf dem Bleche haben. Diese Blätter bäckt man nun aus, was sehr schnell geschieht, weil man sie recht dünn macht, hat inzwischen Rollhölzer oder rund gebogene Bleche zurecht gelegt und legt darauf die heissen, gebackenen Blätter, die sich dadurch biegen. Später bespritzt man auch diese Blätter und gewinnt dadurch eine hübsche Verzierung zu allerhand Aufsätzen.

46. Aufsatz von Bonbon.

Zu solchen Aufsätzen hat man häufig Formen aus Zinn oder Kupfer, in welche man den Caramel hineingiesst. Jedoch kann man auch ohne solche Formen Aufsätze von Bonbon herstellen und muss man dann sich die Schnörkel, die man dazu haben will, auf Pappe zeichnen, dann ausschneiden und dann auf den gestrichenen Bonbonstein legen und mit Spritzglasur einen starken Faden an den äusseren Kanten des Schnörkels ziehen. Hat man das gethan, so nimmt man behutsam den Schnörkel von Pappe aus dem gespritzten Faden heraus, legt ihn etwas weiter und macht es ebenso, bis man genug solcher Theile hat. Hat man gar keine Formen, so muss man alle Stücke, die man gebraucht, in eine solche Einzwängung giessen. Zu diesen Aufsätzen kocht man meistens verschiedene Farben von Bonbon und giesst von jeder Farbe einen Theil der Schnörkel. Beim Giessen dieser Schnörkel muss man eine Pfanne mit etwas enger Tülle haben, damit es nicht so dick herausfliesst. Die äusseren Kanten der Bonbon-Schnörkel bespritzt man mit Spritzglasur und setzt sie dann zusammen mit aufgelöstem Zucker.

47. Macronenaufsatz von 2 Etagen.

Von fester Macronenmasse dressirt man verschiedene Schnörkel, z. B. 6 Stück S zur unteren Etage, 6 Stück C, welche man um $\frac{1}{3}$ kleiner macht, zur zweiten. Dann bereitet man 4 Ringe, nämlich 2 so gross als die Platte, auf der der Aufsatz stehen soll, und 2 kleinere, um zwischen der ersten und zweiten Etage zu liegen. Dies alles setzt man mit flüssig gemachtem Zucker zusammen und bringt dazwischen verschiedenen Zierrath an, als: Mandelblätter, Glasurspähne, Blumen, farbige Mandeln, Silbespillen, grüne Blätter von Papier u. dergl. Oben auf die Krone setzt man ein Blumenkörbchen oder eine Figur.

48. Füllhorn.

In einer Thonform, die man vom Töpfer hat anfertigen lassen, bäckt man von beliebiger Tortenmasse die Figur eines Füllhorns, überspritzt dieselbe mit Schaummasse oder glasirt sie, belegt die Figur am breiten Ende mit Früchten und verziert alles geschmackvoll.

49. Macronen-Pyramide.

Nachdem man die Form geschmiert hat, lässt man auf Feuer etwas Zucker unter beständigem Rühren schmelzen, fange von unten an; wenn man dann die Form entfernt hat, verziere und garnire man dieselbe mit Glasur, Mandelspähnen, Blumen und dergl., oben darauf setzt man gern eine Traganth oder Caramel-Figur.

50. Gateaux oder Felsenzucker.

Koch 2lb Zucker zum Bruch, rühre einen Esslöffel Eiweiss-Glasur hinein, rühre es mit dem Spatel tüchtig durch und giesse den Zucker in die mit Butter bestrichene Form. Man kann auch den Zucker hart werden lassen, und schneidet mit der Säge beliebige Stücke davon. (Ein paar Tropfen Citronensaft zu dieser Masse ist sehr zu empfehlen.

51. Pousier Wachs.

Schmelze 4 oz gelbes Wachs, dann thue ½ Esslöffel voll venetianischen Terpentin dazu, ¼ oz Fass-Unschlitt, rühre Alles gut durch einander, nimm es vom Feuer und mische soviel feine Kreide darunter, dass man es gut bearbeiten kann. Die Figuren werden dann mit Instrumenten von Knochen oder Messing ausgearbeitet. Will man sie nach der Verfertigung glatt haben, so nehme man einen Haarpinsel, tauche denselben in Terpentin-Oel und streiche sie glatt.

52. Glasur-Späne.

Man streiche eine nicht zu feste Spritz Glasur auf Oblate, schneide sie dann in längliche Streifen, lege sie auf gebogene Bleche oder Hölzer, und wenn trocken, garnire man sie recht schön und gebrauche sie zu Aufsätzen, um die Ecken und Winkel auszufüllen. Diese Späne fertigt man auch in verschiedenen Farben an.

IV. Theil.

Thee- und Tafel-Bäckerei.

53. Blätter-Teig.

1 lb Mehl, 1 Ei, 1 oz Butter and soviel Wasser, dass der Teig 1½ lb wiegt; arbeite den Teig tüchtig und lege ihn an einen kalten Platz. Dies ist der Grundteig.

Dieser Grundteig wird mit dem Rollholze federspulenstark ausgerollt, 1 lb Butter darauf gelegt und von allen vier Seiten von dem Grundteige überschlagen, so dass die Butter in der Mitte zu liegen kommt; dies wird dann behutsam ausgerollt, dass keine Butter heraus gequetscht wird, und hat es dann die Dicke eines viertel Zolles erreicht, so wird der Teig wieder vierfach zusammen geschlagen; bei dem Rollen ist es nöthig, den Backtisch mit Mehl zu bestäuben, damit der Teig nicht anhängt, es darf aber nur so wenig wie möglich sein, denn sonst geschieht der Schönheit der Waare Eintrag; vor dem Zusammenschlagen muss das angehängte Mehl abgekehrt werden, man lässt dann den Teig eine viertel Stunde ruhen. Dann wird er noch dreimal ausgerollt und überschlagen. Um sich von der Güte des Teiges zu überzeugen, nimmt man eine kleine Probe (sticht ein Plätzchen heraus) und backt es bei flüchtiger Hitze; schmilzt noch nach unten Butter heraus, so muss der Teig noch einmal ausgerollt und zusammen geschlagen werden; die Probe ist gut, wenn er in die Höhe steigt, sich auf eine Seite legt und trocken aussieht. Der Teig ist nun zum Schneiden fertig.

In jeder anderen Stadt macht man aus Blätterteig Stücke mit anderen Namen und anderer Form, und es würde zu weit führen, die Menge mir bekannter Formen und Namen hier aufzuführen. Ich will nur im Allgemeinen darüber bemerken, dass man verschiedene Ausstecher dazu hat, um den Blätterteig auszustechen; oftmals füllt man denselben mit Marmelade (Gelee darf man nicht nehmen, weil dasselbe beim Backen ausfliessen würde), schlägt ihn zusammen, bestreicht ihn mit Ei und legt ihn in Hagelzucker. Auch wird derselbe nach dem Backen glasirt mit Wasser-, auch mit Eiweissglasur.

54. Mürbe-Teig.

3 lbs Mehl, 2 lbs Butter, 1 lb Zucker, Zimmet, $\frac{1}{2}$ oz Ammonia.

55. Zimmet-Sterne.

1 lb Butter, 1 lb Zucker, 4 Eier, $\frac{1}{4}$ oz Ammonia, $\frac{1}{4}$ pt Milch, 2 lbs Mehl, mit Milch bestrichen und in Hagelzucker gelegt.

56. Anis-Plätzchen.

2 lbs Zucker, 8 Eier, 1 lb Mehl, warm schlagen, 2 Stunden trocknen lassen und backen in mittlerer Hitze

57. Gewürz-Ringe.

2 lbs Krümel, $\frac{1}{2}$ lb Zucker, 2 oz Butter, 6 Eier, $\frac{1}{2}$ pt Molasses, 1 lb Mehl, $\frac{1}{2}$ oz Ammonia, Gewürz.

58. Pumpernickel.
1 lb geschnittene Mandeln, 2 lbs Zucker, 4 lbs Krümel, 18 Eier 2 lbs Mehl, 1 oz Ammonia, Gewürz.

59. Theestengel.
½ lb Butter, 1 lb Zucker, 4 Eier, 1½ lb Mehl, ¼ oz Ammonia, mit Ei bestrichen; heisser Ofen.

60. Chocoladen-Ringe.
1 lb Zucker, 2 oz Butter, 4 Eier ¼ lb geriebene Chocolade, 1 lb Mehl, ¼ oz Ammonia.

61. Macronen-Törtchen.
Belege 18 Rosettenformen mit Mürbeteig, thue etwas Marmelade hinein, schlage 5 Eiweiss zu Schnee, 6 oz Zucker, 3 oz gestossene Mandeln, fülle die Törtchen damit, bestaube sie mit Zucker und backe sie langsam.

62. Anis-Zwieback.
2 lbs Zucker, 18 Eier, warm geschlagen, 1 oz Anis, 2 lbs Mehl untergerührt; auf bestaubten Blechen tressirt, heiss gebacken, wenn kalt, geschnitten und leicht geröstet. Dieses giebt sechs Stangen.

63. Vanille-Bretzeln.
1 lb Zucker, 1 lb Butter, 4 Eier, 2 lbs Mehl, ¼ oz Ammonia, zu Bretzeln geformt, mit Ei gewaschen und in Hagelzucker gelegt.

64. Thee-Kuchen.
1½ lb Zucker, 2 lbs Butter, 8 Eier, ¼ pt Milch, ¼ oz Ammonia, 4 lbs Mehl.

65. Napoleons.
Backe einen dünnen Kuchen von Blätterteig, halb durchgeschnitten; die eine Hälfte bestreiche mit Vanille Crême, lege die andere darauf, mit Wasserglasur glasirt und geschnitten.

66. Crême-Törtchen.
Steche von Pieteig Rosetten aus und tressire einen Rand von Cream Cake-Masse darum, backe und glasire den Rand mit Chocoladen-Glasur und fülle mit Vanille-Crême.

67. Maserinen.
Rosettenförmchen werden mit Blätterteig ausgelegt und gefüllt mit ¼ lb Almond Paste, ¾ lb Zucker, ¼ lb Krümel, und Eiweiss genug, dass es eine weiche Masse giebt, lege ein Streifchen darüber und backe.

68. Leipziger-Kuchen.

Wie oben, nur fülle sie mit ¼ lb gehackten Mandeln, ½ lb Zucker, Eiweiss, lege ein Streifchen darüber, bestaube sie mit Zucker und backe.

69. Marschall-Kuchen.

Aehnlich wie oben; rolle eine Platte Blätterteig, bestreiche sie mit obiger Mandelmasse, schneide in Rauten und backe.

70. Porzellan-Schnitte.

Wie oben, nur statt der Mandelmasse nehme Spritz-Glasur.

71. Schaum-Torte.

Backe einen Boden von Mürbeteig, bestreiche mit Gelee, überziehe sie mit Windmasse und decorire.

72. Thee-Bretzeln.

½ lb Butter, ½ lb Zucker, mit 5 Eiern gerührt, 1 lb Mehl dazu, spritze die Bretzeln auf Bleche, bewerfe sie mit Hagelzucker und backe.

73. Vanille-Bretzeln.

¼ lb Butter, ¼ lb Zucker, ½ lb Mehl, 1 Eiweiss; forme davon Bretzeln, backe und glasire mit Vanille-Glasur.

74. Vanille Thee-Biscuit.

5 oz Butter, ½ lb Zucker, mit 3 Eiern schaumig gerührt, 14 oz Mehl, ¼ oz Ammonia; hiervon steche die Form einer Schuhsohle aus, ¼ Zoll dick, bestreiche sie mit Ei, lege sie in Hagelzucker und backe.

75. Zimmet-Stangen.

Reibe ½ lb Almond Paste mit 5 bis 6 Eiweiss, 1½ lb Zucker dazu, rolle hiervon einen langen, 3 Zoll breiten Streifen aus, glasire ihn mit fester Eiweiss-Glasur, schneide in ¾ Zoll breite Streifchen und backe sie auf bestaubten Blechen.

76. Mandel-Berge.

10 Eiweiss zu Schnee, 1 lb Zucker, ½ lb geschnittene Mandeln, etwas geröstet, formire kleine Häufchen und backe langsam.

77. Congress-Kuchen.

Reibe ¼ lb braune Mandeln mit Eiweiss, thue sie in eine Schüssel, wiege dann ¾ lb Zucker zu, thue etwas Zimmet hinein und rühre die Masse mit so viel Eiweiss schaumig, dass dieselbe dickflüssig wird. Diese Masse fülle alsdann in die mit Mürbeteig ausgelegten Formen, lege von denselben ein leichtes Kreuz darüber, besiebe sie mit Zucker und backe sie langsam aus. Bevor man die Masse einfüllt, kann man auch etwas Marmelade in die Formen thun und dann die Füllung.

78. Devrient.

Backe von ¼ lb Mandeln eine Brodtorten-Masse, fülle davon eine Kapsel etwa ¾ Zoll hoch, backe dieselbe und zerschneide sie in Stückchen von 1½ Zoll Breite und 2 Zoll Länge und überziehe dieselben mit Chocoladen-Glasur. Alsdann backe von Windmasse kleine Böden, ebenso gross, als die oben beschriebenen Stücke, auf 4 Eiweiss 12 Loth Zucker, backe sie gut aus und bestreiche sie dann mit Himbeer-Marmelade und setze sie mit ersteren zusammen.

79. Dominosteine.

Backe eine Mandelkapsel und zerschneide dieselbe in Stücke von 1½ Zoll Breite und 2½ Zoll Länge. Die Hälfte dieser Stücke glasire mit Chocoladen-Glasur, die andere Hälfte glasire weiss und spritze dann Punkte von beiden Glasuren so auf, dass weiss auf Chocolade und Chocolade auf weisse Glasur kommt.

Man kann natürlich dieses Backwerk von anderer Masse machen, auch kann man dasselbe einfarbig glasiren und nur die Punkte zweifarbig machen.

80. Backwerk aus Wienerkapsel.

Aus Wienerkapsel macht man vielerlei Backwerk und eignet sich gerade diese Masse gut dazu. Man kann die Kapsel doppelt zusammen legen, füllen und verschieden glasiren und schneiden, und hat dann Wienerschnitte, auch sticht man mit Ausstechern verschiedenes aus, z. B.:

81. Strohhüte.

Man sticht mit einem grösseren und einem kleineren Ausstecher runde Stücke aus, befestigt den kleineren Theil mit Marmelade auf dem grösseren, überzieht das Ganze mit Apfelsinenglasur und trocknet es ab. Alsdann spritzt man mit Gelee oder Marmelade ein Band um und steckt ein Stückchen Citronat als Feder auf eine Seite.

82. Schmetterlinge.

Ebenso ausgestochen mit einem Ausstecher, der einen Schmetterling vorstellt, mit Gelee, zwei und zwei zusammen gefüllt, glasirt, getrocknet und dann verziert. Von Chocoladen-Glasur spritzt man einen Corpus in die Mitte.

83. Bohnen.

Kann man von Wienermasse ausstechen oder schlägt die Masse zu Mohrenköpfen an und spritzt davon Bohnen, füllt sie ebenso wie jene und glasirt sie weiss oder roth und macht in der Mitte der Bohne ein Pünktchen andersfarbiger Glasur.

84. Aprikosenschnitte.

Von Wienermasse ausgeschnitten, etwa 1½ Zoll breit, 2½ Zoll lang, auf den Rand Tupfen von Windmasse gesetzt, auf ein Brett gelegt und leicht abgebacken, dann in die Mitte Aprikosen-Marmelade eingefüllt, glasirt und verziert.

85. Johannisbrod.

Oval von obiger Masse ausgestochen, Tupfen von Windmasse auf den Rand und ebenso gebacken wie vorhin, dann mit eingemachten Johannisbeeren gefüllt und glasirt.

86. Dieselben auf andere Art.

Von Wiener Kapsel 1½ Zoll breite, 2 Zoll lange Stücke geschnitten und mit Johannisbeeren in Gelee belegt, dann ein wenig Zucker zum Faden gekocht, etwas tablirt und damit überzogen und abgetrocknet. Diese sehen sehr hübsch aus.

87. Krapfen, auch Mohrenköpfe genannt.

Schlage eine Biscuitmasse von ¼ lb Zucker, 6 Eigelb, das Weisse der Eier zu Schnee und mit ¼ lb Mehl untergerührt. Davon werden Plätzchen in der Grösse eines Dollars auf Papier tressirt und gebacken. Nachdem sie gebacken, schneide man sie vom Papier und höhle die untere Seite etwas aus, fülle etwas Vanille-Creme hinein, lege zwei und zwei zusammen und glasire sie mit Chocoladen-Glasur.

Diese Krapfen sind sehr schmackhaft und mit Recht sehr beliebt. Zu bunten Schüsseln kann man diese Krapfen auch weiss und roth überziehen. Der weissen Glasur giebt man den Marasquino-Geschmack, der rothen Vanille-Geschmack.

88. Spritzkuchen oder French Crallers.

Zur Anfertigung der Spritzkuchen gehört, wie es schon der Name besagt, eine Spritze, womit man die Kuchen tressirt, und zwar muss dieselbe einen Stern haben. Die Massen dazu werden sehr verschieden gemacht, doch ist die Zubereitungsweise stets dieselbe. Man wiegt in einen Kessel ¼ lb Butter, 1 oz Zucker und giesst dazu ¼ qt Wasser, setzt dasselbe auf Kohlenfeuer und lässt es kochen. Sobald es kocht, rührt man ½ lb Mehl hinein und röstet dies so lange ab, bis sich die Masse vollständig vom Kessel ablöst, alsdann hebt man den Kessel vom Feuer, schüttet das Abgeröstete in eine Schüssel und lässt es erkalten. Nachdem es erkaltet, rührt man nachgerade 7 bis 8 Eier dazu, thut einige Tropfen Citronenöl hinein und spritzt nun Ringe von dieser Masse auf ein stark mit Fett getränktes Papier, welches so gross als die

Pfanne ist, worin man backt. Hat das Fett oder die Butter nun die nöthige Hitze zum Backen, so legt man das Papier mit den Spritzkuchen nach unten in das Fett; es wird nicht lange dauern, so hebt sich das leere Papier hoch und man nimmt dasselbe heraus und backt nun die Spritzkuchen auf der einen Seite, bis sie gelbe Farbe haben, alsdann wendet man die Kuchen, backt auch die zweite Seite so weit aus, wendet dann die Kuchen nochmals nimmt dann einen heraus und untersucht, ob sie egal hart sind. Dann nimmt man die Kuchen aus dem Fett und bestreut sie mit Zucker und Zimmet.

Beim Backen aller Fettkuchen muss man darauf achten, dass das Fett nicht zu heiss oder zu kalt werde. Im ersteren Falle muss man kaltes Fett zur Hand haben, um etwas dazu zu thun, im anderen Falle verstärkt man das Feuer.

89. Sahnenküchelchen.

$\frac{1}{2}$ lb Schmelz Butter schaumig gerührt, dann $\frac{1}{2}$ lb Zucker, 8 Eigelb, der Schnee von 4 Eiweiss und $\frac{1}{2}$ lb Mehl dazu. Davon tressirt man Plätzchen auf Papier in der Grösse einer Wallnuss, legt ein Stückchen Citronat auf und streuet etwas Mandeln darauf. Diese werden flüchtig gebacken.

90. Theeschlangen.

Reibe $\frac{1}{4}$ lb Mandeln mit einem Ei, wirke dazu $\frac{1}{4}$ lb Butter, $\frac{1}{4}$ lb Mehl, $\frac{1}{4}$ lb Zucker und etwas Zimmet; lass dann den Teig etwas abkühlen, rolle dann davon einen langen Streifen etwa 4 Zoll breit und glasire denselben mit fester Eiweissglasur, schneide dann kleine, 1 Zoll breite Streifen davon, lege sie auf Blech und biege dabei die Enden nach rechts und links. Dieselben werden langsam gebacken.

91. Punsch-Ringe.

$\frac{1}{2}$ lb Butter, $\frac{1}{4}$ lb Zucker und $\frac{1}{4}$ lb braune Mandeln mit einem Ei gerieben, etwas Zimmet, Nelken und einem Gläschen Punschextract oder Rum tüchtig durchgerührt und dann $\frac{1}{2}$ lb Mehl dazu gewirkt. Davon tressirt man Kränze, streicht sie mit Ei und legt sie in Hagelzucker, dann auf Bleche und bäckt sie flüchtig.

92. Windbeutel.

Nimm in einen Kessel $\frac{1}{4}$ lb Butter und $\frac{1}{4}$ Quart Wasser, lass dies zum kochen kommen und rühre dann $\frac{1}{2}$ lb Mehl hinein, rühre dies so lange, bis es sich vollständig vom Kessel ablöst, thue es dann in eine Schüssel und rühre 8 Eier hinein. Von dieser Masse setze mit einem Tressir-Beutel kleine Häufchen auf Bleche, streiche sie mit Ei und backe sie gehörig aus.

93. Chau d'eau Körbchen.

Man macht einen leichten Teig aus 1 ganzen Ei und 3 Eigelb, 3 Löffel Wein, 3 Löffel gute Milch, etwas Zucker und ein wenig Salz, und soviel Mehl als nöthig, damit der Teig wie zu Eierkuchen sei. Nun muss man eine Blechform haben, die ein Körbchen vorstellt, diese streicht man in Butter, taucht sie in die Masse und bäckt es in heissem Schmalz wie bei Pfannkuchen, dann schiebt man das gebackene Körbchen ab und wiederhole das Eintauchen und backen.

Diese Körbchen füllt man nachher mit Chau d'eau, Béses, Schlagsahne, Vanille, Crême u. dergl.

94. Anischius zu Chocolade.

Nimm 1 lb Zucker in eine Schüssel und rühre denselben mit 18 Eigelb schaumig, thue etwas Anis oder auch Muscatnuss dazu, schlage dann das Weisse von den 18 Eiern zu Schnee und rühre denselben mit $\frac{1}{4}$ lb Mehl zu der Masse. Davon mache auf ein gestrichenes und mit Mehl bestaubtes Blech lange Streifen, die etwa 3 Zoll breit sind, streiche sie behutsam mit Ei und backe sie. Nachdem sie gebacken und abgekühlt sind, schneidet man sie in schräge Streifchen, legt sie auf's Blech und röstet sie etwas. Diese Biscuite schmecken sehr gut zu Chocolade und werden in den meisten Conditoreien dazu gegeben.

V. Theil.

Macronen-Bäckerei.

Das Grund-Recept der Macronen ist wie folgt: 1 lb Almondpaste, $1\frac{1}{4}$ lb Zucker, ungefähr 10 Eiweiss, auch kann man 1 oz Cornmeal zusetzen

95. Belegte Macronen.

Hat man die Macronen-Masse bereitet wie vorhin, so tressirt man runde Macronen in der Grösse von einer halben Wallnuss und legt darauf ein Stückchen Citronat oder auch Orangenschale und glasirt dieselbe nach dem Backen. Bei dem Backen muss man recht vorsichtig sein und darauf wohl achten, dass man die Macronen nicht zu heiss bäckt, weil sie dann nicht gehörig aufgehen, aber auch nicht zu kalt, weil die Macronen sonst trocken werden.

96. Gefüllte Macronen.

Von derselben Macronen-Masse tressirt man runde Macronen und bäckt sie aus. Sobald sie aus dem Ofen kommen, drückt man mit einem Stöckchen in die Mitte der Macrone eine Vertiefung und spritzt mit einer Düte Gelée hinein und thut etwas Glasur darüber.

97. Rosen-Macronen.

Diesen kann man, nachdem man die Masse etwas roth gefärbt hat, den Geschmack durch einige Tröpfchen Rosenöl geben, oder man glasirt dieselben nur mit Rosenglasur.

98. Zimmet-Macronen.

Man setzt der Masse etwas Zimmet zu und färbt sie mit etwas Bolus röthlich.

99. Chocoladen-Macronen.

Zu derselben Masse thut man auf $\frac{1}{2}$ lb Mandeln $\frac{1}{4}$ lb geriebene Chocolade, Zimmet und Nelken und verdünnt die Masse noch etwas mit Eiweiss. Nachdem die Macronen tressirt sind, bestreut man sie mit Hagelzucker.

100. Vanille-Macronen.

Der Macronen-Masse etwas gestossene Vanille als Geschmack zu geben und mit Vanille-Glasur nach dem Backen glasirt.

101. Citronen-Macronen.

Eben so, nur etwas auf Zucker abgeriebene Citronenschale, hinzugethan.

102. Bestreute Macronen.

Die Macronen, wenn sie tressirt sind, bestreut man mit gehackten Mandeln und glasirt sie mit Vanille-Glasur. Diese schmecken besonders fein.

103. Bemerkung.

Alle diese verschiedenen Dessins kann man auch verschieden bestreuen und belegen oder füllen. Streuen kann man mit Mandeln, Hagelzucker und geriebener Chocolade. Belegen mit Früchten, Citronat und Orangeschalen.

104. Mandelbogen.

Man hat dazu gebogene Bleche nöthig, die man aus weissen Blechtafeln machen lässt. Die Biegung muss ein

Halbzirkel sein. Man bestreicht eine oder mehrere Tafeln Oblaten mit nicht zu fester Macronen-Masse, bestreut dieselben mit gehackten Mandeln oder Hagelzucker und theilt dann die Tafel in Streifen von 1 Zoll Breite und 4 Zoll Länge, legt diese dann auf den gewärmten Bogen und bäckt sie darauf aus.

105. Mandelbogen und Blätter.

Dieser wurde schon bei den Aufsätzen, bei denen sie unentbehrlich sind, gedacht; doch will ich derselben hier nochmals erwähnen, weil sie in diese Abtheilung gehören. Meistens hat man zu diesen Schablonen, doch kann man sie auch auf das Blech streichen, danach zerschneiden und dann über die Bleche biegen. Die Mandelblätter hat man in verschiedenen Grössen und fertigen sich die Conditoren die Schablonen selbst an. Die Masse dazu ist $\frac{1}{2}$ lb Almondpaste, 12 oz Zucker, 2 oz Mehl, 4 Eiweiss. Verdünnen kann man die Masse mit Wasser und muss sie weicher sein als Macronenmasse.

106. Zimmetstangen.

Man reibe $\frac{1}{2}$ lb braune Mandeln mit 5 Eiweiss fein, thue dann $\frac{1}{2}$ lb Zucker und etwas gestossenen Zimmet dazu. Diese Masse rolle man aus, glasire sie mit Eiweiss-Glasur und schneide dazu Streifen von $\frac{3}{4}$ Zoll Breite und 3 Zoll Länge, die langsam ausgebacken werden; statt der Mandeln kann man Almondpaste nehmen.

107. Mandelschlangen.

$\frac{1}{4}$ lb Almondpaste, 1 lb Zucker, $\frac{1}{2}$ lb Butter, 8 Eier, 2 lb Mehl, $\frac{1}{4}$ oz Ammonia mit Ei waschen und biege in S Form.

108. Mandel-Ringe.

1 lb Almondpaste, $1\frac{1}{2}$ lb Zucker, $\frac{1}{4}$ lb Corn-Meal, mit Eiweiss gemischt und mit Sterntülle auf bestaubten Blechen tressirt.

109. Mandel-Bogen.

1 lb Almondpaste, 1 lb Zucker, 1 oz Corn-Meal, 6 Eiweiss gemischt, auf Oblaten gestrichen, geschnitten und auf halbrunden Blechen gebacken.

110. Macronen-Schnitte.

1 lb Almondpaste, $1\frac{1}{2}$ lb Zucker, 2 oz Corn-Meal, 6 Eiweiss auf Mürbeteig gestrichen, geschnitten, mit gehackten Mandeln bestreut, gebacken und glasirt.

111. Mandel-Bretzel.

1 lb Zucker, 1 lb Butter, $\frac{1}{2}$ lb Almondpaste, 2 Eier, 1 lb Mehl zu Bretzeln geformt, mit Ei gestrichen und in Hagelzucker gelegt und gebacken.

112. Zimmetstangen von Mandeln

Reibe ½ lb weisse Mandeln mit 5 bis 6 Eiweiss ziemlich fest und thue 1½ lb Zucker und etwas Zimmet dazu, reibe dies tüchtig und rolle dann die Masse auf dem Backtisch zu einem langen, 3 Zoll breiten Streifen aus; glasire darauf diesen Streifen mit fester Eiweiss-Glasur und schneide kleine, etwa ¾ Zoll breite Streifen daraus, die auf einem etwas gestrichenen und mit Mehl bestaubten Bleche langsam gebacken werden; statt der Mandeln kann man auch Almondpaste nehmen.

VI. Theil.

Marzipan.

Marzipan unterscheidet sich von Macronenmasse hauptsächlich dadurch, dass kein Eiweiss dazu verwendet wird, sondern nur Wasser. Die Zubereitung des Marzipan ist schwierig und soll er schön sein, so muss er sehr aufmerksam behandelt werden. Es dürfte in Haushaltungen nicht leicht gelingen, Marzipan zu machen, weil daselbst ein steinerner Mörser zum Reiben der Mandeln fehlt, der dazu entschieden nöthig ist.

Die Mandeln werden geschält, öfter gewaschen dann in reines Wasser gethan und darin 12 Stunden gelassen, aus demselben mit einem Schaumlöffel herausgehoben, und so viel, als man mit einem Male reiben kann, möglichst fein gerieben. Wasser braucht man beim Reiben nicht mehr zuzugiessen, da die Mandeln, wenn sie 12 Stunden gewässert, nass genug sind. Hat man auf diese Weise alle Mandeln fein gerieben, so thut man sie in einen flachen Kessel, wiegt auf 6 lb Mandeln 4 lb feingestossenen Raffinatzucker und stellt den Kessel über Kohlenfeuer, fortwährend darin rührend und beobachtend, dass es ja nicht anbrenne. Dies Abrösten des Marzipan setzt man fort, bis er sich vom Kessel löst, oder, wenn man ihn mit dem Finger anfasst, nichts an demselben kleben bleibt. Alsdann bestreut man den Bonbonstein mit Zucker, legt die Marzipanmasse darauf, drückt sie zusammen und hebt sie zum Gebrauch auf.

Will man von dieser eben beschriebenen Masse Gebrauch machen, so nimmt man einen Theil auf die Marmorplatte, wirkt auf 1 lb etwa noch ½ lb feinen Zucker ein und verarbeitet diese Masse dann verschieden.

113. Königsberger Marzipan.

Man rollt den angewirkten Marzipan ¼ Zoll stark aus und sticht mit Ausstechern verschiedene Figuren, als Herzen, Rosetten und Sterne aus; dann schneidet man von demselben Marzipan Ränder etwa ¼ Zoll hoch und befestigt diesen Rand mit Wasser auf den Rändern der ausgestochenen Sachen, dann lässt man sie einige Tage trocknen. Nachdem sie genug getrocknet sind, legt man die angefertigten Gegenstände auf ein Brett und schiebt sie in den heissen Ofen, worin sich die Ränder sehr bräunlich färben, dann nimmt man sie wieder aus dem Ofen heraus, bestreicht hierauf den Boden der Marzipanstücke mit Gelee und thut darüber eine starke Glasur von Rosenwasser, hält es wieder eine Minute in den Ofen und belegt dann die Sachen mit eingemachten Früchten.

114. Marzipantorte.

Die Anfertigung dieser Torte ist fast ebenso wie die der Marzipan-Stücke. Hierbei schneidet man einen runden, öfter auch einen viereckigen Boden aus und zerschneidet diesen zu einem Stern, oder was man sonst für Dessins wünscht. Die einzelnen Stücke werden ebenso mit Rändern versehen, wie vorher gezeigt, und um die Torte herum legt man dann einen etwa einen Finger starken Rand, der die Tortenstücke zusammenhält. Diesen Rand schneidet man mit einer kleinen Scheere oder kneift ihn mit einer Zange aus, wie Conditoren zu haben pflegen. Im Uebrigen behandelt man die Torte wie die Marzipan-Stücke.

115. Marzipan-Confect.

Von angewirkter Marzipanmasse macht man noch mancherlei Figuren, die man im Ofen röstet, wie bei den Marzipan-Stücken gezeigt worden. Man formt Bretzel, Schnörkel, Schlangen, Korkzieher u. dgl., auch füllt man solche Sachen, indem man eine Vertiefung hineinmacht, die nach dem Rösten mit Gelee gefüllt und glasirt wird.

116. Backwaaren von Marzipan.

Man formt von angewirkten Marzipan-Semmeln Bretzeln u. dgl., trocknet sie, bestreicht sie dann mit Eigelb und röstet sie im heissem Ofen ab Diese Sachen sehen den wirklichen Backwaaren sehr ähnlich.

VII. Theil.

Hefen- und Schmalz-Bäckerei.

117. Hefenteig.

¼ lb Press-Hefe 2 qt Milch, mache einen weichen Teig und setze ihn an einen warmen Ort.

118. Grundteig.

Nachdem obiger Hefenteig am Fallen is, setze ¾ lb Butter, ¾ lb Zucker, 8 Eier und mache einen schönen schlanken Teig. Dieses ist der Grundteig, wovon die verschiedenen Sorten Kuchen angefertigt werden.

119. Zwiebäcke.

Werden von Grundteig gemacht, gebacken, geschnitten und getrocknet.

120. Glasirte Zwiebäcke

Wie oben, und mit folgender Glasur glasirt und hellgelb gebacken.

121. Glasur.

1 pt Eiweiss zu Schnee, 4 lb Zucker, ¾ lb gehackte Mandeln mit etwas Vanille untergerührt und glasirt.

122. Muskuchen.

Statt wie vorhin die Füllung mit Aepfeln zu machen, kann man auch Pflaumenmus mit Zucker und Mandeln vermischt einfüllen, oder Kirsch- oder Apfelmus, welch letzterem man etwas Arac zum Geschmack zusetzt.

123. Pressburger Zwiebäcke.

Von dem bereits beschriebenen Grundteig formirt man längliche Zwiebäcke, etwa 4 Zoll lang und 1½ Zoll breit, drückt sie ein wenig flach, lä-st sie aufgehen und bäckt sie aus. Nach dem Erkalten schneidet man diese Zwiebäcke und bestreicht die Aussenseiten mit einer leichten Baisermasse, der man etwas gehackte Mandeln, auch etwas Semmelkrumen zumischt, legt dann die weiche Seite der Zwiebäcke auf's Blech und lässt sie langsam rösten.

124. Plunderbretzeln.

Man nehme von dem Grundteig soviel als man braucht und rolle ihn flach aus, bestreue denselben zur Hälfte mit Zucker und Zimmet und lege gut gewaschene Butter, auf 1 lb Teig ¼ lb, dazwischen, schlage dies zusammen und ziehe den Teig wie den Blätterteig, doch nur dreimal geschlagen. Von dem fertigen Teige schneide man alsdann lange Streifen, rolle dieselben, mit der linken Hand nach oben, mit der rechten nach unten drehend, zusammen und schlage dann eine Bretzel davon. Diese Bretzeln lasse man dann aufgehen, doch dürfen sie nicht warm stehen, bestreiche sie mit Ei, streue geschnittene Mandeln darüber, backe und glasire sie mit Wasserglasur.

125. Martinshörner.

Den Teig behandelt man wie bei den Plunderbretzeln, theilt ihn in kleine Stücke, etwa ¼ Zoll dick, 1½ Zoll breit und 5 Zoll lang, streicht darauf eine Füllung von Mandeln, Zucker und Corinthen (die Mandeln mit Rosenwasser gerieben und auf ¼ lb ½ lb Zucker), schlägt den Teig dann darüber, wickelt ihn auch so auf wie bei den Bretzeln und legt dann Halbmonde davon auf's Blech. Nachdem man sie hat aufgehen lassen, werden sie mit Ei gestrichen, gebacken und dann glasirt.

126. Grieskuchen.

Der Grundteig wird etwa ¼ Zoll dick ausgerollt, mit Butter gestrichen und zum Aufgehen gestellt. Nachdem dies geschehen, streut man etwas Zucker, Zimmet und mit kochender Butter gemischten feinen Gries darüber und backt ihn.

127. Speckkuchen.

Man fertigt einen Kuchen mit Rand, lässt ihn aufgehen, giesst dann 6 bis 8 Eier darüber, streut dann in Würfel geschnittenen Speck darauf, auch etwas Kümmel und Salz. Flüchtig backen.

128. Zwiebelkuchen

Der Kuchen ist wie vorhin. Die Zwiebeln werden den Tag zuvor fein geschnitten, mit Fett weich geschmort und abgekühlt. Zum Gebrauch schlägt man einige Eier dazu, thut etwas Kümmel und Salz hinein, auch wohl etwas Zucker, streicht diese Masse auf den Kuchen und backt ihn gut aus. Muss warm gegessen werden.

129. Kirsch-, Pflaumen-, Heidelbeer- und Apfelkuchen.

Man vertheilt die Frucht auf einem dünn ausgerollten Kuchen gleichmässig, bestreut ihn mit Zucker, auch wohl etwas Zimmet; sehr schön machen sich diese Kuchen, wenn sie mit Vanilla-Crême übergossen und gut ausgebacken werden. Da der Vanilla-Crême ziemlich theuer kommt, so lasse ich hier ein billiges Recept folgen:

130. Crême.

2 qt Milch gekocht und ½ lb Gries hinein gerührt. Dieser Crême muss gefärbt werden mit Eigelb oder Safran.

131. Topf- oder Napfkuchen,

sowie Stollen, Räder-Gebäck und dergl. setzt man dem Grundteig noch etwas mehr Butter, Zucker, Gewürz und Eier zu. Geregelte Recepte lassen sich nicht gut angeben, da der Geschmack zu verschieden ist.

132. Zimmet- oder Kaffee-Kuchen

werden von Grundteig angefertigt, ½ Zoll dick ausgerollt und in mittlerer Hitze gebacken. Viele glasiren den Kuchen mit Rosenwasser-Glasur, andere bestreuen denselben vor dem Backen mit Zucker und Zimmet.

133. Streusel-Kuchen.

Behandlung wie vorhin, nur bestreut man den Kuchen mit folgendem Streusel vor dem Backen: 5 lbs Mehl, 1 oz Zimmet, 1 lb Zucker, 2 lbs warme Butter, gemischt und durch ein grobes Sieb gerieben.

134. Streusel auf andere Art.

1 lb gehackte Mandeln, 1½ lb Zucker, 2 oz Zimmet.

Kaffee-, Zimmet- und Streusel-Kuchen sollten vor dem Backen mit warmer Butter bestrichen werden.

135. Käse-Kuchen.

Nachdem der Kuchen genug aufgegangen, thut man den inzwischen geriebenen Käse (weissen Käse), dem man etwas Zucker, Corinthen und Citrone zusetzt, einen Finger hoch darauf und übergiesst diese Mischung mit zerschlagenen Eiern, Zucker und Butter. Nun backt man den Kuchen gut aus; um dies zu erreichen, thut man wohl, mit einem Messer den Kuchen zu heben, um zu sehen, ob derselbe einen guten Boden hat; ehe der Kuchen am Boden nicht gelbbraun ist, ist er nicht gebacken.

136. Quark-Kuchen.

Wie vorhin. Die Füllung ist: Weisser Käse mit Zucker versüsst, einige Eier mit Corinthen dazu und zuletzt mit gehackten Mandeln und Zucker bestreut.

137. Mohn-Kuchen.

Wie vorhin. Die Füllung besteht aus 1 lb mit kochendem Wasser aufgequelltem Mohn, 2 oz Butter, 4 oz Zucker, 4 Eigelb, gemischt, aufgetragen fingerstark, mit Zucker und Mandeln bestreut und gebacken.

138. Rädergebackenes.

Rühre $\frac{1}{2}$ lb Butter mit $\frac{1}{2}$ lb Zucker schaumig und thue nachgerade 16 Eigelb hinein, reibe auch eine Citrone zu, giesse dann ein Glas Wein hinein und rühre $1\frac{1}{2}$ lb Mehl dazu. Diesen Teig lasse etwas auskühlen, rolle ihn dann ziemlich dünn aus und schneide mit dem Backrädchen einen Zoll breite und zehn Zoll lange Streifen daraus, lege dieselben wie eine Schleife zusammen, backe sie danach in Fett und bestreue sie mit Zucker.

Man erhitzt das Fett so weit, dass, wenn man mit einem nassen Stöckchen hineinfährt, das Fett aufkreischt. Würde das Fett nicht so heiss sein, so zieht es sich in die Pfannkuchen hinein und macht sie fetter, als sie sein sollen und giebt ihnen auch eine schlechte Farbe. Ist das Fett heisser, so können sich die Pfannkuchen nicht genug dehnen, werden zu leicht braun und sind dann sehr unansehnlich. Am besten ist es, wenn man erst eine Probe backt, um sich zu überzeugen, ob das Fett den nöthigen Hitzgrad hat.

VIII. Theil.

Leb- und Honigkuchen-Bäckerei.

Dieser Kuchen, der in manchen Gegenden in grossen Massen verfertigt wird, erfordert einen guten Molasses, den man einige Male aufkochen lässt und dann mit gewöhnlichem Weizenmehl anrührt; auch kann man etwas Honig zusetzen. Dieser Teig bildet dann den Grundteig. Das Mehl darf erst dann in den Molasses gerührt werden, wenn derselbe schon abgekühlt und nur noch lauwarm ist. Derselbe sollte mehrere Tage liegen, bevor er verarbeitet wird.

139. Dünner Honigkuchen.

Mache einen Teig von 3 lb Mehl, $\frac{1}{2}$ lb gelöster Pottasche, $\frac{1}{4}$ lb Ammonia und soviel Wasser, als nöthig. Dann wiege 30 lb Grundteig ab, lege beide Teige unter die Breche und arbeite es tüchtig untereinander. Es darf nicht zu viel Mehl beim Brechen verbraucht werden. Dieser Teig kann dann verwendet werden zu Leb- und dünnem Honigkuchen. Bei dickem Honigkuchen dieselbe Behandlung, nur nimm 1 oz Trieb von jedem weniger.

140. Pflastersteine.

Feinere Lebkuchen und Pflastersteine dieselbe Behandlung, nur werden etwas gehackte Mandeln und Citronat darunter gemischt.

Bei Lebkuchen sollte man erst eine Probe backen, um sich zu überzeugen, ob der Teig genug Trieb enthält, welches man an der Probe ausfinden wird; es ist dann noch Zeit genug, mehr beimischen zu können. Diese Vorsicht ist nothwendig, indem die Pottasche zu unsicher arbeitet.

141. Weisse Lebkuchen.

5 lb Zucker, 10 lb Mehl, $\frac{1}{2}$ lb Lard, 4 oz Ammonia und nicht ganz 2 qt Milch. Dieser Teig darf nicht zu viel gearbeitet werden.

142. Thorner Lebkuchen, Nürnberger, Braunschweiger, Baseler, Augsburger, Französischer, Holländischer Lebkuchen

unterscheiden sich nur durch die verschiedenen Früchte und Gewürze; im Uebrigen dieselbe Behandlung.

143. Citronen-Kuchen.

Wie vorhin, nur 1 lb Lard zu 30 lb Grundteig.

144. Sheveletten.

60 Eigelb, 1 lb Zucker, 1 oz Ammonia, $1\frac{1}{2}$ pt Milch und soviel Mehl als nöthig. Dieselben werden in kochendem Wasser gekocht, indem man eine gewisse Menge in's Wasser wirft; sobald sie heraufkommen, nimmt man sie heraus, fährt so fort, bis sie alle gekocht sind, setzt sie auf Pfannen und backt sie in heissem Ofen. Sheveletten sind runde Ringe, welche dutzendweise zusammengebunden werden und das Bund mit 5 Cents verkauft wird.

145. Braunschweiger Confect.

1 lb Butter, $\frac{1}{2}$ lb Zucker, 2 lb Mehl, $\frac{1}{4}$ lb fein gehackte Mandeln und 4 Eier werden zusammengewirkt und noch $\frac{1}{2}$ oz Ammonia dazu gethan; dann rollt man die Masse dünn und sticht sie beliebig aus. Auch kann man kleine Bretzeln davon machen.

146. Weisser Marzipan.

1 lb Zucker wird mit 4 Eiern etwas gerührt, dann 1¼ lb Mehl, etwas Ammonia und Gewürz dazu gethan und davon ein Teig gebildet. Nun hat man in Holz geschnittene Formen, in welche man den Teig hineindrückt, oder man sticht Figuren davon aus, lässt sie mehrere Stunden trocknen und backt sie im warmen Ofen ab.

147. Wasser-Marzipan.

1 lb Zucker wird in 1 Tasse kochendem Wasser aufgelöst, dann 1¼ lb Mehl dazu gerührt und ein Teig gebildet. Davon sticht man Figuren aus oder drückt die Masse in Holzformen, lässt alsdann die Sachen wieder trocknen, legt sie dann auf ein feuchtes Tuch, damit dieselben von unten feucht werden, bringt sie dann auf Bleche und backt sie langsam ab.

Die beiden zuletzt beschriebenen Backwaaren werden meist nach dem Backen bemalt.

148. Patience. Geduldskuchen.

Schlage den Schnee von 10 Eiweiss und rühre dann mit einem Spatel 1 lb feinen Zucker und dann ¾ lb Mehl darunter. Rühre diese Masse so lange, bis sie etwas flüssig ist, und tressire dieselbe mit einer Düte auf mit Wachs gestrichene Bleche in kleine Plätzchen oder kleine, etwa 1 Zoll lange Biscuits. Alsdann lasse diese Plätzchen einige Stunden trocknen und backe sie kühl ab, dass sie einen hübschen Fuss bekommen. Als Gewürz kann man den Plätzchen Vanille zusetzen.

IX. Theil.

Von der Anfertigung der Schaumsachen.

Um diese Sachen gut herzustellen, ist zuerst auf die grösste Sauberkeit der Gefässe und auf den besten Zucker zu sehen, wer der darin geizen will, fange gar nicht an; die drei verschiedenen Grundmassen unterscheiden sich dadurch, dass die warm geschlagene Masse mehr Glanz hat, die kalt geschlagene besser in der Figur steht und die geriebene dauerhafter ist, sich länger hält, aber nicht so viel ausgiebt.

149. Warme Schaummasse oder gekochte Glasur.

Man nimmt 2 lb Zucker (feinste Raffinade) und kocht ihn sorgfältig mit ½ qt Wasser bis zum grossen Flug, während dessen müssen 10 bis 12 Eiweiss zu einem steifen, festen Schnee geschlagen sein, und unter immerwährendem Schlagen wird dann der heisse Zucker in einem langen Strahl hineingegossen und noch geschlagen, bis sie abgekühlt ist, dann wird sie auf mit zerlassener Butter bestrichene Bleche tressirt.

150. Kalte Schaummasse.

12 Eiweiss werden zu steifem Schnee geschlagen, 1½ lb feiner Staubzucker und ¼ lb feinster, trockener Puder behutsam hinein gerührt und dann auf leicht gestrichene Bleche oder auf Papier tressirt.

151. Gerührte Schaummasse.

Man nimmt 2 lb feinsten Staubzucker und reibt ihn mit mindestens 4 Eiweiss zu einem weissen, flaumigen Schaum, dem man etwas Essigsäure zusetzt.

Werden die daraus gefertigten Sachen nicht hoch genug beim ersten Tressiren, so wiederholt man den Guss auf dieselbe Weise; sollen Goldborten darauf kommen, oder Blumen, oder Traganth, so kommen sie noch auf die feuchte Masse; sollte diese jedcoh zu trocken sein, so bedient man sich einer schwachen Gummilösung oder der Spritzglasur.

152. Figuren, welche aus Schaummasse hergestellt werden können.

Man tressirt gewöhnlich folgende flache Gegenstände daraus, und zwar auf Papier durch die Spritze oder eine starke Düte:

Buchstaben aller Art mit diversen Verzierungen von Spritzglasur.
Vögel in Kränzen, mit Blumen, in Nestern, mit Eiern.
Körbe und Körbchen mit Früchten, Blumen, Thieren, Vögeln.
Vasen mannigfaltiger Grösse und Verzierung.
Füllhörner, verziert, mit oder ohne Blumen und Früchte,
Kronen, verziert mit Spritzglasur und den sogenannten Diamanten. Schwäne machen sich auch sehr gut.
Guitarren und Harfen, Lyra's in vielen Grössen und Verzierungen.
Devisen, als Glaube, Hoffnung und Liebe etc.
Kaninchen und Pudel auf Polstern. Verschiedenes Geflügel.

Mannigfache Verzierungen, sogenannte Züge und alle anderen denkbaren Formen. Fische, Kinder, Larven werden mit Spritzglasur, Goldborten und Brillanten (Zinnspitzen) nach Belieben verziert, man macht sie aber nicht gern grösser als 1½ Zoll im Durchmesser.

153. Conserven-Formen.

Zu Früchten nimmt man im Sommer natürliche Früchte, welche schön ausgewachsen sind, bestreicht die Frucht mit Leinöl und steckt sie bis zum vierten Theil in weichen Thon, macht von Thon einen Rand herum und bestreicht die Frucht noch einmal; nun rührt man etwas Figuren-Gyps mit warmem Wasser an und giesst den Brei auf die Form, nach fünf Minuten nimmt man den Gypstheil ab, schneidet mit dem Messer wie man es haben will, macht einige Löcher an die Seite, bestreicht es wieder mit Leinöl und setzt den Theil wieder auf die Form, fährt mit dem Gypsgiessen so fort, bis alle Theile gegossen sind, macht ein Loch zum Eingiessen des Zuckers hinein und lässt sie recht trocknen. Dann legt man sie acht Tage in Leinöl mit etwas Terpentinöl vermischt und lässt sie an der Sonne trocknen. Alle anderen Formen werden auf die gleiche Weise angefertigt.

X. Theil.

154. Mandel-Auflauf

ist eine compaktere Masse als das Schaum-Confect und wird folgendermassen bereitet: Man nimmt 3 lb feines Zuckerpulver (Raffinade), mischt es mit 2 oz abgeschälten, fein geriebenen, bitteren Mandeln und mit nicht ganz steifem Schnee von 6 Eiweiss zu einer Masse. Diese wird federspulenstark ausgerollt und in die verschiedensten denkbaren Figuren ausgestochen, 1½ Stunde auf mit Mehl bestreuten Blechen trocknen gelassen und dann kühl gebacken. Die Figuren backen sich 1 Zoll hoch und werden mit Wasser oder Eiweiss-Glasur glasirt und beliebig mit buntem Streuzucker oder bunter Spritzglasur verziert.

155. Weisser Auflauf mit Vanille.

Dazu wird der nicht zu steif geschlagene Schnee von 6 Eiweiss mit 3 lbs fein gestossenem Zucker, dem man gern etwas Vanille zusetzt, gemengt, federspulenstark ausgerollt, ausgestochen und wie vorher getrocknet und gebacken. Nun wird er mit verschiedenen Wasser-Glasuren glasirt und mit buntem Zucker und Garnirung verziert.

156. Rother Auflauf mit Rosengeschmack

wird ebenso gemacht, nur mit Cochenille-Farbe gefärbt und werden bisweilen einige Tropfen Rosenöl zugesetzt, auch mit dem Verzieren wird er auf vorige Art behandelt.

157. Chocoladen-Auflauf.

Man setzt auf 3 lbs dieser Masse $\frac{1}{2}$ lb gut geriebene Chocolade zu; die daraus geformten Figuren können mit verschiedenen Glasuren verziert werden, wie die vorigen.

158. Gespritzter Auflauf.

Dieselbe Masse wird mit der Sternspritze tressirt; sie eignet sich besonders zu Nestern (indischen Vogelnestern), wird mit Zucker-Glasur glasirt und mit bunten Zuckern bestreut und garnirt.

159. Traganth-Auflauf.

Man weicht 1 Loth Traganth mit $\frac{1}{4}$ qt Wasser ein, drückt es dann durch ein Tuch oder streicht es durch ein Haarsieb in den Mandelstein, rührt den Traganth mit der Keule recht schaumig und thut nach und nach feinen Staubzucker dazu, giesst auch ein Liqueur-Glas voll starken Sprit hinein und mischt soviel Zucker zu, dass man die Masse ausrollen kann. Dieser Auflauf wird ebenso behandelt wie der Mandel-Auflauf; er wird beim Backen ganz weiss.

160. Baiserschaalen.

Man schlägt 10 Eiweiss zu festem Schnee, rührt 1 lb Zucker dazu, tressirt davon mit einem Löffel oder einer Spritze Häufchen in der Grösse eines halben Apfels, bestreut sie mit Zucker, legt sie sodann auf nasse Bretter und backt sie etwas flüchtig aus; so dass sie inwendig weich bleiben. Nun lässt man die Baiser erkalten, nimmt dann mit einem Löffel dass Weiche heraus, streicht die innere Seite glatt und trocknet die Schaalen recht aus.

Die Schaalen werden, wie bekannt, mit geschlagener Sahne, auch mit Eis gefüllt. Kommen sie nicht bald zur Verwendung, so müssen sie an einem warmen Orte aufbewahrt werden.

161. Spanischer Wind.

Zu 8 zu festem Schnee geschlagenen Eiweiss rührt man 1 lb Zucker, tressirt davon mit einem Löffel längliche Häufchen auf Papier und backt sie recht langsam.

Baiser- oder Windmassen streut man vor dem Backen immer mit etwas Zucker ein, um eine festere Kruste zu erzielen.

162. Porzellan-Bretzeln.

½ lb Staubzucker wird mit 3 Eiweiss schaumig gerührt, dann 6 oz Mehl oder Puder und etwas Citronenöl dazu. Davon macht man 40 Bretzeln, drückt sie auf einem gestrichenen und mit Mehl bestaubten Bleche etwas breit, lässt sie einige Stunden trocknen und backt sie langsam ab. Nachdem sie gebacken, glasirt man sie mit Eiweissglasur.

XI. Theil.

Von den Cremes und Wein-Gelees.

Die Crèmes werden theils von Sahne, theils von Wein bereitet und durch Eier verdickt; aber auch ohne dieselben werden Crèmes bereitet und die Verdickung durch Gelatine bewirkt, oder durch Schaumigschlagen, wie bei der Schlagsahne, die auch dazu gehört.

163. Schlagsahne.

Die Schlagsahne ist der überfüllte dicke Rahm von der Milch, wenn diese etwa 12 bis 16 Stunden gestanden hat und noch nicht sauer geworden ist. Man kann von 10 bis 12 qt guter Milch 1 qt Sahne abfüllen, mehr jedoch nicht, sonst würde sich die Sahne nicht schaumig schlagen und nicht consistent werden. Nachdem die Sahne abgefüllt ist, setzt man sie noch einige Stunden kühl, womöglich auf Eis, schlägt sie dann mit einem Schneebesen in einer Schüssel oder einem Kessel schaumig, versüsst sie mit Zucker und mischt etwas gestossene Vanille hinzu. Wird die Sahne nicht gleich gebraucht, so mischt man den Zucker noch nicht zu, weil sich sonst zu viel Flüssiges absetzt.

164. Schlagsahne mit Pumpernickel.

¼ lb guten Pumpernickel, der noch nicht zu trocken ist, reibt man und mischt ihn zu der eben beschriebenen Schlagsahne, der etwa auf 1 qt ¼ lb Zucker und etwas gestossene Vanille beigemischt ist.

165. Schlagsahne mit Erdbeeren.

Man nehme etwa ½ lb gute Wald-Erdbeeren, reibe dieselben durch ein Haarsieb, damit die Kerne zurückbleiben, mische 1 qt Wasser und ½ lb Zucker der Masse zu und rühre dieses behutsam zu der recht fest geschlagenen Sahne.

166. Crême von Pistatien.

In der Bereitung ist derselbe ebenso wie die Blanc manger. Man nimmt dazu 1 lb Pistatien, die man fein reibt, kocht sie mit 1½ qt Sahne oder Milch und ½ lb Zucker auf, thut 2 oz aufgelöste Gelatine zu und giesst das Ganze durch ein Sieb. Sollte man diesen Crême etwas grüner wünschen, so färbt man denselben mit etwas Spinatsaft.

167. Crême von Marasquino.

1 qt Schlagsahne wird recht fest geschlagen, dann ½ lb feiner Zucker, 1 Weinglas voll Marasquino und 2 oz aufgelöste Gelatine dazu gemischt, in die Form gethan und auf Eis gestellt.

168. Crême von Chocolade.

½ lb feine Vanille-Chocolade wird warm gemacht und dann mit ein wenig Wasser aufgelöst; darauf wird 1 qt Schlagsahne fest geschlagen, ½ lb Zucker, die Chocolade und 2 oz Gelatine dazu gemischt, das Ganze in die Form oder Crêmeschaale gethan und auf Eis gestellt.

169. Crême de Rose.

Derselbe wird nach demselben Verhältniss gemacht wie 167, nur werden einige Tropfen Rosenöl als Geschmack statt des Marasquino und ein wenig Cochenille zum Färben hinzu gethan.

170. Crême zu verzieren.

Die Crêmes werden, wenn sie in grösseren Schaalen sind, meistens mit kleinen Plätzchen belegt, auch mit buntem Zucker bestreut, oder mit eingemachten Früchten belegt. Man kann auch von dem Crême etwas in eine Düte nehmen und besprizt die Schaalen damit, oder man verwendet Gelee dazu, was auch recht gut aussieht. Sehr hübschen Effect macht es, wenn man die Crêmes mit Biscuitstückchen und diese dann mit Gelee belegt.

171. Chocoladen-Crême.

Auch dieser Crême hat dasselbe Verhältniss der Eier und des Zuckers. Man löst nur noch ½ lb Chocolade mit der Milch auf und kocht den Crême damit auf.

172. Citronen-Crême mit Schnee.

Will man den vorhergehenden Crême gern noch etwas ausgiebiger machen, so schlage man einige Eiweiss zu Schnee und ziehe denselben unter, wenn der Crême abgekocht ist. Es ist dieses besonders räthlich, wenn man den Crême in Schaalen füllt.

173. Gelees.

Zu dem Wein-Gelee nimmt man, um das Geliren zu erzielen, theils Gelatine, theils Hirschhorn, theils Hausenblase. Das Letztere ist freilich das Theurere, aber es hat den grossen Vortheil, dass die davon bereiteten Gelees gleich klar sind und keiner weiteren Klärung bedürfen, während die Gelees von Gelatine oder Hirschhorn mit Eiweiss geklärt und dann filtrirt werden müssen, wobei selbstverständlich viel verloren geht.

174. Wein-Gelee von Gelatine.

Man löse 1 oz recht weisse Gelatine mit $\frac{1}{4}$ qt Wasser auf gelindem Kohlenfeuer auf, thue dann den Saft von 3 bis 4 Citronen dazu, 10 oz Stückenzucker, $\frac{1}{2}$ Flasche guten, kräftigen Rheinwein und 2 Eiweiss. Dies Alles koche man unter beständigem Rühren auf, schrecke es mit etwas Wein nochmals ab, lasse es wieder aufstossen und giesse es dann in einen Filtrirbeutel von Flanell oder durch eine Serviette. Es wird nicht gleich klar durchlaufen, man muss es erst öfter wieder zurückgiessen bis es klar durchläuft. Da beim Filtriren sich dieser Gelee leicht abkühlt, so muss man darauf sehen, dass man den Filtrirbeutel an einem warmen Orte und etwas geschützt aufgestellt hat.

Füllt man diesen Gelee in Formen, die nachher gestürzt werden sollen, so muss man $\frac{1}{2}$ oz Gelatine mehr nehmen. Die Formen werden alsdann in warmes Wasser gehalten und lassen sich dann leicht stürzen.

175. Gelee farbig.

Von der obigen Mischung färbt man die Hälfte roth, giesst ein wenig davon in die Form, stellt diese auf Eis, bis der Inhalt gelirt, giesst dann ein wenig von der nicht gefärbten Hälfte darüber, lässt auch dies geliren, und so fort, bis die Form gefüllt ist.

Die flüssige Mischung erhält man warm, damit sie nicht schon vor dem Eingiessen fest wird.

Alle anderen Gelees erhalten ihren Namen durch den beigefügten Geschmack.

176. Blanc Mange.

¼ lb Gelatine, ½ pt Rosenwasser, 2 qts Milch, ½ lb Zucker, ½ pt Mandelmilch, lasse es zum Kochen kommen; wenn lauwarm, fülle es in Formen. Mandelmilch macht man wie folgt: Reibe 1 oz süsse und 3 oz bittere weisse Mandeln mit 1½ lb Zucker und 1 qt Orangeblüthen-Wasser recht fein und lasse es durch ein feines Sieb laufen.

XII. Theil.

Liqueur-Fabrikation.

Das Grund-Recept ist folgendes: Löse 2½ lbs Stücken-Zucker in ¾ qt Wasser auf; alsdann giesse 1 qt Spiritus dazu; alle Liqueure erhalten ihren Namen durch die Beimischung der ätherischen Oele. Diese Oele sollten immer in dem Spiritus gelöst werden, indem sie sich in der fertigen Mischung nicht mehr vertheilen und als Fettperlen obenauf schwimmen würden.

Ich lasse einige der Namen folgen:

177. Kümmel-Liqueur, Pfeffermünz-, Vanille-, Himbeer-, Kirsch-, Kaffee-, Rosen-, Citronen-, Anis-, Nelken-, Zimmet-, Pomeranzen-Liqueur etc.

30 Tropfen ätherisches Oel ist genug zu 1 qt Spiritus. Liqueure müssen, wenn sie nicht ganz klar sind, durch Löschpapier oder Flanell filtrirt, sowie ein Bischen Alaun zugesetzt werden.

178. Kräuter-Bitters.

¼ lb unreife Pomeranzen, ½ oz Quarsia, ½ oz Thymian, ¼ oz Taubenkropf, ½ oz Salbei, ½ oz Wachholderbeeren, 1 oz Zimmet, 1 oz Kümmel, 1 oz Anis, ½ oz Citronenschalen.

Alle diese Kräuter und Gewürze übergiesst man mit 4 qts Spiritus, lässt es 8 Tage ausziehen, giesst es dann ab und versüsst es mit 6 lbs Zucker, der mit 1½ qt Wasser aufgelöst ist; auch zu bitteren Liqueuren hat man jetzt ätherische Oele.

179. Punsch-Extract.

6 lbs Zucker übergiesst man mit 1½ qt Wasser und kocht ihn damit zum Breitlauf. Inzwischen hat man 20 Citronen ausgepresst und lässt den Saft einmal mit aufkochen. Nun lässt man den Zucker kalt werden und giesst 6 Flaschen

feinen Rum oder Arac zu, mischt es gut und füllt es zum Klären in ein Fass. Einen kräftigen Punsch giebt es, wenn man $\frac{1}{3}$ Essenz und $\frac{2}{3}$ kochendes Wasser nimmt.

180. Glühwein-Essenz.

$\frac{1}{2}$ lb Zimmet, $\frac{1}{4}$ lb Nelken, 2 oz Muscatblüthen übergiesst man mit 1 qt Spiritus und lässt es in der Wärme ausziehen.

Einige Löffel dieser Essenz genügen, einer Flasche Rothwein, die mit $\frac{1}{4}$ lb Zucker versüsst ist, das nöthige Gewürz zu geben.

Will man Liqueure ordinärer haben, so setzt man mehr Wasser zu.

181. Bonekamp.

Dieser berühmt gewordene Liqueur wird auf folgende Weise bereitet:

3 oz getrocknete unreife Pomeranzen, 1 oz Pomeranzenschalen, 2 oz Enzianwurzel, 1 oz Kaskarillarinde, $\frac{1}{2}$ oz Kukumerwurzel, $\frac{3}{4}$ oz Zimmet, $\frac{1}{2}$ oz Nelken, $\frac{1}{4}$ oz Rhabarber werden zerstossen und zerschnitten in eine Flasche mit $1\frac{1}{2}$ lb starkem Spiritus, $3\frac{1}{2}$ lbs Wasser, 40 Tropfen Sternanisöl übergossen und $\frac{1}{2}$ lb Zucker zugesetzt. Diese Mischung lässt man 8 Tage lang stehen, schüttelt dieselbe während dieser Zeit einige Male um, presst sie dann aus und filtrirt sie durch Löschpapier.

182. Marasquino di Sara.

4 lbs Zucker löst man mit $\frac{3}{4}$ qt Himbeerwasser, $\frac{1}{4}$ qt Orangeblüthen-Wasser und $\frac{1}{2}$ qt reinem Wasser auf, giesst dann 1 Flasche Baseler Kirschwasser und $1\frac{1}{2}$ qt Sprit dazu.

183. Marasquino-Liqueur.

$\frac{3}{4}$ lb destillirtes Kirschwasser, $\frac{3}{4}$ lb Himbeerwasser, 6 oz Orangeblüthen-Wasser werden über 3 lbs Stückenzucker gegossen und dieser damit aufgelöst, alsdann giesst man 1 qt feinsten Sprit dazu.

184. Rosen-Liqueur.

$2\frac{1}{2}$ lbs Zucker löse man mit $\frac{3}{4}$ qt destillirtem Rosenwasser auf, thue dann 1 qt Sprit dazu, dem man noch 3 Tropfen Rosenöl zugesetzt hat.

185. Vanille-Liqueur.

3 bis 4 Stangen Vanille spalte man und stecke sie in 1 qt Sprit, lasse sie einige Tage an einem warmen Orte stehen und ausziehen. Alsdann löse man $2\frac{1}{2}$ lbs feinen Stückenzucker mit $\frac{3}{4}$ qt Wasser auf, giesse dann den Sprit dazu und

färbe die Mischung entweder mit Cochenille-Farbe roth, odei auch mit etwas Zucker-Couleur hellbraun.

186. Bischoff.

Auf 6 Flaschen Rothwein nimmt man 1½ lb Stückenzucker und lässt ihn darin auflösen, alsdann giesst man ¼ qt Bischoff-Essenz dazu.

Hat man solche Essenz von Orangen nicht vorräthig, so kann man auch die Schalen von einigen grünen Orangen hineinthun und lässt dieselben darin ausziehen.

187. Bischoff-Essenz.

2½ lbs Pomeranzenschalen, gekocht und von den weissen markigen Theilen befreit, zerschneidet man in kleine Stücke und thut sie auf ein Fass, ebenso 1 lb trockene kleine Pomeranzen, die etwas überstossen sind, und giesst darüber 15 qts Sprit. Diese Essenz verwendet man theils zur Anfertigung von Bischoff, theils zu Liqueuren, wie Curacao etc.

188. Cardinal.

6 Flaschen leichter Rheinwein werden mit 1 lb Zucker versüsst und mit einigen Löffeln voll Cardinal-Essenz angebittert. Ein genaues Verhältniss lässt sich dabei nicht angeben, weil der Wein zu verschieden und mehr oder minder für das Bittere empfänglich ist. Man muss dabei seinem Geschmacke folgen. Hat man keine Essenz vorräthig, so kann man auch hier sich gleich der Orangen bedienen, wie bei dem Bischoff.

189. Limonade-Extract.

2 lbs Raffinade-Zucker kocht man zum kleinen Faden, auch kocht man die fein abgeschälte Schale einer Citrone mit. Inzwischen hat man 10 Citronen ausgepresst und den Saft durch ein feines Sieb gegossen; diesen Saft giesst man in den Zucker, sobald er die Probe hat, giesst das Ganze nochmals durch ein Sieb und verwahrt den fertigen Extract auf Flaschen an einem kühlen Orte.

190. Höllen-Punsch.

1 lb Zucker wird mit 2 Flaschen Rothwein kochend gemacht, dann in eine Terrine gegossen und 1 Flasche Arrac hinzugefügt und mit einem brennenden Fidibus angezündet und brennend in die Gesellschaft gebracht.

XIII. Theil.

Von den Glasuren.

Zur Anfertigung von Glasuren bedarf man in der Regel ganz feinen Zucker, der durchaus mehlartig und egal ist. Zu den Wasserglasuren und gewöhnlichen Eiweissglasuren genügt es, den Zucker durch ein offenes, feines Haarsieb gesiebt zu haben, zu der Spritzglasur muss man aber ein so feines Sieb als nur möglich und darum auch sehr trockenen Zucker haben, weil etwas feuchter Zucker das Sieb gleich verstopfen würde. Solche feine Siebe müssen auch durch eine sogenannte Trommel verschlossen sein.

191. Wasser-Glasur.

Wasserglasur ist nur eine feine Mischung von dem feinen Glasurzucker mit Wasser in einer breiartigen Consistenz. Die Glasur trägt man auf kaltes Backwerk mit einem Messer auf, auf warmes Backwerk, wie Kaffeekuchen u. dergl., auch mit einem Pinsel. Bei kaltem Backwerk muss die Glasur im Ofen etwas abgetrocknet werden, bei warmem Backwerk ist dies jedoch nicht nöthig. Dieser Glasur kann man mit Oelen oder Essenzen jeden beliebigen Geschmack geben. Am besten eignet sich Rosenwasser, Orangeblüthenwasser und Vanille-Essenz dazu.

192. Rosen-Glasur.

Derselbe Zucker, mit Rosenwasser angemischt, oder etwas Rosenöl als Geschmack und roth gefärbt.

193. Citronen-Glasur.

1 Citrone auf Zucker abgerieben und in ein wenig Wasser geschabt, dann den Saft einer Citrone und soviel feinen Zucker, als nöthig, um die breiartige Consistenz zu erlangen.

194. Apfelsinen-Glasur.

Man reibe eine Apfelsine auf Zucker ab und schabe das Abgeriebene in etwas Wasser, presse dann auf ein Sieb den Saft der Apfelsine und einer Citrone und mische dazu soviel Zucker als nöthig.

195. Chocolade-Glasur.

Etwas complicirter als die anderen Glasuren ist die Chocolade-Glasur. Man erwärmt $\frac{1}{2}$ lb Chocolade, thut sie in eine

Casserole, giesst $\frac{1}{4}$ qt heisses Wasser zu und wiegt 1 lb Zucker darauf, dies arbeitet man recht durcheinander, dass die Chocolade sich gehörig auflöst, giesst dann noch etwas Wasser nach und kocht nun die Glasur zum Faden, tablirt sie dann gut ab und überzieht noch warm das zu Glasirende und trocknet die Glasur im Ofen etwas ab.

196. Gekochte Glasur.

Man kocht geläuterten Zucker zum schwachen Faden und trägt auf die zu glasirenden Sachen diesen Zucker mit einer Bürste oder festem Pinsel auf. Diese Glasur, der man beliebigen Geschmack geben kann, wird meist zu feinem Pfefferkuchen angewendet und bekommt einen hübschen Glanz und feines Ansehen.

197. Eiweiss-Glasur.

Gewöhnliche Eiweissglasur rührt man von Eiweiss mit Glasurzucker an und rührt sie recht schaumig. Geschmack kann man dieser Glasur beliebig geben, auch die Farbe, die man meist mit dem Geschmack harmonirend darstellt.

198. Chocolade-Glasur von Eiweiss.

Der angerührten Eiweissglasur von 2 Eiweiss setzt man $\frac{1}{4}$ lb gewärmte Chocolade zu, rührt dieselbe tüchtig unter und verdünnt die Glasur dann mit Läuterzucker.

199. Spritz-Glasur.

Zu dieser wichtigen Glasur nimmt man den feinsten Zucker, sogenannten Staubzucker, rührt von 2 Eiweiss und diesem Zucker einen ziemlich festen Brei an, thut einen Theelöffel voll Essigsäure hinein und rührt damit so lange, bis die Glasur ganz schaumig und so fest ist, dass sie, wenn man sie auf einander legt, nicht aus einander fliesst. Der Name dieser Glasur sagt schon, wozu sie verwendet wird. Man garnirt damit alle Torten und Backwerke, indem man sie in kleine gedrehte Düten füllt und durch eine kleine feine Oeffnung spritzt. Aber auch Confecte kann man von dieser Glasur machen und ihr dann einen Geschmack durch Essenz geben.

Zu gröberen Garnirungen bedient man sich des Gummibeutels oder der Garnir-Spritze.

200. Ersatz für Eiweiss.

Löse $\frac{1}{4}$ lb Gelatine oder Leim in 1 qt warmes Wasser, halte das Wasser warm bis Alles aufgelöst ist. Will man nun Eiweissglasur machen, so gebraucht man diese Lösung statt Eiweiss. Lasse die Essigsäure fort und setze ein Bischen pulverisirten Alaun zu.

XIV. Theil.

Ueber den Traganth.

Der Traganth ist ein Gummi und durch Wasser löslich. Er besitzt viel Zähigkeit, besonders in Verbindung mit dem Zucker. In der Conditorei wird er jetzt weniger gebraucht als früher, da die Arbeiten daraus durch andere Zucker-Figuren, auch Chocolade Figuren verdrängt worden sind. Immerhin ist er nicht ganz zu verdrängen, und es würde ein Fehler sein, wenn er hier nicht erwähnt würde. Die Arbeiten aus Traganthteig erfordern meistens viel Geschicklichkeit, besonders Figuren aus freier Hand gearbeitet.

201. Traganth-Lack.

Löse 2 oz Gummi mastic in $\frac{1}{4}$ pt Terpentin auf und halte ihn gut verschlossen.

202. Bonbon-Lack.

3 oz Sandarac, 1 oz venetianischen Terpentin mit starkem Spiritus aufgelöst. Man achte darauf, dass er die Dichtigkeit von Syrup habe.

203. Chocolade-Lack.

$\frac{1}{2}$ lb Benzoe pulverisirt man, schüttet es in eine Flasche, übergiesst es mit 1 qt Sprit, stellt es warm und schüttelt es öfter um, damit sich Alles gut auflöse. Nachdem es aufgelöst ist, filtrirt man es durch Löschpapier und hebt es zum Gebrauch auf. Wenn man damit lackiren will, bedient man sich eines weichen Pinsels.

204. Der Traganthteig.

Man weiche 2 oz Traganth in $\frac{1}{2}$ qt Wasser ein und lasse ihn darin 24 bis 36 Stunden stehen. Alsdann muss man ein starkes leinenes Presstuch haben, wodurch man den Traganth presst, damit das Unreine, was der Traganth etwa enthält, darin zurück gehalten wird. Nachdem man den Traganth durchgepresst hat, thut man ihn in den recht rein gewaschenen Mandelstein, reibt ihn tüchtig und thut nach und nach feinen Staubzucker hinein, bis der Traganth recht weiss ist und sich etwas trocken anfühlt. Nun kann man den Traganth in einen Topf thun und zum Gebrauch aufheben. Will man ihn verwenden, so nimmt man einen Theil davon auf eine Marmorplatte und wirkt ihn mit dem feinsten Zucker zu einem festen Teige. Auch kann man den Traganth mit Puder anwirken, besonders wenn er zu Sachen verwendet werden soll, die voraussichtlich nicht genossen werden.

205. Die Verarbeitung des Traganthteiges.

Wie ich schon vorhin bemerkt habe, erfordert die Bearbeitung des Traganths eine nicht ungewöhnliche Geschicklichkeit, besonders wenn es sich um Figuren handelt, die bossirt werden müssen; es lässt sich also nicht erwarten, dass hier eine Beschreibung davon stattfinde. Die Arbeiten aus Traganth sind sehr vielfältig, und wenn sie auch nicht mehr so willig Käufer finden, so werden sie von Conditoren immer noch gern gearbeitet. Ausser den Figuren, die schon erwähnt wurden, werden nun viele kleine Spielereien gearbeitet, die besonders in mehreren Grössen angefertigt werden und die man Traganth-Dragee nennt.

Zu dem grösseren Dragee fertigt man Thiere und aus Formen geschnittene menschliche Figuren auf kleinen Postamenten, die gemalt und lackirt werden.

Zu dem mittleren Dragee macht man kleine Bücher, Würfel, Aepfel, Rüben, Blumen, Tauben, Dominosteine, Kaninchen etc. Zu dem kleinen Dragee macht man Bohnen, Gerstenkörner, kleine Muscheln, Schnitzelbohnen, Aepfelchen, Seifenkugeln etc.

Zu diesem Traganth-Dragee verwendet man Traganth, der ganz mit Zucker angewirkt ist, da diese Sächelchen oft von den Kindern genossen werden.

206. Formen zu Traganth.

Die Formen, die zur Traganth-Verarbeitung gebraucht werden, macht sich ein geschickter Conditor selbst. Man modellirt den Gegenstand, den man vervielfältigen will, entweder von Thon oder auch Traganth, auch benutzt man dazu Gegenstände aus der Natur. Man legt den zu formenden Gegenstand auf eine mit Oel gestrichene Platte, achtet darauf, dass er genau aufliegt, bestreicht ihn mit Oel, stellt von Pappe einen Rand darum, lässt dann Schwefel zergehen und giesst dann diesen über das Modell. Nachdem der Schwefel erkaltet, nimmt man die Modelle heraus und die Formen sind fertig zum Gebrauch.

XV. Theil.

207. Garniren und Schablonen.

Im Besitz von dieser Scheibe ist der Zirkel in der Bäckerei nicht durchaus nothwendig ; man lege diese Scheibe auf den schon glasirten Cake oder Torte und markire sich das erwählte Muster; die Puncte, welche Löcher vorstellen, werden hierzu gebraucht, indem man die Spitze einer Bleifeder hindurchsteckt, diese Scheibe ermöglicht es, den Cake in einem Moment gleichförmig einzutheilen und den Mittelpunkt zu finden. Dieselbe sollte ungefähr ein Fuss im Durchmesser haben. 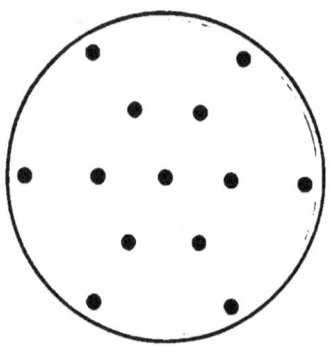 Ausser dieser Scheibe schneidet man sich Ovals, Sterne, Lyras, Harfen, Füllhörner, Fruchtkörbe, Schmetterlinge, Blumenkörbe, Schultaschen, Blumen-Vasen, Squares, grade und gebogene 4, 6, 8 und mehr Ecken in verschiedenen Grössen. Das Schablonenschneiden besteht hauptsächlich darin, dass man das Papier mehrfach zusammenlegt und das erwählte Muster schneide. Nachdem man das Muster in Papier geschnitten, überträgt man dasselbe auf Pappe, schneidet dasselbe recht glattkantig nach dem Muster und die Schablone ist fertig zum Gebrauch; man lege dieselbe dann auf den schon glasirten Cake oder Torte und streicht mit einer Bleifeder sehr leicht um die Kanten der Schablone.

208. Ornaments aus Spritzglasur.

Die Anfertigung von Burgen, Wasserfällen, Tunnels geschieht auf folgende Weise :

Nachdem man sich die verschiedenen Theile des Aufsatzes gezeichnet hat, so lege man eine leicht geschmierte Glasplatte auf die Zeichnung, nehme die Garnirspritze und folge der Zeichnung; wenn trocken setze man die einzelnen Theile vermittels Spritzglasur zusammen, garnire die Kanten und Ecken, setze eine Figur oben darauf und decorire mit Papier und Traganth, Blätter, Rosen und Blumen. Stellen die Aufsätze Burgen, Kirchen oder Häuser vor, so legt man die Gardinen aus Gauze oder buntes Papier auf die Glasplatte und garnirt oben darauf; können aber auch später angemacht werden.

209. Aufsätze auf Gauze.

Wie oben, statt der Glasplatte bedient man sich der Gauze, welche man über die Zeichnung spannt und garnirt; wenn trocken schneidet man die Gauze an den Kanten schön ab und verfährt wie oben. Diese Aufsätze sind sehr stark und machen einen guten Eindruck. (Siehe Illustration). Zuweilen ist es auch nothwendig, dass die einzelnen Theile auf beiden Seiten garnirt sein müssen, dieses ist sehr einfach, indem man die Sachen, wenn trocken, umdreht und verfährt, wie schon erklärt.

210. Tafel-Aufsätze.

Das Feld der Aufsätze ist unendlich gross, denn für den geschickten Arbeiter gibt es überhaupt nichts, was nicht täuschend nachgeahmt werden könnte, und es würde zu weit führen, hier eine vollständige Erklärung folgen zu lassen, dennoch möchte ich die verschiedenen Massen erwähnt haben, aus welchen die einzelnen Theile der Aufsätze angefertigt werden. Marzipan, Macronen, Caramel, Traganth, Spunsugar, Almondpaste, Confectioners Paste, Nougat, grained Sugar, Glasur, Meringue, Felsenzucker, Papiermaché, Pastillage u. s. w. Zum decoriren der Aufsätze gebraucht man ferner Glasur und Mandelspähne, Papier und Traganth-Blätter, Rosen, Blumen, Brillanten, Silberpillen, carmelirte Früchte, Gold- und Silber-Schaum, Bronze, Streu- und Hagelzucker in allen Farben, Gauze, Glanz- und mattes Papier in den verschiedensten Farben, rohe Seide oder Spunsugar verwendet man für Fontainen und Wasserfälle, Baumwolle für Schaum, Spiegelglas für Stillwasser, und gefärbtes Gras und Moos; um die Kanten des Spiegels zu verhüllen, wird auch mit Vorliebe zwischen FelsenZucker angebracht, um die Riffe und Vorsprünge täuschend darzustellen. Aufsätze, welche durch Ringe zu einer höheren Figur gebracht werden, z. B. Bienenkörbe, Mandelberge, Macronen-Aufsätze, füllt man gerne mit Schlagsahne-Crême, Bonbons oder Meringue; bei dem Serviren nimmt man den oberen Theil des Aufsatzes ab. Ferner möchte ich erwähnt haben, dass man bei feineren Aufsätzen gerne Spieldosen, Feuerwerk u. dgl. anbringt; um Eisenbahnen, Bergwerke und Fahrstühle in Bewegung zu setzen, bedient man sich einer alten Alarm-Clock, aus welcher man natürlich das Stundenrad herausnehmen muss.

XVI. Theil.

Früchte in Dunst.

211. Blanchiren.

Blanchiren ist ein technischer Ausdruck und bezeichnet das Weichkochen derjenigen Früchte, die im halbreifen Zustande eingemacht werden sollen. Bei dem Blanchiren kann man auf die Farbe der Früchte einwirken, indem man den Früchten, die grün sind und recht grün bleiben sollen, etwas Salz oder Alaun zusetzt.

212. Behandlung.

Hat man die Gläser, Flaschen oder Büchsen mit der betreffenden Frucht gefüllt, so übergiesst man sie mit Läuterzucker, dann nimmt man doppelte Schweinsblase und bindet dieselbe recht fest über, und zwar so, dass wenn man die Blase überzieht und mit der linken Hand festhält, mit der rechten Hand darauf drückt (um möglichst wenig Luft in der Flasche zu lassen) und gleich wieder tüchtig anzieht und einen Bindfaden recht oft umschlingt. Alsdann setzt man die Gläser oder Flaschen in einen Topf oder Kessel, thut etwas Heu darunter und auch darum, giesst dann so viel Wasser in den Kessel, dass es bis an den Hals der Flaschen geht, setzt es auf's Feuer und bringt es langsam zum Kochen. Kocht es, so lässt man es 16 bis 20 Minuten kochen, setzt dann den Kessel ab und lässt die Gläser darin erkalten, verpicht dieselben noch und verwahrt die Gläser an einem kühlen Ort bis zum Gebrauch.

Sind die Früchte in Blechdosen eingelegt, so werden dieselben von einem Klempner zugelöthet und dann ebenfalls gekocht. Ebenso bei dem neuen Verschluss mit Gummi.

Wird der Verschluss durch einen Kork bewirkt, so bindet man denselben vermittelst feinen Drahts oder Bindfaden fest. Ist der Kork grösser als ein gewöhnlicher Weinflaschen-Kork, so legt man ein rundes Blech, so gross als der Kork ist, mit Flaschenpech über den Kork und verbindet es dann ebenfalls.

213. Birnen in Dunst.

Die schönste Birne dazu ist die Muscateller-Birne. Man schält dieselbe wenn sie noch hart ist, blanchirt sie in Alaun-wasser, kühlt sie ab, legt sie dann in die Gläser, giesst Zucker über und verfährt weiter, wie schon erwähnt.

214. Erdbeeren in Dunst.

Man wählt dazu Erdbeeren, die nicht zu gross sind, doch auch nicht so klein, wie Holz-Erdbeeren. Man pflückt die Beeren von den Stielen, legt sie in Gläser, giesst Zucker über und verfährt wie oben.

215. Himbeeren in Dunst.

Die Himbeeren zupft man ebenfalls von den Stielen, legt sie dann in die Gläser, giesst Zucker über verbindet die Gläser und kocht sie dann.

216. Kirschen in Dunst.

Die Kirschen, die sich am besten dazu eignen, sind die Glas- oder Weichselkirschen. Man zupft die Stiele von den Kirschen, legt sie in die Gläser oder Büchsen und giesst geläuterten Zucker, der den kleinen Faden hat, darüber, sodass das Glas bis auf 1 Zoll voll ist. Alsdann verschliesst man die Gläser recht gut und kocht sie wie schon vorhin erläutert worden.

217. Bemerkung.

Alle hier nicht angebenen Früchte können auf die gleiche Weise behandelt werden, das heisst sie müssen blanchirt werden.

XVII. Theil.

218. Gelees und Marmelade.

Hat man den klaren Fruchtsaft, so rechnet man gewöhnlich auf 1 lb Saft, $\frac{3}{4}$ lb Zucker. Man nimmt dazu guten Melis und setzt den Saft mit dem Zucker auf's Feuer, am besten auf's Kohlenfeuer, welches man recht in Gluth setzt. Nun lässt man die Mischung unter öfterem Umrühren zum kochen kommen, schäumt ab, wiederholt dieses recht oft und kocht die Mischung etwa 10 bis 15 Minuten. Nun taucht man den Schaumlöffel ein und beobachtet, wie die Tropfen davon abfallen. Fliesst die Masse in kleinen Tropfen ab, so ist der Gelee noch nicht gut, fliesst sie schon in dickeren Tropfen ab, die sich beim Abfliessen zusammenziehen und in kleinen Lappen herabfallen, so ist dies die richtige Geleeprobe. Zur grösseren Sicherheit giesst man einige Tropfen auf kaltes Porzellan, stehen dieselben recht rund und zeigen sich auch als Gelee, so darf man ja nicht weiter kochen, weil sonst der Gelee bräunlich und zähe wird. Ferner findet man die Probe leicht, wenn auf das Kochen des Gelee's achtet. Im Anfang steigt der Gelee sehr hoch, so bald er im Steigen nachlässt, ist die Probe nahe. Weil nun aber der Gelee stark steigt, so muss man sich hüten, zu viel in den Kessel zu nehmen, weil er sonst leicht übersteigt.

219. Marmelade.

Marmelade nennt man dasjenige Fabrikat von Früchten, wozu man das Mark der Früchte verwendet. Zu geringen Marmeladen lässt man auch wohl die Kerne der Himbeeren oder Johannisbeeren in dem Marke zu feinen Marmeladen muss man aber durch ein Haarsieb geriebenes Fruchtmark haben. Man nimmt auf 1 lb Mark $\frac{1}{2}$ bis 1 lb Zucker.

Die Probe bei Marmelade von Johannisbeeren und Himbeeren ist dieselbe wie bei Gelee. Bei festeren Marmeladen, als die von Aprikosen, Aepfeln, Kirschen thut man gut, etwas davon auf Papier zu schütten, schlägt es stark durch. so muss man weiter kochen, bis keine wässerigen Theile mehr durchschlagen. Wohl muss man sich hüten, Marmelade zu weich zu kochen, sie ist sonst dem Verderben sehr leicht ausgesetzt.

220. Apfel-Gelee.

Man nimmt einige weinsaure Aepfel, schneidet sie in Viertel, thut sie in einen Kessel, giesst so viel Wasser darauf, dass sie überdeckt sind und kocht sie damit weich. Alsdann schüttet man die Aepfel auf ein Haarsieb, lässt den Saft gut ablaufen und kocht denselben mit 10 oz Zucker auf 1 lb Saft zu Gelée. Dieser Gelée nimmt verschiedene Farben an und sieht gefärbt sehr gut aus, auch kann man demselben verschiedenen Geschmack geben, als Citronen, Apfelsinen-Geschmack etc., durch Zusatz von abgeriebener Schaale. Der Rückstand der Aepfel wird durch das Haarsieb gerieben und zu Marmelade verwendet.

221. Himbeer-Gelee.

Man nimmt auf 1 lb Himbeeren $\frac{3}{4}$ lb Zucker, setzt dies auf's Feuer und lässt es unter öfterem Umrühren zum Kochen kommen. Nun giesst man die Masse auf ein Haarsieb und lässt den Saft ablaufen, den man zu Gelee kocht. Der Rückstand giebt noch ein ganz gutes Compot.

222. Johannisbeeren-Gelee.

¾ lb Zucker zu 1 lb Saft, und koche zu der angegebenen Probe.

223. Kirsch-Marmelade.

Die schönste Kirsch-Marmelade bekommt man von sauren Kirschen. Man setzt die Kirschen, nachdem man die Stiele abgezupft hat, in einem Kessel auf's Feuer, rührt sie tüchtig um, damit es bald Saft giebt, und lasse sie kochen, bis sie ganz zerkocht sind. Alsdann reibe man das Fleisch der Kirschen durch ein Drahtsieb, so dass nur die Kerne zurückbleiben, und koche von dem Mark unter Zusatz von ¾ lb Zucker auf 1 lb Mark Marmelade.

224. Erdbeer-Marmelade

ist in der Zubereitung dieselbe, wie die Himbeer-Marmelade. Man nehme dazu nur Wald-Erdbeeren und setze etwas Johannisbeeren zu.

225. Himbeer-Marmelade.

Man reibt die Himbeeren durch ein Haarsieb, so dass die Kerne zurückbleiben und kocht nun von diesem Mark, indem man auf 1 lb Mark 1 lb Zucker nimmt, Marmelade nach angegebener Probe.

226. Johannisbeer-Marmelade.

ist ebenso wie Himbeer-Marmelade.

227. Pflaumen-Marmelade.

Die Behandlung ist ebenso wie bei der vorher beschriebenen Marmelade, nur kann man hier noch weniger Zucker nehmen.

XVIII. Theil.

Croquant-Aufsatz.

228. Erklärung zu Tafel XVIII.

Obgleich dieser Aufsatz etwas complicirt, ist die Aufstellung doch nicht so schwierig, wie es den Anschein hat, wenn auch hierzu, wie aus der Beilage ersichtlich, viele Theile anzufertigen sind. In verhältnissmässig kurzer Zeit ist dieser Aufsatz dennoch zu vollenden. Die Bestandtheile dieses Aufsatzes bestehen aus Croquant und Macronen-Masse, diese beiden Hauptfactoren sind bei Aufsätzen solcher Verwendung,

wie man also sieht, unzertrennbar, indem bei Anwendung
Beider alle nur erdenkbaren Varietäten aufstellbar sind. Bei
alleiniger Anwendung von Croquant fallen die Aufsätze gewöhnlich steif und plump aus, weshalb ich auch, durch langjährige Erfahrung darin unterstüzt, diese Zusammenstellung
immer verwende und somit bestens empfehlen kann.

Nachdem man sich die Anzahl der einzelnen Theile in
genauer Grösse nach der Beilage und wie schon öfters beschrieben angefertigt hat, schreite man zur Zusammenstellung, wobei der Fuss, bestehend aus 3 Ringen, zwei unten
und einer oben, mit 18 kleineren aufrechtstehenden Ringeinlagen herzustellen ist, doch achte man ja darauf, dass auf
jeder Seite, da der Aufsatz sechseckig ist, 3 dieser kleinen
Ringe, wie aus der Zeichnung ersichtlich, zu stehen kommen.
Hierauf kommt nun der etwas nach innen gewölbte Unterbau, bestehend aus 6 doppelten C zu Trägern bestimmt; die
Nischen dieses Unterbaues sind mit geschweiften Croquanttheilen nach beigegebenem Muster zu arbeiten und auszufüllen, hierauf kommt sodann ein Ring mit Croquant-Boden,
worauf alsdann der Tempel zu stehen hat. Der Tempel selbst
besteht aus einem sechseckigen Innenbau von Croquant mit
einem Vorbau, ebenfalls von Croquant, welcher auf den an
den Ecken placirten Säulen ruht, und sind letztere von Macronen-Masse anzufertigen. Auf diesen Vorsprung oder
Vorbau kommt der Kranz, aus 2 Macronen-Ringen bestehend,
mit einem nochmaligen Boden, worauf dann zuletzt der
Schluss, genau nach der Beilage angefertigt, zu ruhen hat.

Die beiden Gallerien sind von Spritzglasur nach bereits
öfter beschriebener Manier auf befettetem Tafelglas mit
Dessin-Unterlage anzufertigen, und ist es zu empfehlen, diese
Glasursachen zu verschiedener Verwendung vor Allem in
Angriff zu nehmen damit dieselben Zeit haben, während der
anderen Zubereitungen im Trockenschrank zu erhärten. Ebenfalls fertige man immer einige Theile, hauptsächlich solcher
Glasursachen, mehr an, damit man bei entstehendem Bruch
nicht in Verlegenheit kommt. Die anderen Garnituren sind
von Spritzglasur vor Zusammenstellung anzubringen, und
richte man sich hierbei nach der Zeichnung.

Nougat-Tempel.

229. Erklärung zu Tafel I.

Dieser äusserst elegante Aufsatz, zu allen Gelegenheiten
passend, ist seines vollendeten, schönen Baues wegen sehr
zu empfehlen; auch ist seine Anfertigung überaus leicht, da

nach genau hergestellten Modellen gearbeitet werden kann. Der Aufsatz, einen Tempel mit 6 Oeffnungen darstellend, besteht aus Croquant und Macronen-Masse, bestehend aus 2 Etagen, 3 Ringen verschiedener Grösse mit 16 resp. 32 aufrechtstehenden Einlagen, worauf ein Croquant-Boden liegt, der den Tempel, welcher aus einem Stück Croquant ausgeschnitten und bis zu den sich berührenden Enden aufgerollt wird, zu tragen hat. Das Aeussere des Tempels besteht aus 6 halb aufgerollten Säulen und ebenso vielen Thürbogen, welche auf diesen ruhen. (Bei allen diesen Anleitungen resp. Beschreibungen richte man sich immer nach der Zeichnung, woraus alles genau ersichtlich und wonach, ohne zu irren, gearbeitet werden kann). Ist nun die Aufstellung soweit vorgeschritten, richte man den Kranz, bestehend aus 2 ungleichen Ringen (d. h. der obere muss etwas vorspringen) und 16 Einlagen her, welcher, vollständig fertig, sodann aufgesetzt und befestigt wird. Hierauf wird nun ein Croquant-Boden angesetzt, worauf eine Gallerie anzubringen ist. Das Schlussstück, bestehend aus 5—6 geschweiften S, auf einem oder mehreren Ringen ruhend, wird schliesslich mit Caramel verbunden, auf dem Boden aufgestellt, und der Aufsatz ist fertig. Wenn gewünscht, kann man noch eine vergoldete Kugel und einen Amor anbringen, wiewohl der Abschluss auch ohne die Anbringung von Kugel und Amor vollständig gelungen ist, weshalb solche ganz gut fortbleiben können.

Die Garnirung ist mit Spritzglasur auszuführen, wobei auch einige caramelirte Kirschen und Silberperlen zum Fuss und Kranz angebracht werden können. Von Vortheil ist es, alle Aufsätze auf eine Platte mit erhöhtem Fuss und Spitzenrand zu placiren; sie kommen so besser zur vollen Geltung resp. präsentiren sich besser.

Grundriss und Zeichnung findet man weiter hinten in ⅙ der natürlichen Grösse. Der Leser wird aus obiger Erklärung begreifen auf welche Weise man die Aufsätze anfertigt. Da nun der grössere Theil der Aufsätze in dieser Weise zusammen gestellt wird, so kann man diese Instruction als einen Führer und Leiter annehmen.

XIX. Theil.

230. Das Mischen der Farben.

Unschädliche Farben sind jetzt überall im Handel zu haben, und es wäre zum Ueberfluss, wenn wir die Farben hier nochmals folgen lassen wollten. Dennoch will ich das Mischen und Zusammenstellen derselben erklären: Schwarz und roth macht braun; gelb und blau macht grün; roth und gelb macht orange; roth und blau macht violet; schwarz und weiss macht grau; grün und schwarz macht dunkelgrün und roth und weiss macht hellroth.

231. Farben-Harmonie.

Die folgenden Farben sind von Künstlern als die bestharmonirenden anerkannt: Silber und blau, silber und grün, gold und braun und gold und weiss oder rosa.

232. Vom Zuckerfärben.

Nonpareille und Hagelzucker färbt man auf folgende Weise: Man schüttet den zu färbenden Zucker in einen Kessel oder eine Schüssel und erwärmt ihn, dann giesst man von der dickflüssigen Farbe etwas zu, rührt es tüchtig durch einander, womöglich bis es trocken ist; die Farbe darf hierzu nicht zu dünn sein, weil sich sonst der Zucker auflöst.

Technische Ausdrücke.

Die technischen Ausdrücke, die hier im Buche gebraucht sind, bedeuten:

Tabliren, zum Flug gekochten Zucker an den Seiten der Kasserole mit einem Löffel reiben, damit er abstirbt, trübe und dadurch weich werde.

Tressiren heisst die verschiedenen Massen in die gehörige Form bringen.

Karmeliren heisst Gegenstände mit Karmel überziehen.

Garniren heisst Torten und Backwerk mit Spritzglazur oder Gelee ausschmücken.

Abziehen heisst Crême oder dergleichen mit Eiern zu bestimmter Probe kochen, oder nur abquirlen

I.

Nougat-Tempel. Croquant-Aufsatz.

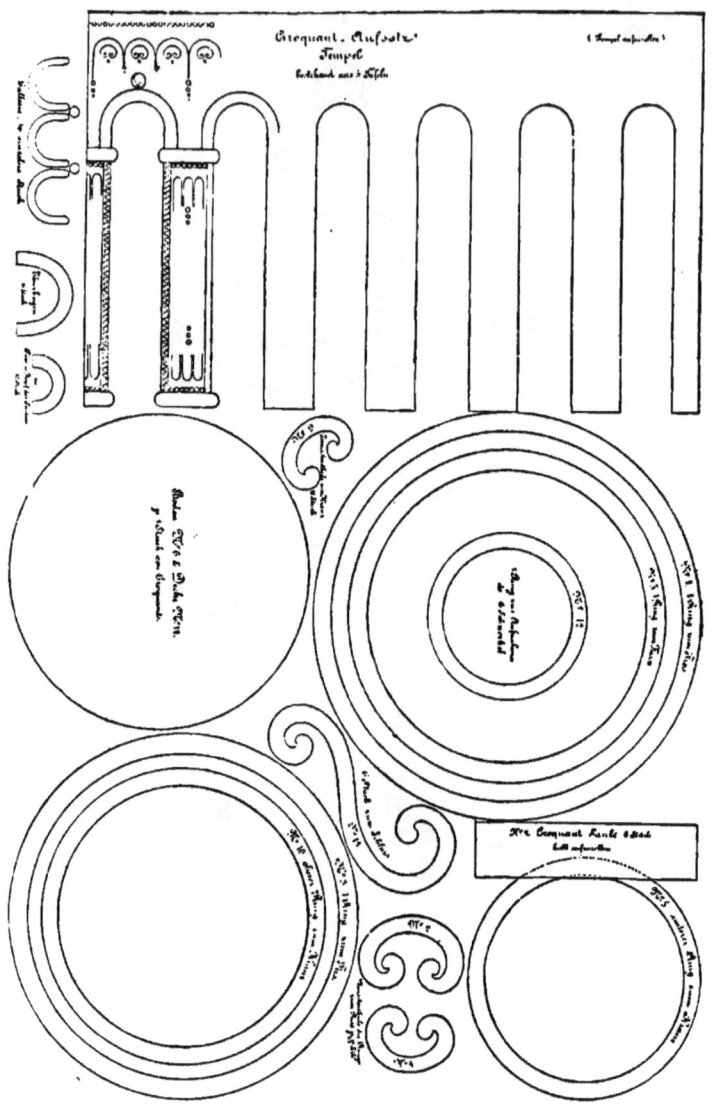

Grundrisse des Croquant-Aufsatzes auf vorhergehender Seite in ⅙ der natürlichen Grösse.

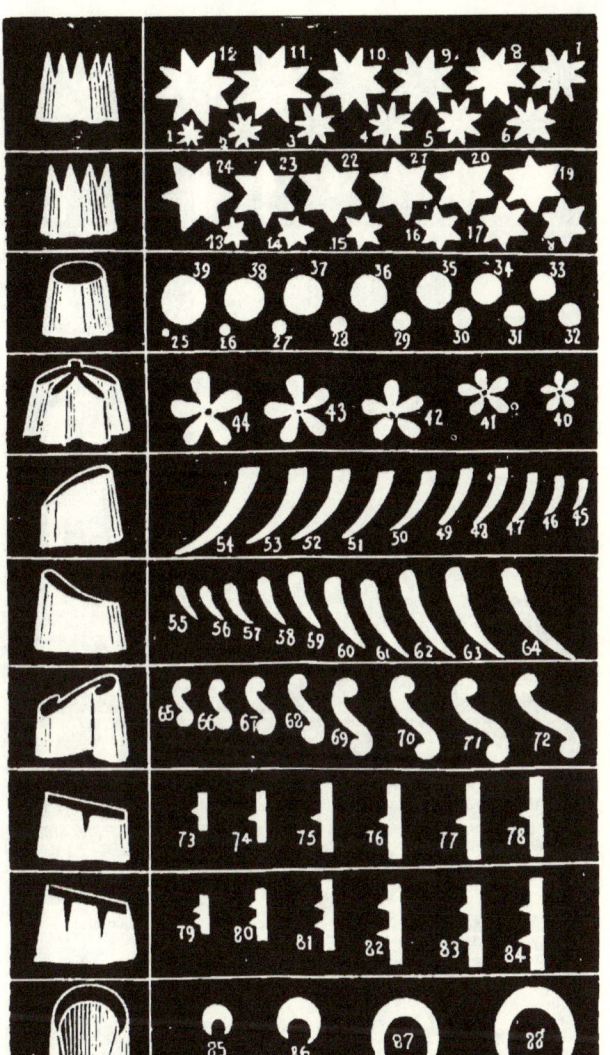

All my tubes are made of German silver and any tube will fit Jumble, Kisses and Ornamenting Machine, also the Jumble, Kisses and Ornamenting Bag.

Price, $1.00 per dozen.

No man can do first-class work without these tubes.

All others are rubbish and not fit to use.

Only a first-class workman knows how a proper tube ought to be.
Price, $1.00 per dozen.

No. 1. Hold the knife steady and turn the cake.
No. 2 shows how to make a proper paper bag.
No. 3 shows how to make roses. First put a star in the centre of the nail head, then add the leaves as shown in cut. The trick of making roses lies in the turning of the nail.

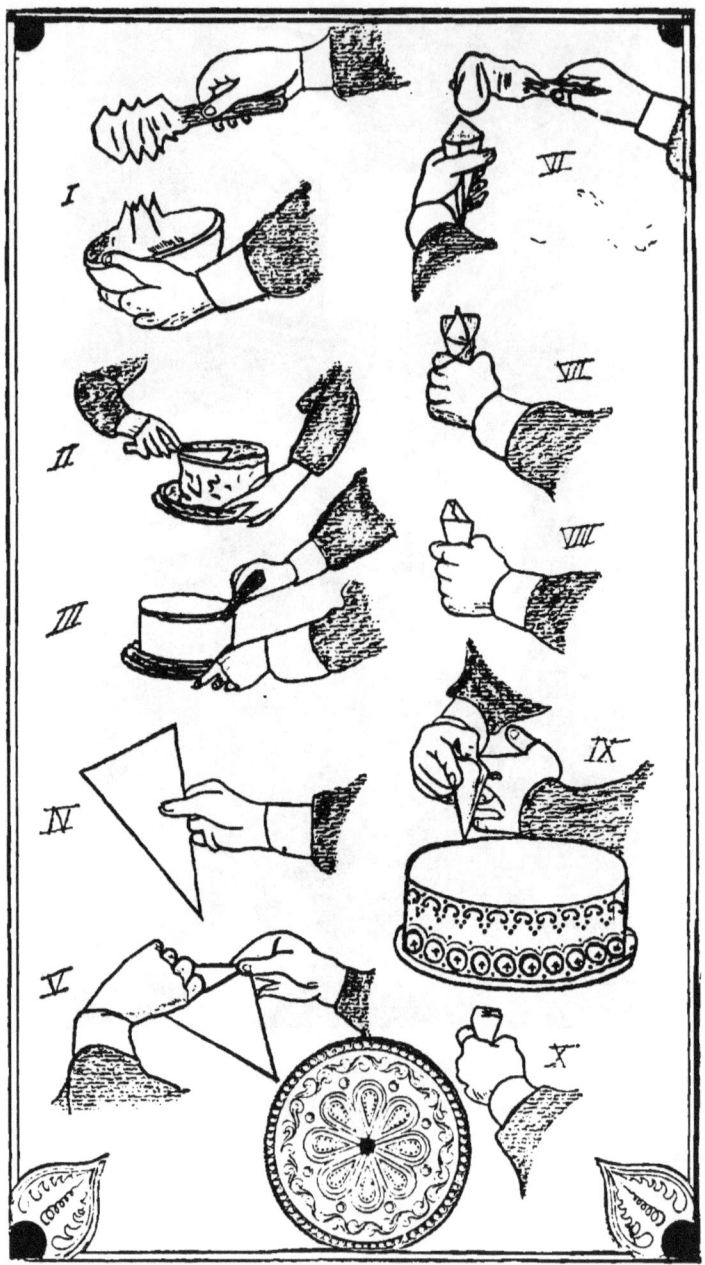

Designs.—Vorlagen.

DESIGNS.

Muſter und Vorlagen zum Dekoriren.

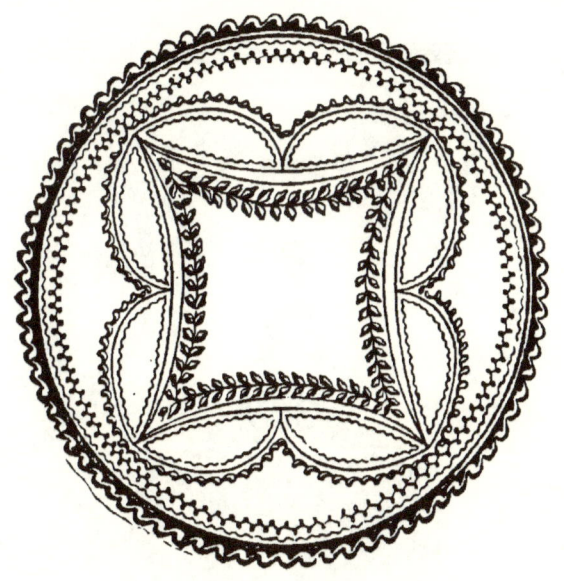

Designs.—Vorlagen.

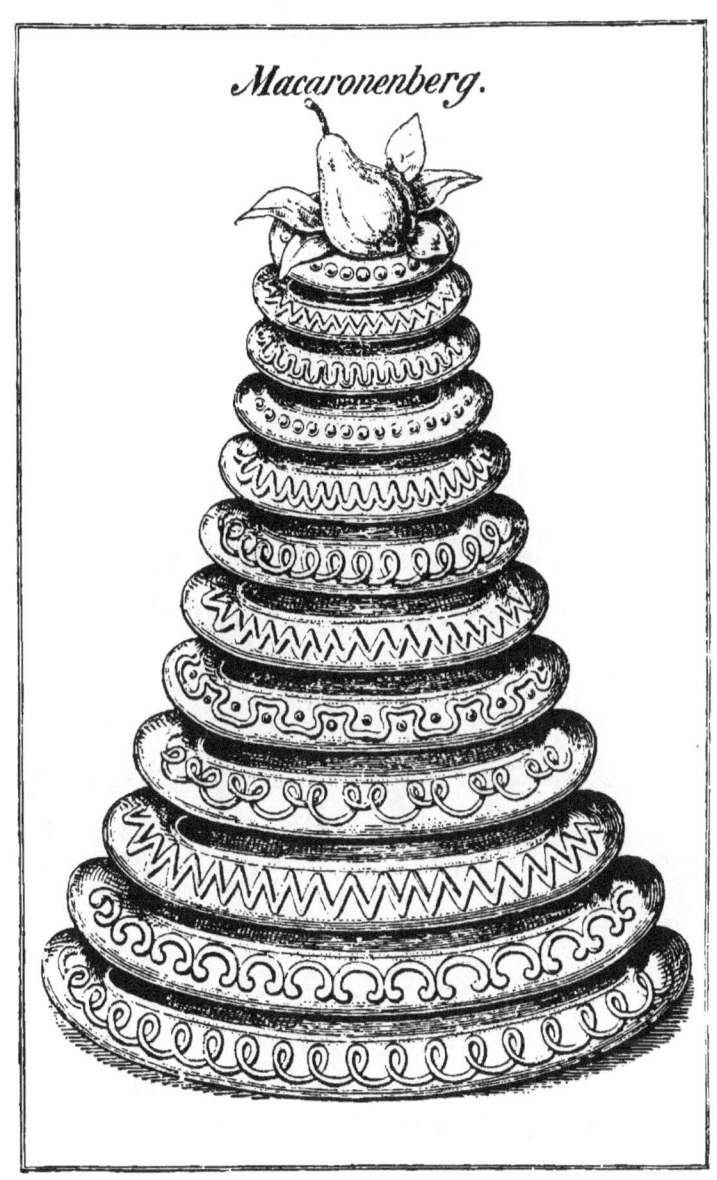

Will man diesen Aufsatz durchsichtig haben, so legt man mehrere Macaronen zwischen die Ringe.

Fisher House.

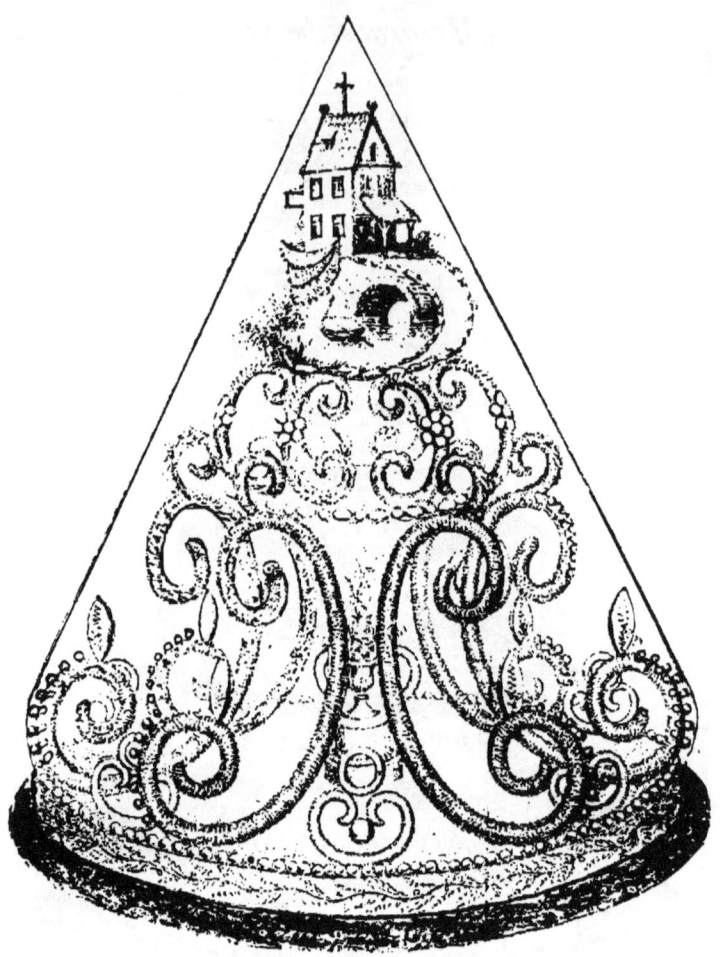

Fischer-Haus.

Die Schnörkel macht man aus fester Macaronen-Masse, das Häuschen von Glasur oder Traganth, das Wasser stellt man durch Spiegelglas her.

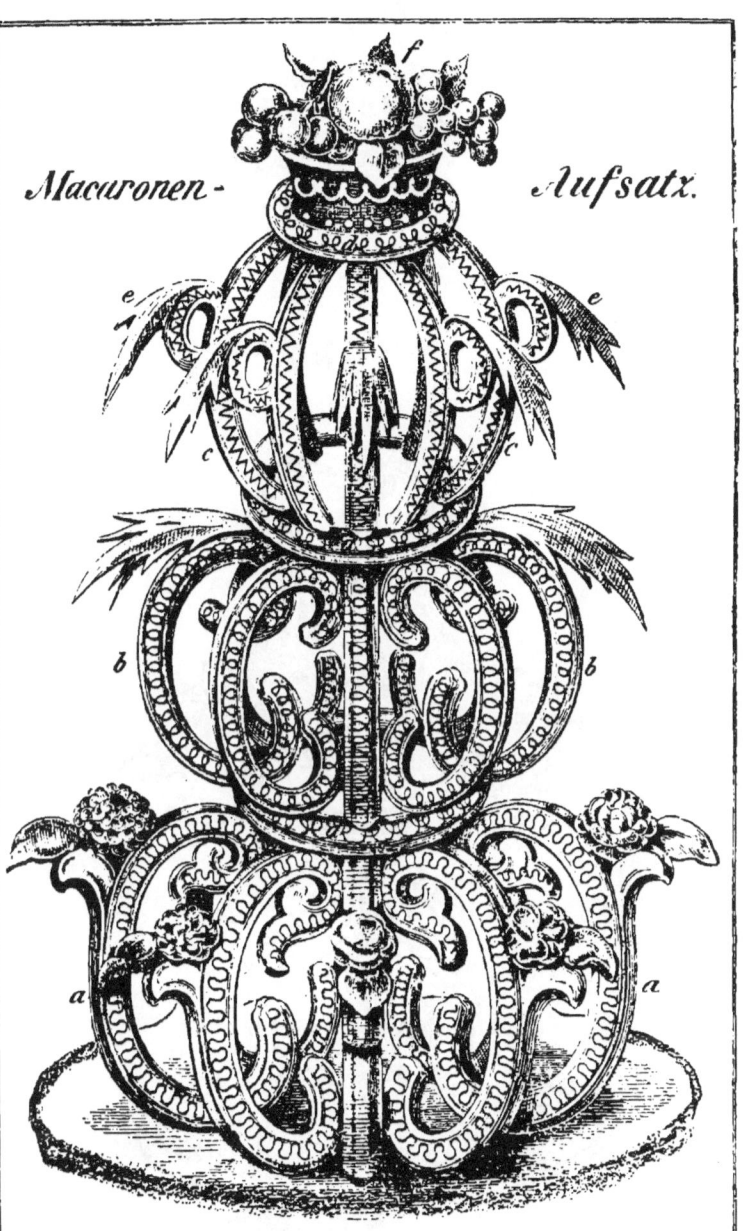

Füll-Horn.

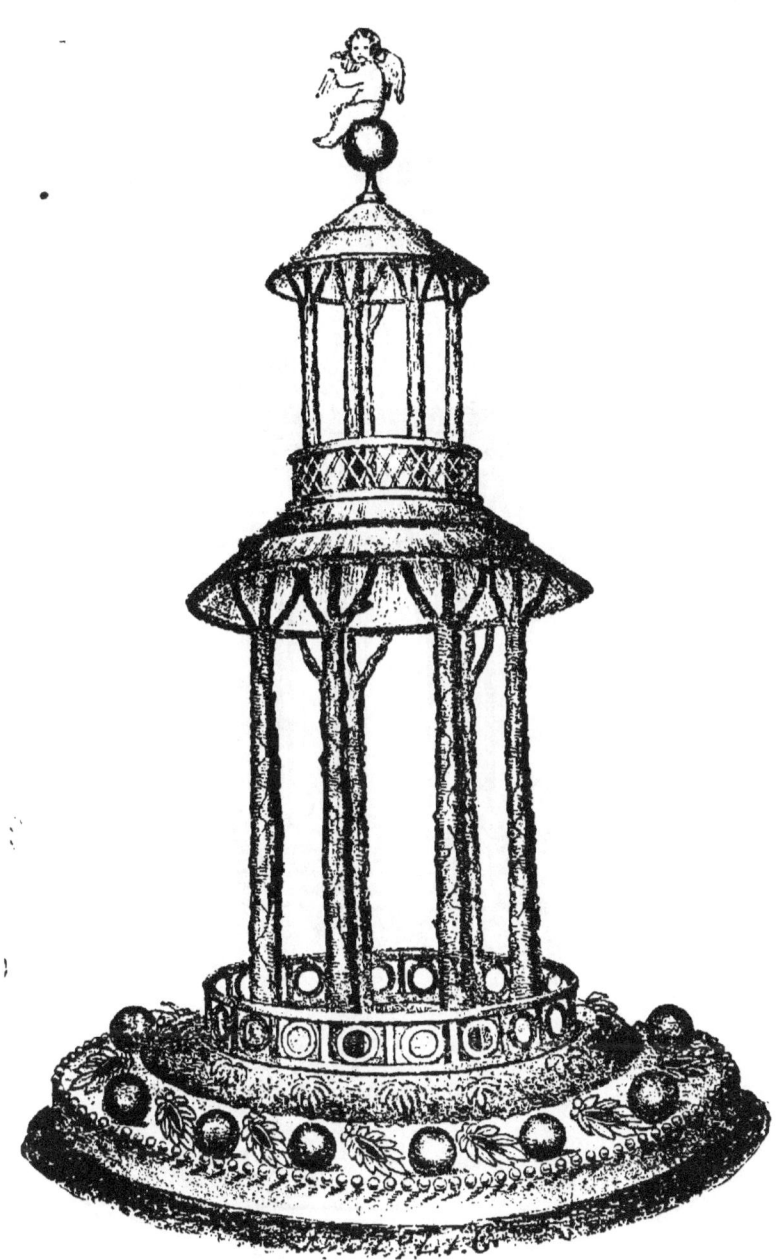

Croquant-Tempel.

XVIII.

Croquant-Aufsatz.

Nougat-Kapelle.

Traganth-Aufsatz.

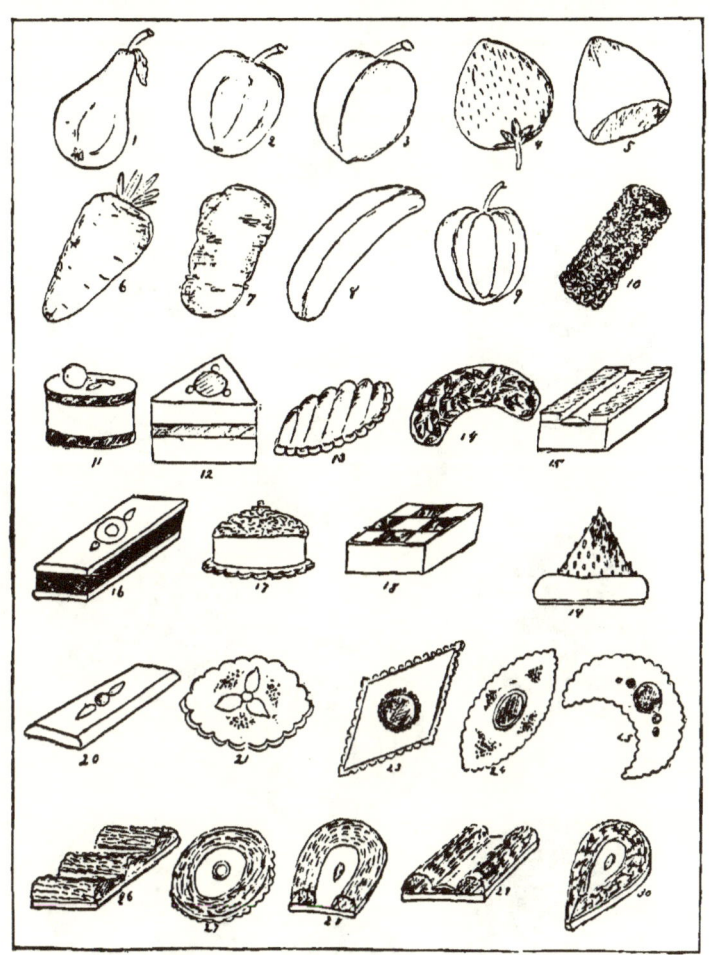

Designs for Fancy Cakes.

Recipes, instructions and information you will find under No. 319 of this book.

Recipes and information you will find in Part III.

Fancy Kisses,

Meringue Beses oder Schaumsachen.

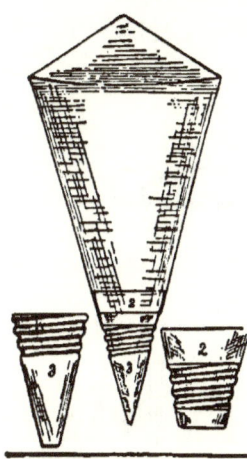

This cut represents my **Little Ornamenter,** which I invented in the city of London in 1876. As others are infringing on my patent I will sell this handy tool with 6 screw tubes and cup, all complete, for **$1.50.**

My **Ornamenting Screw Tubes** are no doubt the best in the market, as each tube will fit the Jumble, the Kisses, the Ornamenting Machine, and also the Little Handy Ornamenter. See illustrations of my art and flower tubes, rufflers, crimpers, leaf and rose tubes.

Set of 12 tubes with screw cup, **$1.00.**
Rubber bags, any size, **50 cts.** each.

Address **H. HUEG,**
P. O. Box 181, Long Island City, N. Y.

I would like to call your attention to my **Improved Ornamenting Machine,** this is the best invention I have ever made. The tubes can be changed from the smallest writing to the largest Jumble tube in a second. It is worked by a spring, is very light and cannot get out of order. This handy tool, with 6 screw tubes, is sold for the small amount of **$2.50.**

My **Kisses and Jumble Machines** are of the same make only larger in size.
Price, with 6 screw tubes and plates, **$1.50** each.

Address **H. HUEG,**
P. O. Box 181, Long Island City, N. Y.

A **Vienna Roll Machine** has been a long felt want, as over two-thirds of the bakers cannot make them and quite a number of first-class workmen have lost their situation on this account. This handy tool is worked by a spring; a boy can make one hundred Vienna rolls in a minute with this machine. Price, **$1.00.**

My **Improved Candy Funnel** will fill three times as much as the old style funnel with less labor. It is worked by a spring, is easy to clean and cannot get out of order. Price, **$1.00.**

Address **H. HUEG,**
P. O. Box 181, Long Island City, N. Y.

ILLUSTRATED

CAKE BAKER

THE ONLY ONE OF ITS KIND.

Containing recipes and information never before in print, also the best and newest recipes now known to the trade,

BY

Herman Hueg,

Practical Cake Baker and Confectioner.

PRICE 50 CENTS.

1892.

This cut represents my **Patent Cream Cake Filler and Cutter.** It will fill and cut 75 Cream Cakes in a minute; is worked by a spring, easy to clean, requires no screwing or fitting and will not dirty the benches or waste cream. No bakery complete without this handy instrument.

Price, $2.50.
H. HUEG, Box 181, Long Island City, N. Y.

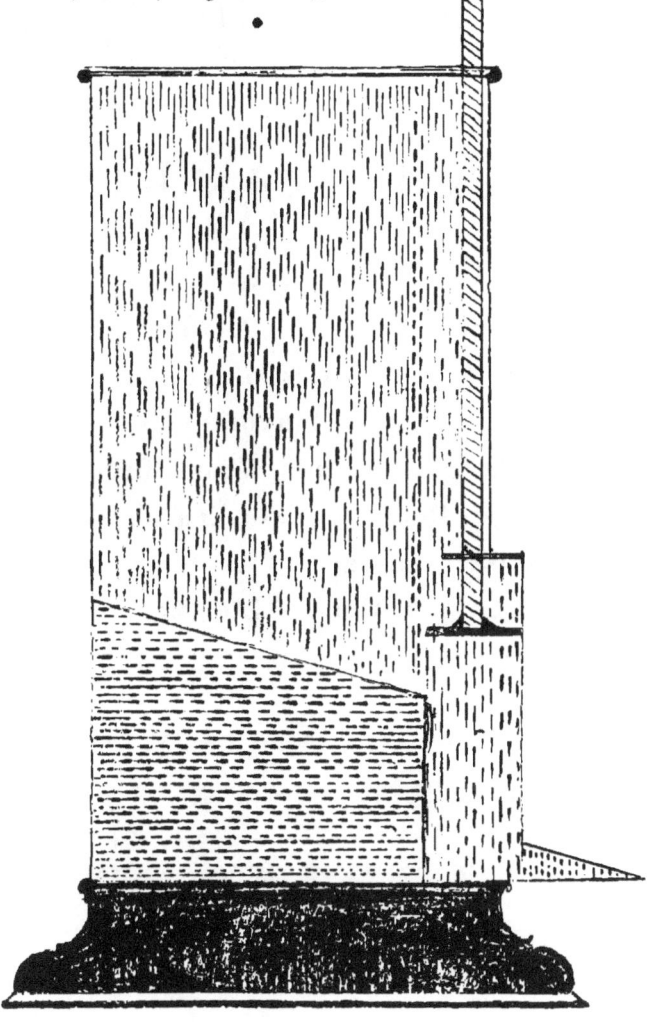

THE PRACTICAL
CONFECTIONER
—AND—
CAKE BAKER.

CONTAINING

One Thousand Practical Recipes and Illustrations for all kinds of Candies, Ice Creams, Syrups, Flavors, Liqueurs, Gum Work, Cordials, Yeast, Bread, Buns, Rolls, Cakes, Crackers, Pastry, Custards, Pies, Icings, Colors, Nougat, Etc., Etc.

BY

HERMAN HUEG,

Practical Cake Baker and Confectioner.

~~PRICE, $1.50.~~

1892.

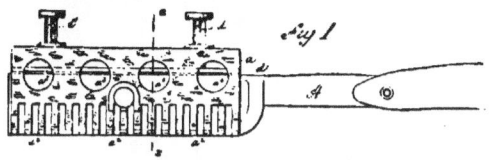

H. HUEG'S PATENT RAZOR GUARD

will fit any razor in the market. By using this Patent Razor Guard the most inexperienced can shave themselves, making shaving a pleasure instead of a misery. All those who cannot shave themselves, or who are afraid to use a razor on their face, this will prove a delightful article. Price, **$1.00**.

Address **H. HUEG.**
P. O. Box 181, Long Island City, N. Y.

PRICE LIST

Patent Cream Cake Filler and Cutter	$2.50
" Candy Funnel	1.50
" Ornamenting Machine, with Screw Tubes	2.50
" Vienna Roll Stamp (Kaisersemmel)	1.50
" Little Ornamenter, with Cup, Bag and Screw Tubes	1.50
" Ornamenting Screw Tubes	0.10
" Large Screw Tubes	0.10
" Jumble Machine, with Plates and Tubes	1.50
" Kisses Machine, with Plates and Tubes	1.50
" Safety Razor Guard	1.00

NEW BOOKS JUST PUBLISHED.

Ornamental Confectionery	$2.00
Illustrated Cake Baker and Confectioner	1.50
Illustrirtes Cake- und Conditor-Buch	1.00
Illustrated Cake Baker	0.50
Geheimnisse der Cake-Bäckerei	0.50
All of the above books, bound in cloth, the whole forming a handsome volume of over 200 pages and 1000 practical recipes	2.50

SEND ALL ORDERS AND COMMUNICATIONS TO

H. HUEG, Box 181, Long Island City, N. Y.

Nougat-Kapelle.

www.ingramcontent.com/pod-product-compliance
Lightning Source LLC
Chambersburg PA
CBHW031442160426
43195CB00010BB/819